HISTORIC
NEW ENGLAND

HISTORIC NEW ENGLAND

A Tour of the Region's Top 100 National Landmarks

By Patricia Harris and David Lyon

Globe Pequot

Guilford, Connecticut

*To the preservationists, historical societies,
and tireless volunteers who keep the lights on and the doors open
at New England's National Historic Landmarks*

Globe
Pequot

An imprint of Rowman & Littlefield

Distributed by NATIONAL BOOK NETWORK

British Library Cataloguing in Publication Information Available
Library of Congress Cataloging-in-Publication Data Available

ISBN 978-1-4930-2456-8 (paperback)
978-1-4930-2455-1 (e-book)

♾™ The paper used in this publication meets the minimum requirements of American
National Standard for Information Sciences—Permanence of Paper for Printed
Library Materials, ANSI/NISO Z39.48-1992.

Printed in the United States

CONTENTS

MASSACHUSETTS

VERMONT

Nickels-Sortwell House, Wiscasset, Maine, p. 226

INTRODUCTION

Within these pages you'll find, among other peculiarities, three submarines, a whaling ship, four windjammers, a Colonial jail, an operating room, a bird sanctuary, a weather observatory, three Shaker villages, a boat building workshop, two lighthouses, a stopover on the Underground Railroad, three carousels, and a terrific public beach. They are all National Historic Landmarks.

We were initially surprised to discover that not all historic landmarks are antique homes of founding fathers or wealthy merchants—although some of them are, and they are often fascinating places. But the sites in the six New England states are surprisingly diverse, which got us thinking about what makes a National Historic Landmark.

In our hunting and gathering past, a landmark was literally that—a mark in the landscape to tell us where we were and how to get wherever we were going. The Old English word originally meant a marker that indicated the boundaries of an estate, a kingdom, or a community. By 1859, the term was being used figuratively for a place or event that marked a turning point in history.

It is this figurative sense that is employed by the National Historic Landmarks program. The places selected for the designation still serve a similar purpose as those ancient boundary stones or blazes on a tree. They mark our place in the cultural landscape and provide guidance about where we all might be headed.

New England has a concentration of National Historic Landmarks greater than anywhere else in the country except New York and California. They reveal a great deal about our regional identity—both what we celebrate and what we feel defines us.

We recognize that much of the country feels that we New Englanders have a puffed-up sense of ourselves, but we have every right to be proud of our many national firsts. That includes the first public arboretum, the first free municipal public library, the first enclosed shopping center, the first well-publicized use of ether for surgical anesthesia, the first independent law school, the first scientific weather observatory, the first bird sanctuary, and even the first nuclear-powered submarine. (If you're scratching your head, those would be the Arnold Arboretum, the Boston Public Library, the Arcade Providence, the Ether Dome, Tapping Reeve Law School, Blue Hill Observatory, Birdcraft, and the USS *Nautilus*, respectively.)

Some of our National Historic Landmarks show how our region grew, from the simple saltbox of the 1686 Jethro Coffin House, the oldest house on Nantucket, to the jewel box of Philip Johnson's Glass House, a seminal example of modern architecture. Likewise, the landmarks trace our industry and industriousness, from Slater Mill in Rhode Island to the thundering mills, locks, and canals of Lowell, to the sheer ingenuity of the perfectly preserved 19th-century mill village of Harrisville, New Hampshire.

Rock-ribbed New England values shaped the character of some of our national leaders. Landmark sites include the birthplaces of four presidents—John Adams, John Quincy Adams, and John F. Kennedy in Massachusetts, and Calvin Coolidge in Vermont—and the childhood home of another, Franklin Pierce in New Hampshire. One of the most powerful of those regional values was the belief in the abolition of slavery. The Prudence Crandall House in Connecticut demonstrates the beginning of the civil rights struggle in education, while the African Meeting House in Boston was a cradle of the civil rights movement in the years before the Civil War. Rokeby farm in northern Vermont is one of the best authenticated stops on the Underground Railroad that carried fugitives to freedom.

The New England landscape inspired many artists and thinkers. Henry David Thoreau went to the woods at landmark Walden Pond. Many of the best American Impressionists painted along the Connecticut coast during their summers at the Florence Griswold House, while Winslow Homer drew strength from the sea and rocky coast of Maine at his studio on Prouts Neck south of Portland. That same coast made Sarah Orne Jewett's heart race in her novels written at her South Berwick home, while poet Robert Frost found his voice building stone walls and watching the shift of seasons on his farm in nearby Derry, New Hampshire. Sculptors Daniel Chester French and Augustus Saint Gaudens built summer studios in western Massachusetts and along the Connecticut River in New Hampshire. Modern dance pioneer Ted Shawn had a summer vision as well, creating Jacob's Pillow at the top of a mountain in the Berkshires.

New Englanders also know how to have fun. We count among our treasured landmarks historic carousels in Watch Hill and Riverside, Rhode Island, and in Oak Bluffs on Martha's Vineyard, still spinning after all these years. Revere Beach, the first public beach in America, is on the subway line from Boston. Our golden age of mountain recreation is alive and well at the Mount Washington Hotel, while the Newport Casino marks the birth of lawn tennis in the United States. Our national preoccupation with the pigskin sport even gets its due at the landmark Yale Bowl.

As the National Park Service defines them, "National Historic Landmarks are nationally significant historic places designated by the Secretary of the Interior because they possess exceptional value or quality in illustrating or interpreting the heritage of the United States." There are more than 2,500 places with this distinction. Often confused with the much longer list of National Historic Places, National Historic Landmarks must meet a much higher standard of significance and go through a rigorous nomination process.

By our count there are about 400 National Historic Landmarks in all of New England, and one of our greatest regrets was that we couldn't include them all. We immediately eliminated those that are inaccessible (or nearly so) to the public, those where there isn't much to see, and all of those that lie on Boston's Freedom Trail or within Minuteman National Historic Park in Lexington and Concord, because they are so extensively documented elsewhere.

We still had to make some very hard decisions to narrow the list to a mere 100. Ultimately, the choices were ours and we apologize to the many worthy sites that we were not able to include. We hope that once you have exhausted our list, you will make your own and keep discovering the places and people that have defined New England.

—Patricia Harris and David Lyon
Cambridge, Massachusetts

Philip Johnson's Glass House, New Canaan, p. 6

CONNECTICUT

Bush-Holley Historic Site, Cos Cob

39 Strickland Road, Cos Cob; 203-869-6899; greenwichhistory .org; open year-round for guided tours; admission charged

The Bush-Holley house in the picturesque Greenwich village of Cos Cob speaks to two key moments in local history: the prosperous late Colonial era when the original owners of the house were the largest slave-holders in Greenwich, and a more romantic period when the roomy structure became a boardinghouse that fostered the plein-air painters of American Impressionism.

The house was originally constructed as a two-story single room on a hilltop overlooking Cos Cob harbor, only 13 miles from the New York border. The strategic location at the intersection of a mill pond and a river that flowed into Long Island Sound was a prime spot for loading and unloading cargo in the New York trade. The original one-room structure was erected in 1728 and a full "salt box" was built alongside it a few years later. When David Bush inherited the property in 1757, he expanded the house to create a proper Georgian mansion that befitted his status as one of the leading citizens of Greenwich. Between 1757 and 1779, Bush joined the two buildings, created a central entrance hall, installed floor-to-ceiling wood paneling in the parlor and parlor chamber, and connected a two-story structure behind the house to create a separate kitchen wing. Fifteen Bush children grew up in the house, and at Bush's death in 1797, the inventory of his property included 10 enslaved adults and 6 enslaved children.

Although records are unclear, the enslaved servants probably lived above the kitchen in the back wing, which was a half story lower during that period. The only heat for the room came from the chimney of the downstairs cooking fireplace. Typically, they would have been given straw mattresses, an extra set of clothing, and some bedding. The last record of enslaved people living in the house dates from 1820, when four enslaved adults were listed.

The Bush family sold the home in 1848, the year that slavery ended in Connecticut, and the spacious building soon became a boardinghouse. New windows and a second-story porch obliterated its Georgian lines but certainly provided guests with attractive harbor views. Josephine and Edward Holley took over the 14-room house on three-quarters of an acre in 1882, and managed to purchase it two years later. At their nearby farm, they had begun taking in artists as boarders, including landscape painter John Henry Twachtman. When they moved into Cos Cob, they deliberately sought an artistic and intellectual clientele of New Yorkers looking to rusticate on the Connecticut coast. Only a short walk from the Cos Cob train station, the Holley House boardinghouse stood less than an hour's train ride from New York City.

Among the early boarders at the Holley House were Twachtman and his good friend J. Alden Weir. They would travel from New York and spend several weeks in the summer happily lugging their easels around quaint little Cos Cob to paint the village, the mill pond, the harbor, and the people. It was a charming country idyll for the big-city artists, and in 1891 Twachtman set up a summer art school in the barn behind the boardinghouse where he could teach his pupils from the Art Students League in New York. Weir joined him a year later, and the school flourished. Over the next 30 years, the influx of painters provided a steady income to many Cos Cob families who could find a spare room to rent to the seasonal visitors.

The layout of the Bush-Holley house and its grounds gives a sense of the artistic camaraderie—of summers spent sketching and painting outdoors or on balconies overlooking the (pre-highway) Strickland Brook, eating and discussing the fine points of aesthetics in the common dining area. The best of the American Impressionists to spend time here, Childe Hassam, was especially fond of painting the daughter of a local tavernkeeper in various settings around the house. Some of these portraits are exhibited in the house and in the exhibitions in the adjoining Storehouse Gallery.

Elmer Livingston MacRae studied in Twachtman's summer classes in Cos Cob from 1896 to 1899. While boarding at the Holley

House, he fell in love with the innkeepers' daughter Constant. They married in 1900, and after Twachtman's sudden death in 1902, MacRae became the principal connection between the boardinghouse and the New York art scene. But the 1913 Armory Show—officially the International Exhibition of Modern Art—changed everything. As new ideas like Fauvism, Futurism, Cubism, and more percolated through American galleries and studios, the charming and colorful Connecticut countryside no longer drew the cream of American painters. After World War I, the Cos Cob art colony effectively faded into obscurity.

The MacRaes continued to live in the Holley House, and Elmer's studio is recreated in a second-floor bedroom. Following his death, Constant Holley MacRae sold the house to the Greenwich Historical Society, and it opened as a museum in 1958.

Birdcraft Sanctuary, Fairfield
314 Unquowa Road, Fairfield; 203-259-0416; ctaudubon.org; sanctuary open daily dawn to dusk; admission by donation

Birdcraft, the first private bird sanctuary created in the United States, was conceived and largely executed by pioneer conservationist and author Mabel Osgood Wright (1859–1934). At a time when the national Audubon movement had stalled and fallen into obscurity, she was instrumental in rebuilding it on the state level. She designed Birdcraft along the radical principles of "bird-scaping" an area with plantings and landscape features that would provide a habitat that encouraged birds.

Born in 1859 in New York, Wright grew up in a rambling house in lower Manhattan when that part of the island was still predominantly rural. She later wrote of how that experience shaped her commitment to nature conservancy. She recalled that in the 1860s, she "ran loose about the ten wide acres at the edge of the village." Birds were taken for granted—as something to eat or creatures whose plumage could be a fashion decoration. But she also recalled that they were "to be listened to in the early hours of dawn and twilight when the notes of the wood thrush or song sparrow carried one away from earth and made the present a waking dream of the worth while."

Wright aspired to become a doctor but was discouraged by her family from attending medical school. She chose to yoke her interest in science to her love of nature and educated herself about the relation of animals and their habitat. In the 1880s, bird plumage on hats was all the rage in fashion, and Wright, like many other nature lovers, was horrified. She began writing naturalist essays, publishing her first, "A New England May Day," in the *New York Evening Post* in 1893. After her collected essays appeared a year later, her publisher asked her to write a field guide to birds. In 1895, she published *Birdcraft: A Field Book of Two Hundred Song, Game, and Water Birds.*

Featuring color reproductions of paintings by John Jay Audubon and other art-ists, *Birdcraft* would become the prototype of the modern bird field guide for a pop-ular audience. In 1897, she collaborated with Elliot Coues to publish *Citizen Bird: Scenes from Bird-life in Plain English for Beginners*, an early and influential guide to the practice of birding. She also wrote stories and books to educate children about birds.

Ironically, by the time Wright published *Birdcraft*, the original Audubon Society, founded in 1886, had foundered and was on the verge of disbanding. In 1896, bird-ers began to rebuild the movement on the state level, starting with the Massachusetts Audubon Society (now Mass Audubon). In 1898, Wright organized the Audubon Society of Connecticut and became its first president. She went on to edit the Audu-bon Society department in the monthly magazine *Bird-Lore*, which later evolved into *Audubon* magazine. She continued as an editor and writer for the magazine until 1910 and a contributor until her death.

Wright decided that the Audubon Society of Connecticut should do more than spread the word. In 1914, she enlisted the assistance of Standard Oil heiress and philanthropist Annie Burr Jennings (1855–1939) to purchase an 11-acre parcel of land near Wright's home in Fairfield to serve as a bird sanctuary. The Audubon Soci-ety of Connecticut, in turn, honored Wright by naming the sanctuary Birdcraft after her famous book.

Wright laid out the guidelines for construction of the sanctuary, including a cat-proof fence encircling the entire property. She specified that it should have a pond dug that would be fed by existing springs, and drew trails so that humans could observe the birds without disturbing them. While the landscape was designed to create a natural environment for birds, the society also constructed a caretaker's bungalow and a rustic building to serve as a museum.

It was a success from the start. In 1914, 16 species nested at Birdcraft in a total of 76 nests. By 1922, both species and numbers of nests had effectively doubled and the human visitation topped 10,000—including 49 school classes. That same year, Birdcraft began banding songbirds to determine if the same birds would return. They did—and the Birdcraft Museum conducts an operation every spring and fall to continue the process of tracking the migrant songbird population. In 1934, Birdcraft also created a special chimney to encourage chimney swifts to nest on the property.

Although the construction of the Connecticut Turnpike and I-95 in 1957 reduced the size of the sanctuary by more than 4 acres, Birdcraft Sanctuary still operates, and during peak migration periods—especially the warbler migration in May—it attracts a striking number of species. Despite some highway noise, the sanctuary has recorded about 120 species of birds.

Standing just 2 blocks north of the Fairfield rail station, it is approached by turning up a driveway through a stone fence. The wrought-iron gate hangs on two square stone piers. The pier on the right is taller because it contains nesting holes near the top. The museum is closed for renovations but the sanctuary is open to visitors.

Philip Johnson's Glass House, New Canaan
Visitor Center at 199 Elm Street, New Canaan; 203-594-9884; theglasshouse.org; open May through November for guided tours by reservation; admission charged

Decades after its completion in 1949, Philip Johnson's Glass House in New Canaan remains resolutely avant garde. Yet its proportions, its transparency, and even its siting on the lot make it arguably a first cousin to a classical Greek temple.

Philip Johnson (1906–2005) was perhaps the most erudite and historically self-conscious of architects. His buildings, though undeniably modern in their particulars, are inevitably grounded in or even inspired by historical structures. Johnson's genius lay in exploiting the essence of a historical form and slyly referencing his source with an architectural gesture. He conceived the Glass House with the insistently horizontal proportions of a Greek temple and used visible vertical beams to hold the glass walls in place in a manner that echoes the classical arcade of columns.

Johnson carried the inspiration even further. The Greeks believed that to approach a temple directly showed hubris to the gods (an affront that, if you weren't careful, could get you chained to a rock for eternity while eagles tore at your flesh), so even the Parthenon can only be approached at an angle. In homage to that concept, Johnson made the Glass House impossible to see in a glance until a visitor is standing out front. The route from the road is even more circuitous than the approach to the Parthenon. A long driveway winds in sweeping curves down a hill on the 49-acre property, pausing at a Donald Judd earthworks sculpture that creates a foreground for the first full view of the house itself.

Shaped rather like the modern ranch houses that would colonize the suburbs in the 1950s, the Glass House is remarkably conventional in its structure—except

that the walls are all glass. It is essentially a single low rectangular box with a central column to carry the main plumbing and ventilation. So the massive brick chimney of the living room fireplace backs up on the plumbing and HVAC of the bathroom, and that central core provides a division that separates the bedroom with desk from the

spacious living room and open kitchen. Radical in its day, it was so influential in the design of both domestic and office spaces (think of the "loft" apartment and the "open office"), that now the layout seems perfectly natural.

The Glass House and the estate that surrounds it show one of the great minds of the modern age at play in the landscape. Visiting on a guided tour feels a little like having a brief conversation with the architect—Johnson himself doing all the talking, of course.

Johnson, who lived in the house with his partner David Whitney (1939–2005), was obsessively neat, which is a useful trait for people who live in glass houses. Although the couple entertained guests every Sunday for lunch, drinks, and conversation in what was Connecticut's longest-running intellectual salon, Johnson didn't want any of them to even lay a sweater down. (There are hidden closets for that.)

Johnson saw the Glass House less as a feature in the landscape than as a pavilion from which to view the landscape. Each wall offers a different but equally pleasing framed view of the lush natural surroundings. Johnson was fond of pointing out that the house had all the features of his grandparents' farmhouse, including a kitchen, dining room, living room, and bedroom. On the other hand, his grandparents probably didn't lounge around in Barcelona chairs designed by Mies van der Rohe.

There were a couple of shortcomings to this icon of modern architecture. The most obvious is lack of privacy. Johnson dealt with it in a characteristic manner for an architect: He built a second structure, the Brick House, that had a private bedroom and study.

The other problem with glass walls is they are terrible for hanging art. Johnson and Whitney were major collectors, and they tended to favor truly outsized works by the likes of Andy Warhol (a close friend) and Frank Stella. Many of the works they owned are actually higher than the mere 10½ feet of the roofline on the Glass House. So Johnson built a bunker-like art gallery where he mounted paintings on wall-sized panels that moved on tracks, like leafing through a book.

When the couple's sculpture collection outgrew the gallery, Johnson designed a separate building to hold some of their smaller pieces that couldn't simply live on the lawns. In all, there are 16 buildings on the property, as Johnson loved an excuse to build something. And as an inhabitant of a Glass House, he ignored both the praise and brickbats of critics, not to mention his sometimes scandalized neighbors. "The Glass House works so well," he famously said, "because the wallpaper is so handsome."

Yale Bowl, New Haven
81 Central Avenue, New Haven; 203-432-4747; yale.edu; see website for game schedule

The Yale Bulldogs football program launched in 1872, making it one of the oldest in the world and one of the most influential in the development of American football from the English game of rugby. When Walter Camp, who became known as the "Father of Football," played halfback for the 1876–1882 Bulldogs, he was already a member of a nascent rules committee for the sport. He proposed a radical shift in the way the game was played. Football, he declared, should dispense with the rugby scrum and continuous play in favor of players on each side lining up on a line of scrimmage. Each play would start when the ball was hiked and end when the ball carrier was tackled. Some scholars of the sport also credit him with cutting the number of players per side from 15 to 11 and introducing yard markers on the field. After Camp, American football was a different game, but Yale continued to dominate the collegiate sport, winning 26 national championships before 1910.

Like any winning team, the Bulldogs had legions of fans, and Yale Field could only accommodate a mere 30,000 of them. So the college built the Yale Bowl, which was completed in 1914. It was said to be the largest amphitheater since the Roman Colosseum opened in AD 80, but the construction technique was straightforward and simple. The designers, engineer Charles A. Ferry and architect Donn Barber, ordered the excavation of an elliptical crater some 28 feet deep and piled up the dirt to create a berm around the perimeter. They created 30 concrete portals to get in and out and simply poured concrete down the interior slopes. The seating capacity of the stadium was expanded to 80,000 at one point but currently stands at 64,000, making it the largest university-owned stadium in its NCAA class. As the first bowl stadium, it has inspired such landmark stadiums as the Rose Bowl in Pasadena, California.

One item of clever scholarship applied to construction of the Yale Bowl would likely have made Archimedes proud. Because Yale plays its main Ivy League rivals in November each year, Ferry and Barber oriented the bowl so that the minor axis of the ellipse points to the sun at 3 p.m. on November 15. As Ferry reported to the

American Society of Civil Engineers, "thus no football player would ever have to look into the sun when Yale plays its big games against Princeton and Harvard." Yale has played Harvard annually since 1875 in what has become known simply as "The Game." The contest alternates between the two schools, and while Yale has won more games over the decades, Harvard has dominated in the 21st century.

As a player in the genesis of collegiate football, Yale also created many of the traditions that go with the game. Its school marching band was one of the first to perform at games, and Yale quickly developed a whole catalog of fight songs, many of which call for the annihilation of the team representing Harvard, or less frequently, Princeton. The best known of the songs were originally sung by the Yale Glee Club and included "Boola" ("When we roughhouse poor old Harvard, / They will holler Boola Boo!") and "Bull-Dog," with words and music by 1913 alumnus Cole Porter.

The Porter song perhaps referred to "Handsome Dan," thought to be the first live mascot of a sports team. There has been an actual bulldog filling the role since 1889. He is selected for his tolerance of loud bands and hyperactive children, and (according to lore) his aggressive stance toward the color crimson (symbol of Harvard) and toward tigers (mascot of Princeton). The first Handsome Dan was stuffed and mounted after he died in 1898 and now resides in a sealed glass case in one of the gymnasium's trophy rooms. Handsome Dan II (1933–1937) died of a broken leg but met a fate similar to his predecessor. He can be seen, also in a glass case, at the Yale University Visitor Center on Elm Street.

Tapping Reeve House and Law School, Litchfield
82 South Street, Litchfield; 860-567-4501; litchfieldhistorical society.org; open mid-April through November; admission charged

By breaking from the United Kingdom, the United States of America was effectively lawless. One of the first challenges in building a new country was to provide a continuity of legal principles. Moreover, there was also a dearth of legal talent because Tory lawyers were forbidden to practice. The Founding Fathers—John Adams, in particular—were concerned that the new country should have "a government of laws, and not of men." That meant some very good men were needed—a cadre of lawyers and judges who could administer and adjudicate both common law and newly enacted statutes.

Tapping Reeve (1744–1823), a distinguished country lawyer from Litchfield in the hill country of western Connecticut, would become one of the founding members of that government of laws. Like many lawyers of his time, he took in clerks—effectively apprentices—who would study his law books in preparation for the bar exam. His first protégé, in fact, was his brother-in-law Aaron Burr (1756–1836), who came to Litchfield to study with Reeve in 1784. He would later serve under Thomas Jefferson as the third vice president of the United States (1801–05).

Reeve's reputation spread widely after the 1781 decision in Brom & Brett vs. Ashley, in which he successfully argued that Elizabeth Freeman, an enslaved woman in Sheffield, Massachusetts, be granted her freedom under the 1780 Massachusetts

Constitution—thereby setting the precedent that led to the abolition of slavery in that state. He was soon taking in so many clerks that, in 1784, Reeve formally founded the Litchfield Law School in a small building next to his own home. He constructed a 14-month curriculum in the law with special attention to American adaptations and enlargements of British Common Law.

The Litchfield Law School was the first independent law school in the country (the College of William & Mary had opened its law school four years earlier). When it opened, there were fewer than 100 lawyers admitted to the bar in Connecticut. Although it never granted a diploma—students received a letter saying that they had read the law at Litchfield and most immediately passed the bar exams in Connecticut and other states—the school would be tremendously influential.

Before the school closed in 1833, Litchfield would train well over 1,000 men from 22 states and 6 foreign countries. Although students from Connecticut, Massachusetts, and New York constituted a slight majority, many came from as far south as Georgia and the Carolinas—including John C. Calhoun (1782–1850), who, like Burr, would serve as vice president (1825–32). In all, the school trained 101 members of the US House of Representatives, 28 US senators, 6 members of the cabinet, 3 justices of the US Supreme Court, 14 state governors, and 13 chief justices of state supreme courts. More than a dozen lawyers who studied at Litchfield ultimately founded university law schools.

The home and law school building of Tapping Reeve, located a few steps from the town green, are operated as a museum by the Litchfield Historical Society. Exhibits and an excellent video conjure up the heady years of the young republic when men flocked from near and far to study in rural Litchfield.

Reeve operated the Litchfield Law School by himself until 1798, when he was elected to the Connecticut State Supreme Court. He hired one of his former students, James Gould, as a fellow lecturer and partner in the proprietary law school. Reeve retired in 1820 at the age of 76, but Gould kept the school going until his own retirement in 1833. By then, the little law school in Litchfield had done its job. Major law schools had sprung up at Yale, Harvard, Columbia, the University of Virginia, and other colleges and universities. After training so many lawyers, Reeve's approach to an American interpretation of British Common Law was enshrined in the increasingly coherent American legal system.

Exhibits range from re-created lecture rooms, complete with desks fitted with inkwells and quill pens, to evocations of the after-dinner arguments among students. Some exhibits also highlight the accomplishments of such distinguished graduates as politician and educational reformer Horace Mann, painter George Catlin, and explorer and diplomat John Lloyd Stephens.

Hill-Stead, Farmington

35 Mountain Road, Farmington; 860-677-4787; hillstead.org; open year-round for guided tours; admission charged

Part art gallery, part historic home, part glorious landscape, Hill-Stead Museum and its 152-acre estate is first and foremost a monument to good taste, talent, and a can-do attitude. The very model of gentility, it was recognized as a National Historic Landmark for a remarkable confluence of art, architecture, and landscape design. In one sense, it is testament to the skill and will of Theodate Pope Riddle (1867–1946), graduate of Miss Porter's School for Girls in Farmington and the first woman to become a licensed architect in both New York and Connecticut.

Theodate Pope—who was christened Effie Brooks Pope but changed her name at age 19 to Theodate to honor her grandmother—was the only child of industrialist Alfred Pope of Cleveland. In 1888, when Theodate was 21, the family spent nearly a year making the grand tour of Europe. Her father was immediately smitten with Impressionist paintings that he saw in France. He shrewdly purchased seminal paintings by Claude Monet and Edgar Degas early in their careers, and he liked to display them in his homes.

The 33,000-square-foot manse on a hill in Farmington was Theodate's doing. After graduating from Miss Porter's, she hired some of the school's faculty to tutor her in architecture. She decided that she wanted to design her family's summer home, so she consulted with the famous firm of McKim, Mead, and White for advice, while indicating firmly in her correspondence that the house was to be a

Pope design. She completed it for her parents to occupy in 1901. Her achievement as an architect flew in the face of convention, which saw architecture as a strictly masculine profession, but she went on to complete a number of other significant commissions, including the reconstruction, restoration, and augmentation of the Theodore Roosevelt birthplace in New York.

Her parents clearly enjoyed the house, and her father filled it with some superb works of art, all displayed in a domestic context. They cover the walls of the drawing room and pop up all over the home to brighten the walls. Alfred Pope had cutting-edge taste for his day, leading him to augment his Monets and Degases with works by Mary Cassatt (a sometimes houseguest), Edouard Manet, Pierre-Auguste Renoir, Camille Pissarro, and James McNeill Whistler—whom he met in 1894 and consulted about new purchases.

A sense of domestic intimacy comes across in the hour-long tours of the house, where guides speak so fondly of the family that you'd think Theodate was a beloved great-aunt and that each had known personally the family butler who served for 60 years. He ruled over the large dining room off the coach entrance where the elder Popes, and then Theodate and her diplomat husband, John Riddle, held dinner parties and dances.

The drawing room, with its Monet haystacks and Degas portraits (one, of a bather, was originally in a bedroom—too scandalous for public display), most delights visitors. The very first Impressionist painting that Alfred Pope purchased, Claude Monet's "View of Cap d'Antibes," hangs prominently over the fireplace.

Theodate's personality really emerges in the library. Before entering, the guide advises, "Close your eyes and smell it—dusty and dry, lots of leather and old pages." Among them are works on the supernatural (Theodate was obsessed with contacting her father after his death in 1913) and volumes by such houseguests as William and Henry James.

Theodate customized the house with deft personal touches, including a closet built into the doorframe of her father's study to hold his golf clubs so he could step outside and hit a few on his personal six-hole course (now a grassy meadow). And although she never had children, she created a personal child's guest bedroom on the second floor, complete with a bathroom fitted with a low sink sized for a small child. Yet for all her "masculine" achievement, she remained ever the lady, as a closet filled with her gowns and parasols attests.

Theodate continued to occupy the house after her father's death in 1913 and continued to have her own adventures. She was one of the survivors of the sinking of the British cruise ship RMS *Lusitania* in 1915. The next year, at age 49, she settled down and married former American diplomat John Wallace Riddle, and they spent more time than ever in Farmington. The gardens and grounds at Hill-Stead received her regular attention, and in 1925 she engaged Beatrix Farrand, one of America's pioneer women landscape designers, to create the lovely Sunken Garden. Recently restored according to Farrand's plan, the Sunken Garden is the site of an annual poetry festival on the grounds.

On her death in 1946, Theodate left behind a 50-page document making Hill-Stead into a museum and spelling out in detail how it was to be displayed and where every work of art was to be hung. She was generous with her wealth—and determined to have the last word as to how it would be shown.

Harriet Beecher Stowe House, Hartford
77 Forest Street, Hartford; 860-522-9258; harrietbeecherstowecenter.org; open year-round; admission charged

Harriet Beechet Stowe (1811–96) was already one of the most famous and influential women in America when she moved to Hartford in 1864. Her husband, theologian Calvin Stowe, had just retired from a decade as a professor at Andover Theological Seminary in Andover, Massachusetts. Hartford was a logical choice because it meant being near family—always a priority for Harriet.

Her sister Isabella was married to John Hooker, one of the two men developing the Nook Farm neighborhood of activists and reformers on Hartford's western edge. The author of *Uncle Tom's Cabin* was a natural fit in this enclave of politicians and writers, journalists and spiritualists, painters, suffragists, and—it went without saying—abolitionists. The Stowes oversaw the construction of an elaborate Victorian Gothic home they called Oakholm, but even America's best-selling author found it too expensive to keep up, so they sold it. In 1873, they moved into the 14-room Victorian Gothic cottage that is now part of the Harriet Beecher Stowe Center.

The new house was actually rather modest for Stowe's means and reputation. She was far better known than Samuel Clemens—pen name Mark Twain (p. 17)—who moved into the 25-room flamboyant Gothic house next door in 1874 and had it decorated by Louis Comfort Tiffany. Although she ultimately wrote more than 30 books, Stowe is remembered primarily for her debut novel, *Uncle Tom's Cabin*, which was serialized in the *National Era*, an abolitionist newspaper, in 1851–52 and issued as a book in 1852.

Displays in the visitors' center trace the impact of the novel. *Uncle Tom's Cabin* was among the first books of the mid-19th century to put a human face on the

horrors of slavery, and if its story of families torn asunder was at points melodramatic and sentimental, it was also an instant international sensation. The book sold 10,000 copies the first week it rolled off the presses. In the first year, it sold 300,000 copies in the US. In Great Britain, it sold 1.5 million in a single year. It was translated into 48 languages before Stowe's death in 1896. She was the literary rock star of her day. The book figured so prominently in galvanizing public opinion against slavery that it is often credited for creating the climate that led to the Civil War.

The tour of Stowe's house focuses more on her achievements and sense of social justice than on the decorative arts and architecture of the Gilded Age—even though Stowe and her sister Catharine Beecher co-authored *The American Woman's Home*, which, among other things, laid out a theory of scientific housekeeping and kitchen design. Ultimately, the tour amounts to a journey through the rooms of a woman whose "family values" (in the best sense of that often-abused phrase) were the lodestone of her moral compass.

The dining room is set for a family meal for four: Stowe; her husband, Calvin; and their adult twin daughters, Hattie and Eliza, who lived in the house until Stowe's death. Guides use the setting to paint a picture of Harriet's own upbringing. Her father, famed evangelist Lyman Beecher, encouraged a lively discussion of the issues of the day at the family table. The Beechers took in students at the nearby Litchfield Law School (see p. 10), and debate was the normal household discourse.

Lyman Beecher encouraged his children to fight for a cause, and Harriet wasn't the only one to take up her father's charge. Brother Henry Ward Beecher became a prominent abolitionist and temperance advocate. Older sister Catharine Beecher founded women's colleges. Younger sister Isabella Beecher Hooker became a leader of the American suffragist movement. Brother Thomas Beecher, also a minister, raised two regiments to fight in the Civil War and served as chaplain to one. (He also performed the marriage ceremony for Samuel Clemens and Olivia Langdon, next-door neighbors to the Stowes.)

The family would relax in the back parlor, with its modest piano and tufted Victorian couch. It served as the family living room, but instead of focusing on an electronic hearth, as it might today, the seating is arranged to encourage round table discussions. Like the Beecher family, the Stowes believed that conversation was the best way to entertain company.

The second level of the house reveals a more personal side of Stowe and her immediate family members. The small room that served as her theologian husband's study holds a dropleaf table where Stowe wrote portions of *Uncle Tom's Cabin* when she and Calvin lived in Brunswick, Maine. She wrote all her works longhand with a flowing, urgent penmanship. Of the estimated 900 original manuscript pages of *Uncle Tom's Cabin*, only 14 survive—9 in various libraries and 5 in the collections of the Harriet Beecher Stowe Center.

The adjoining master bedroom, filled with heavy Empire furniture, has a coal fireplace. A desk is arranged as if Stowe had just stepped away. It's a wonderfully messy vignette, complete with a large wastebasket full of crumpled, rejected drafts—a reminder that Stowe was one of the most prolific writers for publisher Ticknor & Fields. She continued to work until her mind began to fail after her husband died in 1888. Samuel Clemens's account of her dementia at the time is consistent with Alzheimer's disease.

It was a sad end for a woman who clung to memories of all those whom she held dear. Poignantly, the mantle over the master bedroom fireplace is arrayed with photos of Stowe's children. As guides at the Stowe house put it, her life's work was constructed around "the overarching theme of families trying to keep themselves together."

Mark Twain House, Hartford

351 Farmington Avenue, Hartford; 860-247-0998; marktwainhouse .org; open year-round for guided tours; admission charged

Best known by his pen name Mark Twain, Samuel Clemens (1835–1910) wrote that the happiest 17 years of his life were spent in this house at Nook Farm on the west side of Hartford. He and his wife, the former Olivia Langdon (1845–1904), spent considerable effort getting it exactly as they wanted it, right down to the hilltop house lot with sweeping western views.

A decade younger than her husband, "Livy" was the daughter of a wealthy Elmira, New York, industrial family that was also active in social justice causes. One of the two presiding ministers at their 1870 wedding was Harriet Beecher Stowe's younger brother, Thomas, and Olivia was close friends with another Beecher sister, Isabella Beecher Hooker. In 1871, the couple moved to Hartford to be closer to Sam's publisher and Livy's friends at Nook Farm, where Harriet Beecher Stowe (see p. 14) also lived.

Two years later, they used the money from Livy's inheritance to commission the 25-room Gothic Revival brick house, now known as the Mark Twain House, from prominent New York architect Edward Tuckerman Potter. Livy was deeply involved in the details of the house design, working back and forth with the architect on his sketches. In 1881, the couple engaged Louis Comfort Tiffany to carry out the interior design of the public areas of the house. They spent lavishly and lived well, filling the home with a mixture of custom furniture and fine pieces they dragged back from Europe.

As Sam Clemens was fond of saying, "I was born modest but it didn't last."

The couple left the house in 1891 due to financial setbacks and never had the heart to live again in the house where daughter Susy died at age 24. The house was

rescued from demolition in 1929, and over time it has been restored to the Clemens era, complete with many of the original furnishings. Documentary photographs from the era the family lived here have guided restoration, so it truly reflects the tastes and interests of Sam and Livy Clemens.

Tours begin in the room most designed to impress: the central front hall. Here Tiffany covered the walls in a stenciled Moorish pattern that he might have encountered as a young artist painting landscapes in North Africa. Little triangles of reflective silver paint alternate with darker triangles to create patterns that would have jumped and dazzled by gaslight. Throughout the first two floors, architectural details such as coffered ceilings, carved woodwork, and faux leather wallpaper (heavily lacquered embossed paper) add a touch of Moorish fantasy to the basic Gothic style. The house was far brighter than might be expected in a Victorian manse of its era, thanks to generous windows and the clever use of diverted fireplace flues that freed Potter to place windows between rooms over the fireplace mantels.

The front parlor contains both the gigantic mirror the couple had in their Buffalo home and a fine Steinway piano. This is where the family entertained—and where the Clemens girls put on plays and sketches. Sam and Livy's only son, Langdon, had died of diphtheria at the age of 19 months before the family moved to Hartford, but daughters Susy (1872–96), Clara (1874–1962) and baby Jean (1880–1909) all grew up in the house.

The dining room is a model of Victorian propriety, and the family china and silver are used both in the table settings and in the display cases that Livy had adapted from fine antique Boston furniture. There are six seats at the table, since Olivia Lewis

Langdon, Livy's mother, lived with the family through the winters. In turn, they summered at her place in Elmira, New York.

The library gives the most intimate picture of family life. In the bay window nook opposite the fireplace, Sam would tell the children bedtime stories featuring each of the pictures on the fireplace wall and the souvenirs displayed on the mantel. Alas, the library contains none of Clemens's own books. He donated his personal collection to found the Mark Twain Library in Redding, Connecticut, where he lived the last two years of his life. The west wall of the library opens into a conservatory greenhouse that, judging from period photos, was overgrown like a miniature jungle when the Clemens family lived here.

The family bedrooms are all on the second floor. The room originally designated as Livy's sewing room is shown circa mid-1880s, when it became the private bedroom of teen daughter Susy. The other two girls shared a bedroom full of toys and an adjoining "school" room where they took instruction from Livy and private tutors.

The master bedroom is most notable for the giant bedstead of carved Carpathian walnut. It is practically encrusted with angels, and Clemens liked to sleep with the pillows at the foot of the bed so he could awaken to the host of angels on the headboard. He liked to say there were enough of them to look after his whole family. He must have felt betrayed because daughters Susy and Jean both died in their twenties and Livy was just 58 when she died on an Italian trip. Only Clara survived and flourished, living to age 88 and serving as the executor of her father's literary estate.

The sensibility of the house is so feminine and so Victorian that the frontier ruffian savant character that Clemens donned in his public speaking performances seems curiously absent—until the tour arrives at the third floor. At the head of the stairs is the butler's room, and in the corner is the "friends' room" where Sam's buddies who had drunk too much would sometimes spend the night. Most evocative of all is the billiard room. A large billiard table dominates, but one corner is devoted to Sam's writing desk. This is where he wrote the books that made his reputation: *The Gilded Age, The Adventures of Tom Sawyer, The Prince and the Pauper, Life on the Mississippi, Adventures of Huckleberry Finn, A Tramp Abroad,* and *A Connecticut Yankee in King Arthur's Court.*

The room opens out to two covered porches—perfect spots, weather permitting, for an old riverboat man to step out and enjoy a cigar.

Florence Griswold Museum, Old Lyme
96 Lyme Street, Old Lyme; 860-434-5542;
florencegriswoldmuseum.org; open year-round; admission charged

Bruised egos and infidelities aside, historic art colonies always seem like they might have been fun—sort of like summer camp for the gifted, complete with turps and brushes. No American art colony sounds quite as boisterous or possessed of quite such bonhomie as Old Lyme in its early days. And no hostess made such a mark on American art as Florence Griswold (1850–1937), landlady and guardian angel to nearly 200 artists from 1899 into the 1930s.

Her family home was both the spiritual and physical center of the Old Lyme art colony and became a wellspring of American Impressionism. Built in 1817, the late Georgian mansion, with tall Ionic columns forming the front portico, was purchased by Captain Robert Griswold in 1841. It served as his daughter Florence's home from birth until death and has been the centerpiece of the Florence Griswold Museum campus ever since.

Old Lyme was ripe for an art colony when prominent landscape painter and art teacher Henry Ward Ranger blundered into town in 1899. The community on Long Island Sound at the mouth of the Connecticut River possessed an abundance of rustic subject matter as well as beautiful, diffuse seaside light. Best yet, it was on the rail line from New York, so painters could easily escape from Manhattan.

Ranger spent the summer hogging the scenery for himself before letting the rest of the art world know that he had found the American equivalent of Barbizon or Giverny. He declared Old Lyme an ideal setting for American artists returning from Europe with newfangled Impressionist ideas about rendering light and painting in the open air. Just as today, great saltwater marshes lay on the south side of town, while rolling open meadows and deep cedar and oak woods bordered the north. The

village featured handsome Georgian and Federal architecture, and farms divided by long stone walls lined the outlying winding roads. Moonlight and sunlight seemed to shimmer over the landscape. Across the winter of 1899–1900, Ranger recruited fellow New York painters to join him in Old Lyme, where, he said, the landscape was "waiting to be painted."

Like a pied piper, he led them to the Griswold House, where he had spent the summer of 1899. The proprietress, Florence Griswold, had responded to reduced circumstances in the late 1890s by taking in boarders. She was soon the landlady of choice for the exuberant painters who summered in Old Lyme.

Thousands of canvases were completed here over the years, but part of what put the house on the map was that the artist boarders often painted on the doors and on the mahogany panels set into the walls. A committee of artists chose who would paint a panel—and who would not. Being chosen to paint one was considered a mark of status in the Old Lyme art circle. It was also, no doubt, crushing to some aspirants to be passed over. Judging by the panels that remain, it helped to have a sense of humor.

As more artists came to stay, new panels were mounted in the dining room, which today chronicles changing styles in American painting early in the 20th century. (There are 41 painted panels in all.) Among the most striking are those painted by Willard Metcalf, who seemed to return each summer with the regularity of a migrant warbler, and Childe Hassam, who seemed to show up at every place along the Connecticut coast where the light suited his taste.

The passage of time and the shifting tastes of art criticism have singled out Hassam as the most gifted of the group. His use of bright and broken colors to render the shifting and elusive character of light came to define the style of the Old Lyme art colony. A group that started by emulating Ranger's solemn and moody scenery concluded by striving to match Hassam's brilliant colors and muscular brushwork.

Self-guided tours of the house are the highlight of the museum complex. The first floor has been furnished to reflect how it looked around 1910, when artists vied to stay with Miss Florence. The broad center hall functions as a de facto art gallery, with modest-sized framed paintings hanging on the wall and a comely portrait of Miss Florence hanging by the front door. Griswold's bedroom and a guest bedroom are off the hall, and the front of the house is dominated by a parlor where the boarders would gather for card games, heated discussions—or even to listen to Griswold play her harp. Also on the first floor is the dining room with its walls covered by painted panels. The second-floor galleries are filled with photographs, paintings, and sketches that chronicle the significance of the Old Lyme art colony in American art. One atmospheric room is also set up as a combination bedroom-studio.

The museum's civilized grounds cover 11 acres between the banks of the Lieutenant River and the historic gardens that Florence Griswold herself began. From late spring until frost, the flower gardens are a painterly riot of colors and textures, and there's usually someone pitching an easel nearby to paint the blooms.

The museum added a large gallery building, the Robert and Nancy Krible Gallery, in 2002 to exhibit some of its rich holdings of Connecticut art. The previous year, the museum acquired the corporate collection of the Hartford Steam Boiler Inspection and Insurance Company. All the works—more than 150 fifty oil paintings, 31 works on paper, and 2 sculptures—are related to Connecticut by either artist or subject.

Monte Cristo Cottage, New London
325 Pequot Avenue, New London; 860-443-5378; theoneill.org; open limited hours mid-June through mid-August; admission charged

With characteristic self-dramatizing, playwright Eugene O'Neill (1888–1953) railed against the pointless symmetry of his birth in New York and his death in Boston. Between tubercular coughs on his deathbed, he was reported to have cursed, "I knew it. I knew it. Born in a hotel room—and goddamn it—died in a hotel room." But O'Neill's world between the opening and closing curtains was a stage, and he always played his part to the hilt.

It's not an exaggeration to say that he studied for the part during the summers of his boyhood. After a winter on the road touring with Eugene's father, the actor James O'Neill, the family would settle for the summer in this modest gray clapboard cottage perched on a hill overlooking the New London waterfront. The elder O'Neill bought the circa-1840 house in 1884 and spent parts of 16 years enlarging and renovating it until, finally, in 1900 the O'Neills moved in. It was the closest thing to a permanent home that the playwright-in-the-making would know until his adult years.

Like the father figure, James Tyrone, in *Long Day's Journey into Night*, James O'Neill had been acclaimed in his youth for his classical and Shakespearean roles. Also like Tyrone, the elder O'Neill hitched his career to a lucrative melodrama that he toured around the country. His role was Edmond Dantes in *The Count of Monte Cristo*, and the family's bread-and-butter dramatic vehicle supplied the name for the house. The cottage was supposed to be the family's respite from the long months on the road. From the evidence of Eugene's plays, it's not clear whether it represented an escape or a torturously claustrophobic form of summer confinement.

Although Eugene O'Neill never lived at Monte Cristo Cottage as an adult, the home and the troubled family life that played out in its small rooms colored the rest of his life and work. In fact, it was both the setting and inspiration for the coming-of-age comedy *Ah, Wilderness!* and for his brooding masterpiece *Long Day's Journey Into Night*, which was not published or performed until after his death.

One room of the house has been converted into a display area for family photographs along with playbills and publicity shots of various productions of *Long Day's Journey Into Night*. (The Scandinavians seem to have a special affinity for the dark melancholy of the play.) But visitors hardly need to study the stills because the house itself may be the best place to appreciate the playwright's most thinly veiled autobiographical work. The Eugene O'Neill Theater Center opened the cottage as a museum to the Nobel and Pulitzer Prize–winning playwright in 1982, and it has been furnished according to O'Neill's own set directions and sketches for the play.

With its upright piano and Victorian furniture, the front parlor has the stiff formality of a room that saw little use. More striking is the back sunroom with wood-paneled walls and ceiling that guides often call the "Long Day's Journey Room." The family spent most of their time in the sunroom, and it was O'Neill's choice as the set for *Long Day's Journey Into Night*. Large windows face east, giving the room a lot of light in the morning, but casting it into deep shadows in the afternoon. True to O'Neill's stage directions, it is comfortably furnished with wicker couch and chair, a glass-front bookcase with well-worn volumes, a rug with "inoffensive" design, and a round table with a green-shaded reading lamp and four chairs pulled up around it. It's almost impossible not to expect actors to enter at any minute and launch into the opening scene.

It requires more imagination to picture what family life would have been like in the upstairs bedrooms. The master bedroom is filled with dark wooden furniture in a combination of the heavy Empire style and more rustic spindled Victorian. Ella O'Neill would sneak off to the small locked room next to the master bedroom to inject herself with the morphine she had become addicted to after Eugene's birth. It gave him one more thing about which to feel guilty and adds to the dark fatalism of the autobiographical play.

Eugene's own room is furnished simply. His desk from Provincetown, where he enjoyed some of his first recognition as a playwright, sits below the front window. The green desk chair was a gift from his third wife, Carlotta Monterey. Although the neighborhood has been built up since the O'Neills' time, the window still affords a lovely view across the lawn to moored boats. Overlooking its history, any real estate agent would list it as a "cheery cottage with harbor views."

USS *Nautilus*, Groton
Historic Ship *Nautilus* and the Submarine Force Museum
1 Crystal Lake Road, Groton; 800-343-0079 or 860-694-3174;
ussnautilus.org; open year-round; free admission

The US Navy may have worked out the kinks of mechanical designs for modern submarines with the *Albacore* (see p. 179), but the nuclear power plant and the resulting design changes to a sub's interior were pioneered at the Electric Boat shipyard and the New London Naval Submarine Base on the Thames River. The USS *Nautilus* (SSN-571) was the world's first operational nuclear-powered submarine, and in her short years of service (1954-80), she racked up many firsts. For all her accomplishments, she also revealed a number of design shortcomings that led to improvements in subsequent generations of nuclear-powered subs. Today she berths in the river alongside the Submarine Force Museum and receives approximately 250,000 visitors each year. Touring the vessel caps off the museum's journey through the saga of submarine warfare.

Appropriately, the museum begins its history of submarines with the 1776 invention of the *American Turtle* by David Bushnell of Saybrook, who created the stealthy undersea vessel to place gunpowder charges against the hulls of British warships. (There's a full-scale model at the Connecticut River Museum in Essex.) Hardly a submarine by modern standards, Bushnell's creation could have as easily been called the American Diving Barrel. It was constructed of oak staves over a rib structure, with a rudder off the back and a hand-cranked propeller on the front. On top, Bushnell mounted a screw augur so the operator could drill a hole in the target vessel's hull to attach the bomb. The museum's re-creation shows a very stressed-looking mannequin crammed into a cutaway model.

The majority of the historic exhibits focus on the underwater boats of World War II and the role of the Silent Service and the Invisible Men during the armaments buildup of the Cold War. Even to visitors old enough to remember the days of duck-and-cover, the extensive exhibits on US-Soviet military posturing seem like period pieces. But the timeline tracing the development of nuclear-powered subs under Admiral Hyman Rickover captures the era's sense of urgency.

The keel for the *Nautilus* was laid in Groton in 1952, and Mamie Eisenhower christened the 319-foot sub in January 1954. Her nuclear power plant allowed *Nautilus* to remain submerged far longer than diesel-electric submarines, and she immediately broke records for longest submersion and longest transits without surfacing. On August 3, 1958, the *Nautilus* became the first vessel ever to reach the North Pole, swiftly cruising over the pole beneath the ice. Two years later, the *Triton*, another Electric Boat vessel, completed the first submerged circumnavigation of the globe, taking 84 days to travel 41,519 nautical miles.

Short videos next to instrument panels give something of the feel of navigating and maneuvering the vessels and firing their weapons. In one darkened alcove, small fry can handle controls for diving and surfacing—and firing missiles. In what almost seems like a clip from *Dr. Strangelove*, a video loop shows a missile bursting from beneath the waves to disappear into the sky, bound for an unseen distant target. Preschoolers jabbing at the buttons invariably shriek with glee at each launch.

Encapsulated in a behemoth metal tube sliding through the inky depths, the submariner learns to listen. A touch-screen display in a side room dominated by decommissioned torpedoes provides landlubbers with an aural snapshot of the underwater world. At a finger tap, "Sounds of the Sea" produces the rumble of an undersea earthquake, the drone of overhead aircraft, the high-pitched twitter of beluga whales (aptly nick-named "canaries of the sea"), the raucous squawking of orcas, and of course the haunting symphonic songs of humpback whales. You can almost hear that music resonate on the metal hull.

The self-guided tour of the *Nautilus* brings home both the ingenuity of space management and the claustrophobic sacrifices of submariners. It becomes immediately clear that backpacks are prohibited not just for security reasons, but for safety and comfort. Films like *The Hunt for Red October* might suggest that submarines are relatively roomy, but this first-generation nuclear sub is as tight as the World War II diesel vessels that preceded her. As families clamber through the sub, the grammar school kids seem best suited for the scale of the rooms and the narrow apertures between compartments.

The tour includes crew quarters, the navigation room, and the pilot controls, but no visit to the engine room or the reactor (long since removed). Since the entryway is in the bow, the first stop is the torpedo tubes, literally feet from fold-down bunks for the crew. (It's hard to say whether the torpedoes or the sailors slid more tightly into their beds.) The walk-through is paced by the recorded tour, with a new narration beginning as you climb through the narrow hatches between sections or go up and down steep stairs. The spaces are so tight that most landlubbers don't linger. Mannequins are scattered throughout to make the vessel seem inhabited, and even they look cramped. The sub would go to sea for months at a time, but most visitors find 10 minutes quite long enough.

Landmark Vessels of Mystic Seaport, Mystic
75 Germanville Avenue, Mystic; 888-973-2767; mysticseaport.org; open year-round; admission charged

Calling itself "the Museum of America and the Sea," Mystic Seaport brings together historic ships and boats and more than 60 original historic buildings to re-create the touch and feel of a 19th century New England seafaring village. The pioneer living history museum employs a number of craftsmen to demonstrate the skills necessary to sustain a maritime community and is widely considered the largest maritime museum in the world. Few villages ever boasted the variety of vessels at Mystic Seaport, which reflects all kinds of maritime activity along the New England coast. Established in 1929 as the Marine Historical Association, the museum covers the waterfront (so to speak) with 15 vessels, 4 of which are National Historic Landmarks.

Charles W. Morgan

When the *Charles W. Morgan* encountered whales on Stellwagen Bank east of Cape Cod in the summer of 2014, it wasn't the first time the broad-beamed caravel had sailed among cetaceans. This time, however, she came without harpoons. Built by Jethro and Zachariah Hillman's New Bedford shipyard, the *Morgan* is the last surviving wooden whale ship of about 2,700 registered American whaling vessels and the oldest commercial ship still afloat. She made 37 voyages lasting from nine months to more than three years before her last crew came ashore in 1921. After an initial restoration, she was displayed in South Dartmouth, Massachusetts, at Whaling Enshrined (an organization created to save the ship) before being towed to Mystic in 1941 to become the anchor exhibit for Mystic Seaport.

Named for her original owner, Charles Waln Morgan, the *Morgan* was launched in July 1841, outfitted at Rotch's Wharf in New Bedford for the next two months, and embarked on her first voyage in September. She stopped in the Azores to take on supplies, then rounded Cape Horn and sailed north via the Galapagos Islands to Alaskan waters. In mid-December, the ship took its first whale on the Kodiak Grounds. She shuttled back and forth between Alaska, Peru, and the Galapagos before heading home to New Bedford. The *Morgan* made home port on January 2, 1845, after killing and processing 59 whales in her trypots. In that first voyage, she brought home 1,600 barrels of sperm whale oil (the most prized for candles), 800 barrels of right whale oil, and 5 tons of bone and baleen. The voyage of three years and three months brought back a cargo that sold for more than $53,000—roughly $1.7 million today.

Over her working lifetime, more than 1,000 whalers of various nationalities served aboard the *Charles W. Morgan*—usually 30 to 35 at a time. Although she was more than 106 feet long and 27 feet wide, with a depth of 13.5 feet, the quarters for the crew were very small, as the trypots and below-decks barrel storage took up most of the vessel. During her career, she brought back 54,483 barrels of whale oil and 152,934 pounds of whalebone and baleen.

For the first three decades the *Morgan* spent at Mystic Seaport, she was embedded in sand to avoid sinking, but was finally restored to seaworthy condition in 1968. An even more thorough $5 million restoration between 2008 and 2013 enabled the *Charles W. Morgan* to undertake her first voyage under sail in more than 90 years in 2014.

From shore, the three-masted ship with her square rigging looks like a massive vessel, but once you file aboard and start dodging the other visitors, it quickly becomes apparent how little space is available on deck. Below decks only gets worse, as the head room is very limited. This was hardly a cruise ship. Most of the crew spent their time on deck, weather permitting, fighting boredom until the terrifying moment came to lower a whale boat into the water and give chase.

L.A. Dunton

If the *Morgan* was primarily a hunting vessel, the *L.A. Dunton* was a fishing vessel, pure and simple. One of the last of the Gloucesterman fishing schooners, she was built in 1921 by the Arthur D. Story Shipyard in Essex, Massachusetts, and was initially powered entirely by sail. (An auxiliary engine was installed in 1923.) The 123-foot vessel was named for Louis A. Dunton, a sailmaker who was part of the consortium that financed her construction. The two-masted wooden-hulled schooner fished New England waters for haddock and halibut until she was sold in 1934 into the Grand Banks fishery off the coast of Newfoundland. The new owner

installed a wheelhouse and altered the rig to sail her as a ketch. The *L.A. Dunton* continued to fish the Grand Banks into the 1950s.

After the *Dunton* was acquired by Mystic Seaport in 1963, the museum removed her engine and restored her rig and stern to their original specifications. Subsequent restorations have brought her back to her appearance in the 1920s. Because the vessel served as a coastal cargo vessel briefly after leaving the fishing trade, some of her interior joinery was altered. Nonetheless, she now represents the kind of barebones vessel that dominated the cod fishery for generations. The large midships compartment in her spacious hold was reserved for the catch, while up to 15 crew could bunk in the forward hold and 5 next to the captain's cabin in the aft hold.

Sabino

The oldest wooden-hulled coal-fired steamboat still afloat, the *Sabino* was built in the W. Irving Adams shipyard in East Boothbay, Maine, in 1908 as a river ferry. She was christened *Tourist* at launch and plied the Damariscotta River. Sunk in an accident in 1918, she was salvaged and sold to a company that gave the rebuilt vessel its current name, *Sabino*, after a Wabenaki sagamore. Between 1921 and 1927, she saw service on the Kennebec River. In her most extended service, she sailed as a ferry between Portland, Maine, and the islands of Casco Bay from 1928 into the late 1950s.

The 57-foot vessel has a truly romantic quality and is surprisingly roomy for a steamboat, thanks in part to being driven by a screw propeller that doesn't require the deck apparatus of a side wheel. In the 1970s, the repaired *Sabino* began offering leisure cruises on the Merrimack River in Massachusetts between Salisbury Beach and Newburyport in one direction and between Newburyport and Merrimack in the other. She operated daytime and evening jazz cruises until 1974, when she was leased to Mystic Seaport to determine her appeal for museum visitors. Although the ocean transit nearly proved the boat's undoing, since she was not built for heavy seas, she was repaired on arrival and served for many years as a popular attraction, with 30-minute and 90-minute cruises offered between Memorial Day and Columbus Day.

In December 2014, she was moved into Mystic Seaport's Henry B. duPont Preservation Shipyard for a complete overhaul. Although the hull and superstructure were fully restored, the steam boiler proved more of a problem. No steamboat boiler manufacturers remain in business, and a boiler maker who can reconstruct the unusal boiler has yet to be found. The boiler was not original, having been replaced in 1941. Repairs, however, proved sufficient to return the *Sabino* to service in the summer of 2017.

The 75-horsepower, two-cylinder steam engine did turn out to be in fine condition. It is original to the vessel and was constructed in 1908 in Noank, very near Mystic Seaport.

Emma C. Berry

One of the oldest surviving commercial fishing vessels in the US, the *Emma C. Berry* was constructed six miles downriver from Mystic Seaport at R. & J. Palmer shipyard in Noank. The classic design for small-crew fishing of in-shore waters, she was built as a sloop smack in 1866 for Captain John Henry Berry, who named her for his daughter.

Noank shipyards were famous all up and down the Atlantic seaboard for building this type of vessel, which carried a live well at midships to circulate sea water and keep the catch alive until it could be landed. At an overall length of 46 feet (including the fixed bowsprit), *Emma C. Berry* initially served as a mackerel seiner, carrying a sloop rig with two headsails and a gaff sail for light weather. She served many masters over the years and was rerigged as a schooner in the late 1880s. In 1916, a gasoline engine was installed. At the end of her fishing career, she served mainly as a lobster carrier, ferrying the catch to port in her well. She was abandoned on the mud flats of Beals Island, Maine, around 1924 but was raised from the mud and made watertight to serve a few years as a coastal freighter.

The *Emma C. Berry* got a reprieve from her ignominious decline in 1931 when wooden boat enthusiast F. Slade Dale purchased the boat and restored her to sailing condition. Dale carried out an extensive restoration in 1963 and kept the

vessel until 1969, when he donated it to Mystic Seaport. The museum then dug into the shipyard records and restored the vessel's deck, horn timbers, spar ironwork, and sloop rigging to bring her back to 1866 form as a Noank sloop smack, even painting her according to the fashion of the times. Although seaworthy, she functions primarily as a floating exhibit at the wharf by the oyster house at Mystic Seaport.

Prudence Crandall Museum, Canterbury
1 South Canterbury Road, Canterbury; 860-546-7800; ct.gov/cct; open early May through October; admission charged

Connecticut made a strong start on public education. In 1700, it was the first colony to mandate the instruction of all its children, requiring each community of 70 families or more to hire a full-time teacher. By the early years of the Republic, education in Connecticut was a fertile mix of public grammar schools and private academies for those who sought more than a rudimentary mastery of reading, writing, and ciphering.

The path to enlightenment, however, was not always smooth. Sometimes it took enormous resolve and personal courage to advance the idea of universal education. Now recognized as Connecticut's official state heroine, Prudence Crandall (1803–90) embodied that faith and commitment—remaining steadfast in her mission in the face of personal and legal adversity.

Born to Quaker parents in Rhode Island, she was educated at the Friends Boarding School in Providence after her father moved the family to the small town of Canterbury in eastern Connecticut. Crandall was already an experienced teacher when she set up the Canterbury Female Seminary in 1831 in a handsome "Canterbury type" Federal house on the town green, now preserved as the Prudence Crandall Museum.

Her intention was to educate the daughters of the local country squires, allowing them to absorb some of the intellectual niceties without having to travel too far from home. All was well—until the fall of 1832, when she admitted 19-year-old Sarah Harris as a day student. Daughter of a local African American farmer, Harris had already attended integrated district schools, studying side by side with some of the girls who had become Crandall's pupils.

Her application letter to Crandall's school resonates with poignancy nearly two centuries later. "Miss Crandall, I want to get a little more learning, if possible, enough to teach colored children and if you will admit me to your school, I shall forever be under the greatest obligation to you," Harris wrote. "If you think it will be the means of injuring you, I will not insist on the favor."

Had all gone smoothly, there would be no Prudence Crandall Museum and she might be just another forgotten 19th century teacher. But Crandall admitted the young woman and quickly learned that Canterbury was an intolerant place. The parents of her other students withdrew their daughters rather than have them learn next to a woman of color.

Crandall traveled to Boston to meet with leading abolitionist William Lloyd Garrison, who assisted with contacts throughout the free African American communities of the Northeast to help her recruit new boarding students. She would resist the bigots by operating a school for "young ladies and little misses of color." Her first out-of-state student arrived from Providence in April 1833, and she soon had enrolled students from as far away as Boston, New York, and Philadelphia.

The Canterbury folk threatened Crandall with fines and, on at least one occasion, one of her students was threatened with a whipping. The student's response was that she would take the whipping as long as she could get an education. Both sides dug in their heels.

At that time, Connecticut was the largest slave-holding state in the North and responded by passing the "Black Law." It forbade people of color entering Connecticut from another state for an education without the express consent of the town. Crandall was arrested and spent a night in the county jail in Brooklyn. She was released the next day and continued to instruct 17 students.

In August 1833, a corner of the school building was set on fire, but the students were able to extinguish the flames before any major damage was done. Crandall faced a series of three court trials. She was initially convicted, but the conviction was overturned and the case against her was dismissed in July 1834. A woman and a group of 20 or so young women of color had prevailed over hatred. But victory was short. On September 9, 1834, a mob attacked the school, broke the windows, and threatened all within. The next day, Crandall closed the school rather than subject her charges to danger.

The "Black Law" was eventually repealed in 1838, and Connecticut finally outlawed slavery in 1848. For her own part, Crandall married a Baptist preacher later in 1834 and moved with him several times until his death in Illinois in 1874. She then reverted to her birth name and moved with one of her brothers to Elk Falls, Kansas. She is celebrated there as a forerunner in the battle for civil rights in public education that ultimately led to the landmark *Brown v. Board of Education* decision by the US Supreme Court.

The house where Crandall taught school remained in surprisingly original condition over the years, and while school-specific artifacts of the 1832–34 period are few, the architecture and scholarly displays do a good job of conjuring the hopes and fears of the day. Meticulous research has reconstructed the lives of many of the students and shows them as highly motivated women of an emerging African American middle class.

Roseland Cottage, Woodstock
556 Route 169, Woodstock; 860-928-4074; historicnewengland .org; open for guided tours June through mid-October; admission charged

There was never any question that Henry and Lucy Bowen—and their descendants—were in the pink. In fact, their summer home in Woodstock, modestly called Roseland Cottage, has been painted 13 different shades of pink since it was completed in 1846. The Gothic Revival structure sits across the street from the town common. With sharply peaked gables capped by ornamental pinnacles, pronounced vertical clapboards, ornamented chimney pots, and general gingerbread-house demeanor, it is pretty much impossible to miss. Operated as a museum by Historic New England, Roseland Cottage speaks volumes about Yankee aspirations in

Victorian-era America as well as the confluence of entrepreneurial business with social and moral reform movements.

Henry Chandler Bowen (1813–96) was born and raised in rural Woodstock but moved to New York at age 20 to seek his fortune. He clerked for six years for Arthur and Lewis Tappan silk merchants before he and a partner set up their own silk wholesaling business on Broadway in Manhattan. In 1844, he married Lucy Tappan, daughter of his former boss, Lewis Tappan. They had their first child within a year and ultimately had seven boys and three girls.

Once they were well established in New York, the Bowens decided they wanted a summer retreat from the heat and noise of the city. Ever the prodigal son, Henry chose to return to Woodstock. Enamored of the theories of Andrew Jackson Downing (a popular writer who championed Gothic Revival buildings in picturesque pastoral landscapes), they commissioned English-born architect Joseph C. Wells to design a fashionable architectural confection.

Roseland is hardly Downton Abbey. But the 6,000-square-foot, five-bedroom "cottage" with soaring ceilings is quite grand for a country town like Woodstock and established Bowen as the local country squire. The interiors were just as over-the-top as the blushing pink exterior. Stained glass windows with Gothic arches and Gothic-inspired furniture provided multiple allusions to chivalry and Christian religious traditions as passed down in the English style. The tone of the ground floor, in fact, is as much liturgical as domestic.

That was fitting for Bowen, a stern Congregationalist who frowned on alcohol, tobacco, and any form of card games. He was also an ardent foe of slavery, citing the bravery of Prudence Crandall in neighboring Canterbury (see p. 32) as igniting the abolitionist flame in his breast as a young man. Bowen's silk business went bankrupt in 1859 in part because southern buyers refused to patronize a company led by such an outspoken foe of slavery. He was one of a trio of high-minded businessmen who underwrote the publication of the antislavery magazine *The Independent*. In fact, he devoted the last quarter century of his life to editing the progressive magazine that later advocated for women's suffrage, temperance, and peaceful international relations.

Although Bowen never ran for office, he was very active in politics—initially as a Whig and then as a prominent supporter of the Republican Party. Roseland Cottage made the perfect venue to entertain friends and political connections, and his guests included several US presidents. He had plenty of space to entertain. The Gothic Revival carriage barn, also built in 1846, even had a bowling alley, and the vast lawns provided space for outdoor entertainment. For more intimate walking and talking, the Bowens had planted a boxwood parterre garden of nearly 3,000 square feet. It has been restored to its original 1850 design with 21 flowerbeds planted with colorful annuals.

Sadly, Lucy Bowen died in 1863 from complications after giving birth to their tenth child, who also died as an infant. In 1865, Henry married Ellen Holt of nearby Pomfret, who became mother to the brood of nine surviving children and bore a

son in 1868. With the family getting ever larger, Bowen expanded Roseland and some of the outbuildings in the 1870s and 1880s, adding the distinctive Lincrusta wall coverings in the public areas of the ground floor. The deeply embossed combination of sawdust and linseed oil became a hallmark decoration of Gothic Revival architecture, and Roseland Cottage has some of the best preserved and most extensive applications of the product in the world.

There's a Victorian sumptuousness to the decoration of the house, with its richly colored and heavily patterned carpets and reflective wall and ceiling coverings. Much of the

furniture is original and was in continuous use by family members until the last grandchild living there died in 1968.

After the expansion, Henry and Ellen Bowen used the summer home even more extensively for entertaining. (Henry bought another nearby estate to handle the overflow of grown children and grandchildren.) The Bowens' grand Fourth of July parties, which took place yearly from 1870 to 1895, were famous. The blockbuster affairs featured groaning tables of food, festive music, and stemwinder patriotic orations. Among the politicians to attend were presidential candidates John C. Fremont, James G. Blaine, and William McKinley, and US presidents Benjamin Harrison, Rutherford B. Hayes, and Ulysses S. Grant. History does not record Grant's reaction to the house rules banning whiskey and cigars.

Kingscote, Newport, p. 58

Flying Horse Carousel, Watch Hill
151 Bay Street, Watch Hill; 401-348-6007; open June through Labor Day; admission charged

A traveling carnival's loss proved to be Watch Hill's everlasting gain. The oldest known example of a carousel where the horses are suspended from chains and struts and swing outward by centrifugal force, the Flying Horse Carousel was built sometime between 1867 and 1876 by C. W. Dare (later the Charles W. Dare Company) of New York. In 1879, a carnival left it behind at Watch Hill, where it has been a fixture of Westerly's seaside resort community ever since.

Located in a wooden pavilion at the end of Bay Street at the entrance to the village beach and the Napatree Point peninsula, the Flying Horse Carousel is one of the most delicate of the surviving historic carousels. Its two ranks of horses are suspended from chains attached to their hindquarters and poles affixed to the pommels on their saddles. Restorers have speculated that the horses were originally suspended by two chains but had been modified because poles gave the horses more stability. Nevertheless, they still seem to "fly" as they swing outward after a revolution or two. The horses come in two sizes and the riders come in one: small. To avoid wear and tear on the mechanism, which is less robust than a platform carousel, riders must be 12 years old or younger, under 5 feet tall, and preferably under 100 pounds. (For a contemporaneous example of a C.W. Dare platform carousel, see the Flying Horses Carousel in Oak Bluffs, p. 156.)

In its early years, the Watch Hill carousel was literally horse-powered by a calico horse in harness that spent its summers walking in circles around the perimeter. Water power was installed in 1897, and the entire mechanism was electrified in 1914. A hand-cranked organ originally provided the music, but by the end of the 19th century, it was replaced by a mechanical band organ programmed from paper rolls. Since 1975, the music has been recorded, with speakers hidden inside the band organ housing.

Even as other carousel builders such as Charles I. D. Looff (see p. 53) and the Philadelphia Toboggan Company created increasingly intricate and ornate carousel figures, the

Dare company's horses remained simply carved and naively painted. The bodies were created from a single block of wood while the legs were carved separately and attached. Each horse has a simple leather saddle and bridle, and the manes and tails are authentic horsehair. All the leather and horsehair pieces have been repeatedly replaced over the years, and the horses are repainted as needed. The agate eyes, however, are original. All the horses originally had metal stirrups, but they were removed during a 1975 restoration to help preserve the painting on the figures. Children are now belted onto their steeds.

In addition to the 20 horses, the carousel started life with three fixed double-seat chariots for the very young or for children intimidated by the outward swing of the horses on chains. When the hurricane of 1938 hit the New England coast, the barrier beach of Watch Hill was devastated, and the carousel was flung into pieces. But all the horses survived intact and were unearthed from the sand dunes where they were buried by the force of the storm. But the chariots were not restored to the carousel for fear that the supporting sweeps had been too damaged in the storm.

Restored several times over the decades, the carousel has been a fixture in the lives of many generations. A mechanism that dispenses metal rings is lowered when the carousel is spinning. Most rings are painted iron, but one is made of brass, and the child who grabs the brass ring wins a free ride.

The carousel even inspired a book. French children's author Paul Jacques Bonzon was so smitten by its charm that he wrote a story, "Le Petit Cheval du Bois," in 1960. Translated into English, the story was published in 1976 as an illustrated book, *The Runaway Flying Horse*.

Block Island South East Light, New Shoreham
Mohegan Trail, off Spring Street, New Shoreham, Block Island;
401-466-5009; newenglandlighthouses.net/block-island-southeast
.html; open for tours in summer; admission charged

New England lighthouses are justly celebrated as archetypes of the maritime beacon. Most are white columns (with or without barber pole stripes) with rotating lights in their multiwindowed caps. But Block Island's South East Light was built to be different, and it is one of the few lighthouses on the New England coast designated a National Historic Landmark.

Erected in 1874 after a number of coasting vessels were lost off Block Island in heavy weather, South East Light and its keeper's house were designed to be showpieces for the US Lighthouse Service. Constructed solidly of brick on granite foundations in the Victorian Gothic style, they are standing proof that the architecture of sharp peaks and pyramidal forms is especially suited to withstand the fiercest weather. Although the legendary hurricane of September 1938 destroyed a barn and the oil storehouse on the site, it did little more to the lighthouse and keeper's house than smash the windows, send some shingles flying, and shut down the electricity. The keeper had to turn the lens by hand for several days. The outhouse was also a victim of the storm, so the keeper's house finally got indoor plumbing as part of the repairs.

First lighted on February 1, 1875, the lighthouse was placed on the Mohegan Bluffs of Block Island, which sits in the middle of major sea lanes about 12 miles south-southeast off the coast of Rhode Island. The bluffs stand roughly 160 feet above the ocean, so the five-story lighthouse (67 feet high) projects far out to sea. The octagonal tower tapers as it rises to the cast-iron parapet and open gallery around the 16-sided lantern chamber. Originally, the pyramidal roof was cast iron, but was replaced in 1994 by a 16-sided copper roof with a ball ventilator inside and a lightning rod on the top.

South East Light originally showed a fixed white light magnified by a first-order Fresnel lens. It was easily mistaken for the light on another ship. The ship pilots' association petitioned the Coast Guard to make it more distinctive, so in 1929 the light was changed to blinking green. The actual light has varied a lot over the years. At first it was a four-wick system that burned lard. It was converted to kerosene in the

1880s and was finally electrified when the light became green. To accommodate the rotation necessary for a blinking light, the lantern house was modified in 1929 so a new complex first-order Fresnel lens could float on a bath of liquid mercury and turn without friction. In 1990, the Coast Guard deactivated the light and transferred its duties as a navigational aid to a much less sexy nearby steel tower.

At the time that the light was deactivated, it was already threatened by the erosion of the Mohegan Bluffs. Built more than 300 feet inland, it was just 55 feet from the cliff edge. With the Army Corps of Engineers supervising, Expert House Movers and International Chimney Corporation jacked up the combined 40-million-pound structure and foundation and pushed it all back 360 feet along metal tracks on rolling beams. Before the 1993 move, the Coast Guard removed the original lens and the environmentally hazardous mercury bath. (International Chimney has since assisted the similar relocations of Highland and Nauset Lights on Cape Cod and Sankaty Light on Nantucket.)

Ownership of the lighthouse complex was transferred in 1990 to the nonprofit Block Island Southeast Lighthouse Foundation, which now maintains the structure. Following the move, the Coast Guard installed a first-order Fresnel lens taken from the decommissioned Cape Lookout Light in North Carolina. South East Light was relighted in August 1994 and continues to wink its green beam through the night haze, warning ships to stay off the rocks and steer a course for the canyons south of Long Island.

The base of the lighthouse tower now contains a small museum and gift shop. The tower is open for tours in the summer.

Gilbert Stuart Birthplace, Saunderstown
815 Gilbert Stuart Road, Saunderstown; 401-294-3001; gilbertstuartmuseum.org; open for guided tours May through September (limited hours through mid-October); admission charged

If ever an Early American artist were up to snuff, it would be Gilbert Stuart, born in 1755 in a room above a snuff mill in the woods of Saunderstown. His Scottish immigrant father built the mill and the house above it in 1750. The mill ground dried and cured tobacco leaves into powdery snuff, a common way of using tobacco in the late 18th century. The elder Stuart's mill was the first of its kind in the American colonies, as the snuff industry was centered in England and the Low Countries. Despite greater proximity to raw materials, the snuff mill failed, and the Stuart family moved to Newport when Gilbert was 6 years old. The birthplace has been preserved as a house and mill museum that also evokes the power of Stuart's art to provide the icons of a new country.

Stuart traveled far from his modest beginnings. While in Newport, he began to develop his artistic skills, creating his first painting, *Dr. Hunter's Dogs*, at age 14. One of his father's friends, Scottish painter Cosmo Alexander, took on Stuart as a student, and they traveled together, painting all the while, in South Carolina and Scotland. When Alexander died suddenly, Stuart used all his resources to get back to Newport with only the clothes on his back. Yet a few years later, at age 20, Stuart

moved to London and entered the circle of American expatriot painter Benjamin West, whose specialty was landscape, which "he painted by the yard," as Stuart wryly observed. The younger painter focused on portraiture and was soon recognized by the Royal Academy.

Still, making a living as an artist was difficult, and Stuart and his wife fled to Ireland in 1787 ahead of debt collectors. With the dust settled on the American Revolution, Stuart returned to the United States in 1793, living first in New York, then 10 years in Philadelphia, where he painted many of his portraits of George Washington. In 1805, he moved to Boston, where he died in 1828, leaving an estate of less than $400. He was buried on Boston Common.

His birthplace museum occupies an unusually scenic spot in the Rhode Island woods, and the property looks much as it did when Stuart was a lad, with a mill pond impoundment, the gambrel-roofed barn-red clapboard building that holds both living quarters and snuff mill, and, across the mill stream that is the source of the Narrow River, a working grist mill that the family built shortly before they moved away. Tours include demonstrations of how both mills operated. Much of the building is shown as a re-creation of colonial life, but the restored wooden mill wheel on the side of the house is certainly unusual for its time.

The house was built like an inn with eight bedrooms in all and large living and cooking areas. The room where Stuart was born is shown as a birthing room, complete with a narrow bed supported by ropes on its frame, and a reproduction of *Dr. Hunter's Dogs* hanging on the wall. Many other Stuart reproductions hang in the house, which is filled with Colonial-era furniture. None of the pieces is definitively original to the house, but one of the upstairs beds may be from the Stuart family. The portraits of 18th and 19th century ladies and gentlemen seem very much at home in the surroundings.

Stuart painted more than a thousand portraits in his career. Many were society commissions, but the first six presidents also sat for him, as did First Ladies Martha Washington, Abigail Adams, Dolly Madison, and Louisa Adams. Most Americans carry reproductions of his most famous painting, the bust of Washington on the one-dollar bill. Stuart never finished the original oil, which he kept as his model from which to paint copies after Washington's death. (He is said to have called it his hundred dollar bill, which is the price he charged per copy.) It is now owned jointly by the Museum of Fine Arts, Boston, and the National Portrait Gallery in Washington, D.C.

The museum tour also includes a demonstration of the sluice gate for the mill-way, explanation of the fish ladder built to accommodate the spring spawning of river herring, and admission to the modern facility that holds an excellent art gallery. Exhibitions rotate frequently, but sometimes include original paintings by Gilbert Stuart and his daughter Jane (1812–88). Two nature trails pass a pair of historic graveyards, an archaeological dig at the site of an early farm, and a scenic overlook above Carr Pond, the mill impoundment.

Slater Mill, Pawtucket
67 Roosevelt Avenue, Pawtucket; 401-725-8638; slatermill.org; open for guided tours March through November; admission charged

It's no stretch to say that modern America started in Pawtucket, Rhode Island, when Samuel Slater's water-powered machines for spinning cotton fiber into thread unleashed the Industrial Revolution. It's probably also no stretch to say that he helped pioneer industrial espionage. Still known today in the United Kingdom as "Slater the Traitor," he was born in Derbyshire, England, in 1768 and apprenticed in a state-of-the-art spinning factory at the age of 15. By the time he was 21, he had

mastered not only the operation but also the designs of the machines that had put the United Kingdom in the vanguard of textile technology and manufacturing—specifically the Arkwright water frame and the spinning mule.

Attracted by American bounties for textile mechanics, Slater lied about his occupation (British law forbade the emigration of skilled textile workers) and shipped off to New York. By January 1790, he arrived in Pawtucket in the employ of Providence merchant and investor Moses Brown.

Working with Sylvanus Brown on patterns for the mechanical parts, Slater was able to faithfully reproduce the Arkwright machines from memory. By 1793, Slater Mill in Pawtucket, Rhode Island, was a reality and Pawtucket was on its way to becoming New England's first mill town. The pretty, park-like setting of the Slater Mill Historic Site on the bank of the Blackstone River compresses a century of furious industrialization on "America's hardest working river" into a tale told by three buildings.

The guided tour begins at the oldest structure on the site, a gambrel-roofed cottage owned by Sylvanus Brown (no relation to the wealthy Moses Brown). The cottage was built in 1758 and was restored and reset on its present foundation in 1973. Interpretation focuses on how difficult and time-consuming it was for households to make their own cloth before the advent of industrialization. The guide demonstrates how to card wool, spin it on a spinning wheel (the woman of the house would walk 100 miles a year spinning wool on a "walking wheel"), and then how to weave rough cloth on a hand loom (usually a man's job).

The yellow-clapboard Slater Mill looks more like a barn than a factory, but when it was built in 1793, Pawtucket carpenters had never constructed a factory. The first successful cotton spinning mill in America, it continued to produce cotton thread until it finally closed in 1905. In the early years of operation, all the workers were children aged 7 to 14, who were small enough and nimble enough to dodge in and around the exposed working parts to tend the machines.

As the need for workers expanded, the children were joined by women in what came to be called the Rhode Island System. A half hour before dawn each day, the factory bell would ring to alert the workers. If they did not arrive at the factory by the second bell, which rang at dawn, they were fired. America's first strike took place here over the problem of timekeeping, and the company built a clock tower to show the hours.

Apart from the Rhode Island System, Slater Mill's main achievement was technological—building machines that put a tight and consistent twist on the cotton fibers to make strong thread. Initially, these spools went out to hand weavers to finish into cloth, for the great weaving innovations made in Waltham and Lowell (see p. 102) were still decades in the future. (Although they date from much later than the rest of the factory, a few power weaving looms are also shown here.)

The third building on the site is the 1810 stone structure of the Wilkinson Mill. It is dedicated to the technological innovations of Slater's brother-in-law, David Wilkinson, who is considered the father of machine tools in America. Wooden bobbins, metal gears, tools, and replacement parts for the cotton mill were made here.

The mill is powered by a huge gravity wheel, which is turned by the weight of the water that catches in its blades rather than by the speed of the flow. Before bringing a group into the mill, the guide will raise the water gate, which is sealed in mud, to let the river flow onto the mill wheel's blades. It makes a monstrous croaking and creaking as the wheel begins to turn, powered by 4,000 pounds of water catching in its blade to spin the 16,000-pound breastwheel. The energy of the wheel is conveyed through massive gears and leather pulleys to the power tools on the floor above. It seems a bit like a Rube Goldberg scheme, given its complexity, but all that power made it possible to perform precision machine work in metal. Wilkinson invented the screw cutting lathe, and his workers—skilled male master craftsmen and apprentices, as opposed to the women and children at the mill next door—produced the first commercially successful power looms in America.

Wilkinson was a better inventor than businessman, and his company went belly up around 1830, although the site continued as an active machine shop into the 20th century. Most of the tools in the machine shop now actually date from the late 19th century. But thanks to Wilkinson's innovations, Pawtucket became the first major machine building center in the country.

John Brown House, Providence
52 Power Street, Providence; 401-273-5707; rihs.org/museums/ john-brown-house; open year-round; admission charged

John Quincy Adams, who had visited a few nice domiciles in his day, called the home of Providence merchant and statesman John Brown (1736–1803) the "most magnificent and elegant house I have ever seen on this continent."

That was exactly what Brown, a formidable and ultimately controversial figure, intended. He and his brothers, Nicholas, Joseph, and Moses, were major players in creating what would become Brown University and relocating its campus to their family land. John Brown laid the cornerstone of the university's oldest building in 1770 and served as the school's treasurer for 21 years. He was a founder and first president of the Providence Bank and helped stir the pot for the American Revolution by joining other Providence Sons of Liberty in 1772 to board the British customs schooner *Gaspee* and burn her to the waterline.

John Brown made his fortune in real estate development, a partnership in a foundry that built cannons for the Revolution, and in trade. The trade would prove the most controversial, as he followed in the footsteps of his father and uncle by engaging in the Triangle Trade, which included sending ships to enslave Africans and sell them in the Caribbean. A fervent supporter of slavery—in direct opposition to his Quaker younger brother, Moses, an equally fervent abolitionist—John Brown was the first person to be prosecuted under the Slave Trade Act of 1794, and was forced to forfeit his ship, the ironically named *Hope*. Nonetheless, he was elected to Congress in 1798.

In 1786, at the height of his wealth and influence, Brown began building Providence's first mansion. Designed by his brother Joseph, an amateur architect, it was the largest house constructed in Rhode Island up to that time. It took two years to complete the three-story late Georgian manse of brick walls trimmed with brownstone, a hipped roof with balustrade, and a central entry pavilion.

Joseph consulted a number of 18th century British architectural pattern books and pulled out all the stops for the interior embellishments. The house is a showpiece of the period style. The traditional Georgian floor plan begins with a central hallway flanked on each side by two rooms. The staircase,

which rises two flights, features beautifully finished twisted balusters and a curved railing, likely commissioned from Newport cabinetmakers. Two ornate Ionic columns at the front of the hallway support classical sculptural busts. The crown moldings and pediments above each doorway are boldly scaled and lavishly elaborate. The rooms themselves have similar detail with pronounced baseboards and chair rails. There are 12 mantels in the house, of which 11 are original. Several feature carved friezes, and those in the downstairs parlors also have either columns or pilasters.

The house stayed in the family until 1850 and was purchased in 1901 by banker and industrialist Marsden J. Perry, who expanded the back of the house and introduced modern plumbing, central heating, and electricity. John Nicholas Brown (a great-grandson of John Brown's brother Nicholas) purchased the house in 1936. In 1942, the family donated it to the Rhode Island Historical Society. Carefully preserved and restored to Colonial décor, often featuring Brown family pieces, it functions as the Society's headquarters and as a historic house museum.

The informal front parlor is displayed as if a funeral were about to take place, complete with a coffin in front of the marble fireplace and a cover on the mirror. The formal front parlor on the other side of the hall is set up with a tea table and a portrait of George Washington, who is said to have come here for tea.

Many of the rooms reflect Brown family taste. The family had saved some panels of the original wallpapers in the house, and the Rhode Island Historical Society used them to create reproductions of the late Georgian French papers with classical figures, garlands, and swags in repeat patterns. They are light, bright, and rather fanciful—very much in keeping with the Chippendale and Hepplewhite furniture.

The dining room sideboards hold elaborate cut crystal side by side with Chinese export porcelain. John Brown's ship *General Washington,* dispatched from Providence in 1787, was one of the first American ships to engage in trade in Canton.

But one of the most striking rooms in the John Brown House was not part of the original building. A lavishly ornamental Arts and Crafts bathroom with decorative tiles, stained glass, and ceramic wall murals was added by Marsden Perry. The amazing decorative work is almost upstaged by the ingenious shower—a cage of pipes surrounding the bather with tiny water jets.

When John Nicholas Brown purchased the house in 1936, he also made his mark by installing an elaborate mural wallpaper in a downstairs room. "The Inauguration of Washington" was drawn by Nancy Vincent McClelland, one of America's first female interior designers and a noted antiques expert. A group of artists hired through the Works Progress Administration scaled her sketches into full-sized cartoons to create six reproductions. The installation is bright, colorful, and unabashedly patriotic. No doubt the original John Brown would have approved.

The Arcade, Providence
65 Weybosset Street, Providence; 401-454-4568; arcadeprovidence .com; retail shops and most restaurants open Monday to Saturday; free admission

Shopping malls pretty much litter the landscape these days, but Providence had never seen anything like the Westminster Arcade when it was completed in 1828. Stretching between Westminster and Weybosset Streets in the downtown business district, it is often cited as the first enclosed shopping mall in the United States and an exemplar of Greek Revival–style commercial architecture.

Now called simply the Arcade, or the Arcade Providence, it was designed by Rhode Island–based architects Russell Warren (1783–1860) and James Bucklin (1801–90), who left a legacy of fine Greek Revival buildings, including churches and homes, throughout the state. For the Arcade, they drew on the model of the covered markets of European cities to grace Providence with a structure of gravity and dignity. History does not record what the first shops in the Arcade offered, but even picking up a newspaper or a pair of shoelaces must have felt like an event. Both façades of the building resemble Greek temple fronts—with six enormous Ionic columns 3 feet in diameter and 45 feet high. Shoppers would climb a short flight of stairs, walk past the columns, and through a deep portico to enter the building. Once inside, the ground floor and two upper levels ringed with cast-iron railings were

flooded with light from a skylight stretching 32 feet by 188 feet along the length of the building.

At an estimated cost of about $145,000, the Arcade was built to last. The granite was mined from the farm of James Olney in nearby Johnston, and Olney even carved his initials into one of the columns. In addition to the granite, the architects specified other fireproof materials, including concrete, brick, cast iron, and tin for the roof. The Arcade did, in fact, survive fires and hurricanes and was a fixture in downtown Providence well into the 20th century. Residents still have memories of stopping in for lunch on a weekday or making a special trip for Christmas shopping.

But the architects and builders could not protect the structure against changing lifestyles and economic downturns. As people moved to the suburbs, where new malls offered acres of convenient parking, it seemed as if the Arcade might have outlived its usefulness. It was rehabilitated and reopened in the 1980s, only to close again in 2008. Many feared for the fate of the downtown stalwart, and the building was even placed on the Providence Preservation Society's list of 10 most endangered properties. Fortunately, developer Evan Granoff realized that the Arcade could be a trendsetter once again. Following a $7 million, multiyear renovation, it reopened in 2013 as a mixed-use commercial and residential property.

The ground floor has space for about 14 shops and restaurants that eschew the typical mall suspects in favor of places with more quirky, local flavor. But the 48 micro-loft apartments on the second and third floors really made Providence sit up and take notice. Designed for young professionals, recent graduates of the city's several universities, and others seeking a return to urban living, most of the units range between 225 and 300 square feet. Compact and well-designed, they include dishwashers and refrigerators, but no stoves.

The lofts tapped into the "tiny house movement"—a practical and philosophical trend that favors a simplified lifestyle with a lighter impact on the environment. Even before they opened, the micro-lofts had attracted a long waiting list. The designs

were also included in the exhibit "Making Room: New Models for Housing New Yorkers" at the Museum of the City of New York.

In 2014, the Arcade received a National Preservation Award from the National Trust for Historic Preservation, which just goes to show that everything old can be new again.

Crescent Park Looff Carousel, Riverside
700 Bullocks Point Avenue, Riverside; 401-433-2828; open weekends from week after Easter through Columbus Day, more days July and August; admission charged

In the early years of the 20th century, America could boast an estimated 4,000 hand-carved carousels, though only a small percentage of these avatars of a simpler age have survived. In New England, many of the carousels that still operate were created by Charles I. D. Looff, who pioneered carousel design in the US and defined what aficionados call the Coney Island style. The Crescent Park Looff Carousel represents the pinnacle of his artistic expression.

Looff (1852–1918) was born in Holstein in southern Denmark shortly before the region was annexed by the German Confederation. As the son of a wagon builder and master blacksmith, he learned how to work both wood and metal. With war on the horizon in central Europe, he emigrated to the United States in 1870. Looff found work as a furniture carver—and as a dance instructor, where he met his wife. In his spare time he began to carve carousel animals in their apartment from scrap wood he brought home from work. In 1876, he assembled his horses into a platform carousel at Lucy Vanderveer's Bathing Pavilion. It was the first carousel—and first amusement ride—at Coney Island.

Buoyed by this initial success, Looff opened a large factory in Greenpoint, Brooklyn, and began producing carousels and other amusement park rides, employing

master carvers Charles Carmel, John Zalar, and Marcus Illions, among others. Their work was characterized by flamboyant horses that gleamed with inset glass jewels and reflective gold and silver leaf—the so-called Coney Island style.

In all, Looff installed three carousels at Coney Island, and the amusement park's popularity inspired imitators. In 1886, Crescent Park was established on Narragansett Bay in the tiny summer village of Riverside in East Providence, Rhode Island. Naturally, the developer wanted a Looff carousel, and the Brooklyn company was happy to oblige with a three-rank version that sat at the head of a 400-foot pier serving the passenger steamboats cruising the bay. In 1895, Looff's Brooklyn factory manufactured the large and elaborate carousel that still operates in Crescent Park. That same year, Looff moved his business operations to Riverside in the summers.

From the outset, Looff intended the Crescent Park carousel as a tour de force. The 66 highly detailed figures assembled in four rows include 4 chariots, 56 "jumping" horses, 5 stationary horses, and a single camel. Each figure is unique. When the city of New York took his Brooklyn factory property to create a public park, Looff moved his entire operation to Riverside in 1905 and modified the Crescent Park carousel to include the "jumping" mechanism. Most of the current figures are thought to date from the 1905–10 period when Riverside was the base of the Looff operations and the Crescent Park carousel served as the company's showpiece. New customers were invited to Riverside to select the figures that they wanted duplicated for their carousels.

Looff himself relocated to California in 1910, leaving three of his children behind to run the Rhode Island business. He established another factory in Long Beach. In 1916, two years before his death, he and son Arthur developed the Santa Monica Pier, complete with an ornate carousel inside a grand building now called the Santa Monica Looff Hippodrome.

Back in Rhode Island, son Charles purchased Crescent Park and ran it during the 1920s. In 1930, his sister Helen and her husband purchased the Crescent Park carousel, which continued to operate until the park closed in 1977. Local fans kept the carousel off the auction block, and the city of East Providence has owned it ever since. Slow but careful restoration has returned the carousel to its glory days. The Andreas Ruth & Sohn band organ, which Looff imported from Waldkirch,

Germany, continues to supply the music using a Wurlitzer music roll system in place of the German card system. The signature hippodrome building has also been restored, including the tinted Sandwich Glass clerestory windows.

In 1985, the Rhode Island General Assembly proclaimed the carousel to be Rhode Island's "State Jewel of American Folk Art." The carousel, in fact, is simply irresistible. As families stroll up the long pathway to the pavilion, little kids can't contain themselves. Leaving parents and grandparents in the dust, they break into a sprint, lured by the magical, mystical strains of the mechanical band organ. With each revolution of the carousel, the arc of childhood passes before an observer's eyes: uncertain toddlers held in place by doting grandparents, spunky preteens leaning as far as they can to grab the brass ring, and chastely flirtatious teenagers cuddling in the chariots.

Original US Naval War College, Newport
686 Cushing Road, Newport; 401-841-4052; usnwc.edu/About/ NWC-Museum.aspx; open year-round by advance reservation; free admission

"Ain't going to study war no more," goes the refrain in a spiritual dating back to pre–Civil War days, but on Coasters Harbor Island in Narragansett Bay, just two miles from downtown Newport, the Naval War College takes the position that one of the best ways to prevent future wars is to study wars of the past.

As the United States began to flex its international muscle in the late 19th century, the navy decided that its highest-level officers needed postgraduate education in the theory and practice of war. On October 6, 1884, the Secretary of the Navy issued General Order No. 325: "A College is hereby established for an advanced course of professional study for naval officers, to be known as the Naval War College." The island off Newport was chosen because many on the committee tasked to find a home were familiar with the location. Newport had housed the Naval Academy during the Civil War, when approaching Confederate troops threatened the Annapolis, Maryland, campus.

The navy moved first into the island's chief building, which had been used as a quarantine lodging for persons suspected of having smallpox, a reformatory, and finally as the Newport Asylum for the Poor. It later came to be known as Building #10. Construction of other facilities began immediately, and the war college moved out of the asylum building after three years.

Most of the campus of the Naval War College is off-limits to civilians and even to members of the military who are not stationed here or invited to study here. But the Naval War College Museum, now occupying the old Newport Asylum for the Poor, is open to the public. It receives about 40,000 visitors per year. Reservations are required and must be made at least a day in advance for US citizens and two weeks in advance for foreign nationals. Once visitors arrive, they must show identification at the gatehouse and pick up a temporary vehicle pass that must be displayed at the entry gate checkpoint.

The war college represents the highest level of professional education in the US Navy, and its graduates have been chiefs of at least 20 foreign navies. The museum, however, focuses a little closer to home—specifically on the naval history of the Narragansett Bay. Exhibits on Newport during the Revolution cover a side of the war generally left out of textbooks. The British navy occupied Newport's strategic harbor until 1779 so they could control the northeast entrance into Long Island Sound. As soon as His Majesty's ships were driven out, they were replaced by our allies, the French. Either way, hard-strapped Newporters had to find firewood and food for all those sailors.

The museum shows a detailed scale model of the *Duc de Bourgogne*, the flagship of the squadron that carried the Comte de Rochambeau from France to fight for the American revolutionaries. In fact, the museum is filled with striking ship's models, including the sloop *Providence*, the first command of young Continental Navy officer

John Paul Jones, and the warship *Bonhomme Richard*, the famed vessel put at Jones's disposal in 1779 by Louis XVI of France.

Scale models give way to actual weapons in the torpedo exhibition. Even before the war college was established, the navy had taken over nearby Goat Island in Newport harbor in 1869 as a torpedo research station and had developed the first torpedo model by 1871. From relatively crude explosive devices slingshotted from their launch vessels, the torpedoes grew to increasingly sophisticated, self-powered weapons. Examples in the exhibit illustrate the difficulties of design. The magnetic detonator on the Mark 14 torpedo, for example, malfunctioned early in its deployment, sinking three US submarines during World War II.

Visitors continue to the second deck (or to landlubbers, second floor), where Alfred Thayer Mahan delivered his influential talks on sea power in the 1880s. His thinking on geostrategy helped launch a naval arms race in Europe and remains influential today. It is one of the reasons why the building was first listed on the National Register of Historic Places.

Strategic thinking remains the forte of the Naval War College. Models of the gymnasium-sized war games maneuver boards show how hypothetical strategies used to be practiced in the days before computer modeling. A 20-minute film recounts the history of the Naval War College and explains how the various components of the college operate, including the Naval Command College international program that integrates naval officers from around the world in studies with officers of the US Navy. As the video makes clear, those studies are "as much about peace and diplomacy as about war."

The Mansions of Newport
Preservation Society of Newport County; 401-847-1000; newportmansions.org

Already prosperous by the middle of the 18th century, Newport became fashionable in the 1830s, when shipping magnates and merchants from the South discovered the cool breezes of Narragansett Bay. Faced with a shortage of hotels, summer visitors began building modest cottages intended to last for just a single season. With the harbor area already taken, the captains of industry erected their manses along Bellevue Avenue and other strategic and scenic points on the rocky promontory on the southern tip of

Newport. As the scale and permanence of those structures began to escalate, Newport became famous for "cottages" that would more accurately be called mansions.

While some residents stayed for the full four-month summer season, the fashionable period in Newport was from mid-June until the first of September, and true social butterflies alighted here only from late June through July. In August they moved on to Saratoga, New York, for the races, and in September and October to the Berkshires of western Massachusetts for fall foliage.

At its most extreme, the disparity of social status between the summer people and the townspeople was appalling, with the summer folk referring to the locals as "our footstools" and going to great lengths to keep them away from Bellevue Avenue, off the private beaches, and out of the yacht marinas unless they were serving as crew. The social season was known for elaborate balls and dinners—even lavish picnics. Competition among hostesses reached its apogee during the decade on each side of 1900, when a single ball could cost more than $100,000 and, in one infamous instance, a dinner party of considerable expense was given for 100 dogs and their masters.

When the Theodore Roosevelt administration finally put some teeth in the Sherman Antitrust Act of 1890, it became unfashionable to make such blatant displays of conspicuous consumption. The federal income tax of 1913 effectively ended the building craze, but by then Newport already had more than its share of grand houses to rival the hereditary estates of Europe. By the early 20th century, many of the properties had become white elephants that were too expensive to heat and maintain. But Americans remain fascinated with the lifestyles of the rich and famous, and the Preservation Society of Newport County has been able to preserve a number of the properties as house museums. Here are five that help trace the history of the "cottage" society.

Kingscote
253 Bellevue Avenue, Newport; open March to October; admission charged
In 1839, when Florida cotton plantation owner George Noble Jones (1811–76) decided to build a summer home in Newport, he ushered in the "cottage era." British-born architect Richard Upjohn (1802–78) was charged with designing a romantic and fanciful home to be placed on Bellevue Avenue, as the farm path on the outskirts of town was called. Upjohn was celebrated for his Gothic Revival churches, and his design for Jones did not disappoint with its roofline of multiple gables and chimneys and its painstaking detail. The Gothic arches, vaguely medieval windows, towers, and multiple porches made it resemble a medieval tent city pitched to host a jousting tournament. The entry foyer, with its procession of three Gothic arches, wood-paneled ceiling, and strip parquet floor, evokes the liturgical associations of Upjohn's churches. The restraint and proportion of Georgian manses may have suited Newport's old money, but new money demanded a better show.

The Jones family left Newport at the outbreak of the Civil War, and Kingscote was sold in 1864 to William Henry King, a China trade merchant. When his nephew David King (1839–94) inherited the house in 1876, he installed gas lighting and began renovations. In 1880, he hired McKim, Mead and White to enlarge the structure to keep pace with the larger and more elaborate cottages erected in Kingscote's wake. The firm draped Victorian exuberance atop the strong Gothic Revival bones of the house. The addition included an opulent new dining room that skillfully blended Colonial American details in the woodwork with some exotic, Asian-inspired ornamentation. The dining room included an installation of opalescent glass bricks created by Louis Comfort Tiffany as well as cork tiles to cover the ceiling and create a frieze on the wall. The expansion also added new master bedrooms and a nursery but maintained the general Gothic Revival appearance of Upjohn's smaller footprint. The King family continued to use the house until 1972, when the last in the line left it—complete with original family furnishings and personal collections—to the Preservation Society of Newport County.

Chateau-Sur-Mer
474 Bellevue Avenue, Newport; open March to October; admission charged
When China trade merchant William Wetmore (1801–1862) commissioned a mansion in Newport, he had it built as a year-round home. He was a hardy Vermonter who, like the northerly ducks and geese that winter in Narragansett Bay, considered Newport quite comfortable in all seasons. Wetmore engaged Newporter Seth C.

Bradford (1801–78) as architect-builder, and Bradford outdid himself, creating a grand granite palace in the Italianate villa style. Completed in 1852, it eclipsed all the "cottages" he had built before. Chateau-sur-Mer was enlarged in the 1870s to maintain its status as the largest and most ornate structure in Newport until the Vanderbilt houses were constructed in the 1890s.

Social historians often cite Chateau-sur-Mer as ushering in Newport's Gilded Age—both in the design aspirations of the great house and in the lavish entertaining that took place here. Although his much younger wife seems to have vanished from the historical record shortly after they moved from New York City to Chateau-sur-Mer, the recently retired Wetmore threw himself into a vigorous social life. In 1857, he hosted a "Fête champêtre" on the grounds. The elegant picnic for 2,000 of his closest friends was described by the *Newport Daily News* as "without doubt incomparably the grandest private entertainment ever given in the country."

When William Wetmore died in 1862, his oldest surviving child was George Peabody Wetmore (1846–1921), who was educated at private schools in Newport and went on to graduate from Yale College in 1867 and Columbia Law School in 1869. But his interests lay elsewhere. He was governor of Rhode Island as well as a US senator and one of the organizers of the Metropolitan Opera.

When George and his wife Edith took off for an extended trip to Europe in the 1870s, they charged architect Richard Morris Hunt (1827–95)—one of the first Americans to study at the École des Beaux Arts in Paris—with remodeling and redecorating Chateau-sur-Mer. The ballroom is one of the few rooms relatively unaltered from Bradford's original Italian Renaissance model design.

Given carte blanche, Hunt made the manse a showpiece of French Second Empire style. He added a new three-story wing, a carriage porch entry, and a four-story tower to the original Italianate villa. At the top of the central Great Hall, stained glass windows spill light into the levels below. Hunt also designed the impressive entrance gate to the estate with posts modeled on Egyptian obelisks. The Wetmores later hired Ogden Codman, then fresh off a triumphant redesign of rooms in the Breakers for Cornelius Vanderbilt II, to create the ladies' reception area, called the Green Room, in the Louis XV style. The dining room and library created by Hunt follow Italian Renaissance Revival models and were actually fabricated in Italy, disassembled, and shipped over for installation. Their carved wall panels, ceilings, and custom furniture declare both the evolved taste of the owners and their means to install only the very finest examples of craftsmanship.

A virtual chronicle of changing fashions in high Victorian style, the house remained in the Wetmore family until George and Edith's daughter, also Edith, died in 1966. Three years later, the estate was purchased by the Preservation Society of Newport County.

Marble House
596 Bellevue Avenue, Newport; open year-round; admission charged

The first of the spectacular Vanderbilt mansions, Marble House was a 39th birthday present to his flamboyant wife, Alva (1853–1933), from William K. Vanderbilt (1849–1920), grandson of the railroad magnate Cornelius Vanderbilt. Alva had already cajoled her husband into building a grand mansion in New York, where she schemed her way into the old money "Four Hundred" of high society, and insisted that her husband build her a summer cottage in Newport next door to Caroline Astor's Beechwood.

Nothing would do but to hire Richard Morris Hunt, the architect who designed houses for all the "best people" of the age. Fully understanding Alva Vanderbilt's aspirations for new wealth to be recognized as American aristocracy, Hunt took his inspiration from the Petit Trianon at Versailles and built a 52 room mansion between 1888 and 1892. The "cottage" was named for its principal building material—500,000 cubic feet of marble in all and 100,000 cubic feet of white marble in the façade alone. Nearly two-thirds of the reported $11 million price tag was spent on the stone. The interior marble is principally yellow and pink, yet the ballroom, which is gilded from top to bottom and is hung with golden chandeliers, is even more dramatic. Alva clearly articulated her desires to Hunt, hoping that Marble House would be her "temple to the arts."

In some ways, it was a temple to Alva—a grand stage set where she could hold court as a leading hostess in Newport society. While Hunt provided the spaces, Jules Allard et Fils of Paris did the interior decorating. Indeed, when Allard created a French salon for the Vanderbilts' Manhattan townhouse, it launched a craze for French 18th century interiors in New York. Allard worked his magic again for Marble House, re-creating a Versailles dining room on the ground level, complete with a room-length dining table and set of chairs so weighty that servants had to pull them from the table before guests could be seated. (The side chairs weigh about 75 pounds, the armchairs 100.)

The Gold Room, Alva's pride and joy, radiates wealth and power in a pastiche in the style of the Sun King, Louis XIV. The extraordinary quality of the carved

woodwork and the fine crystal chandelier (hanging from the mouth of Apollo) is almost overwhelmed by the gold leaf that covers nearly all the woodwork. The fireplace surround is a bronze copy of a Michelangelo statue, and acorn and oak leaf symbols of the Vanderbilt family abound throughout the room.

William K. did get his own grand room where he could display his collection of medieval armor. The church-like Gothic Room features stained glass windows, a mock-cathedral fireplace, and carved Gothic Revival furniture.

Up the grand central staircase, the marble walls on the second level are actually faux painted rather than real stone, since the house had to be finished on a deadline for Alva's birthday. The nature of the marriage is captured by the couple's respective bedrooms. William K.'s small room was boldly masculine, with a desk more prominent than the bed or any other furnishings. Alva's bedroom was a giant Louis XIV confection in a pinkish lavender with silk brocade on the walls and an elaborately carved ceiling.

The Vanderbilts divorced in 1895, just three years after the cottage was completed, and Alva moved down the street to the 52-room Belcourt mansion, where

she continued playing the Newport hostess as wife to Oliver H. P. Belmont, William K.'s former best friend. She retained custody of the two boys in the divorce—having already married off daughter Consuelo as a dollar princess to the Duke of Marlborough. She also kept Marble House, which she used as a giant storage closet.

After Belmont's death in 1908, Alva reopened Marble House. Her sons William K. Jr., who became a pioneer in auto racing, and Harold, a fine yachtsman who would go on to successfully defend the America's Cup three times, were already out on their own by this time. On moving back to Marble House, Alva had a marvelous caprice of a Chinese tea house built on the back lawn and threw herself into the cause of women's suffrage until the ratification of the 19th Amendment in 1920. Thereafter, she lived principally in France until her death in 1933. Marble House was sold in 1932 to Frederick H. Prince, and the Preservation Society acquired the property in 1963 from the Prince estate with generous assistance from Harold Vanderbilt, who also donated many of the family furnishings that had been dispersed to other houses.

The Breakers
44 Ochre Point Avenue, Newport; open year-round; admission charged

The grandest of the Newport Gilded Age mansions was constructed for Cornelius Vanderbilt II (1843–99), the older brother of William K. Vanderbilt of Marble House. Their grandfather, Commodore Cornelius Vanderbilt (1794–1877), had established the family fortune by investing in steamships, then by wresting control of the New York Central Railroad. In 1885, the same year he took over at the railroad, Cornelius II bought a wooden house in Newport called the Breakers. It burned in 1892, and the following year he commissioned Richard Morris Hunt, who had designed Marble House for his brother, to come up with something even grander.

That was a 70-room Italian Renaissance–style palazzo that drew its inspiration from 16th-century palaces of Genoa and Turin. It would be Hunt's final achievement before his death in 1895, and he opened the tap on the Vanderbilt wealth to engage a huge team of artisans and some of his favorite decorators. Jules Allard et Fils assisted with furnishings and features, ransacking Europe for the best available examples and reproducing what they could not buy outright. Vienna-born sculptor Karl Bitter—who had burst on the scene in New York at age 21 by winning a competition for the Astor memorial bronze gates at Trinity Church—designed and executed most of the relief sculpture. Ogden Codman from Boston decorated the family quarters.

Allard completely fabricated the Music Room and Dining Room in his Paris studios, then took them apart and shipped them to Newport to be reassembled. Codman was so grateful for the tour-de-force rooms that he allowed Allard to incorporate the initials "AF" in the painted designs of the Music Room ceiling.

There is really no other way to describe the dining room except as palatial. At 2,400 square feet, it is the largest and most ornate room in a house of large and ornate rooms. A dozen towering Corinthian columns in pink alabaster support the enormous carved and gilded cornice that forms the transition to the vaulted ceiling. The goddess Aurora thunders across the ceiling in her four-horse chariot, bringing the dawn. A pair of enormous Baccarat crystal chandeliers (each of which has both gaslights and electric bulbs) provide the real light for dining. All that glitters actually is gold in this room, which is trimmed with a mixture of 18-, 22-, and 24-carat gold leaf glued to the walls and woodwork.

In contrast to the Italian Baroque creations of Allard, Hunt designed the Billiards Room in a Renaissance interpretation of classical Roman style. The walls are constructed of beautifully mottled silvery Cippolino marble that contrasts with the gold-toned rose alabaster of the arches. Mosaics make up much of the decoration, from the floors with their motif of spouting whales to the classical mosaic portrait of a goddess at her bath on the ceiling. Throughout the room, semiprecious stones form mosaics of acorns. The handsomely carved billiards table looks like it could have come from the palace of Lorenzo de Medici—had Lorenzo played billiards.

Multitalented artist John LaFarge designed the stained glass skylight over the grand staircase. It was originally installed in the family's Manhattan townhouse but was removed to Newport when the New York manse was renovated in 1894.

Bedrooms on the second and third floors continue the opulence, with Codman's interpretation of Louis XIV style on the second floor, where the family slept, and Louis XVI style in the sitting room and guest bedrooms of the third floor. The 18-foot ceilings allowed Codman to stack servants' quarters two high on the third floor for a total of 30 small rooms.

The youngest of the Vanderbilts' seven children, Gladys, inherited the house when her mother, Alice, died in 1934. (Her father, Cornelius II, had died of a stroke in 1899 at age 55.) Gladys was, like her cousin Consuelo, a dollar princess who had married the Hungarian Count Laszlo Szechenyi. The countess was fond of Newport and was a strong supporter of the Preservation Society of Newport County. In 1948, she opened the Breakers to help raise funds for the society, which purchased the house from her heirs in 1972.

The Elms
367 Bellevue Avenue, Newport; open year-round; admission charged

The Vanderbilts may have had more money (and more flair for scandal) than anyone else in Gilded Age Newport, but it's possible that the Berwinds had more fun. Coal baron Edward Julius Berwind and his wife, Herminie Torrey Berwind, daughter of an American consul to Italy, hailed from Philadelphia and spent much of their time in New York. In 1888, they purchased a quaint Victorian cottage on Bellevue Avenue as a summer getaway, but found themselves lusting for something a little more suited to Mr. Berwind's status as a captain of industry. In 1898, they hired Horace Trumbauer of Philadelphia to create a lavish mansion modeled after the 1750–52 Chateau d'Asnières-sur-Seine outside Paris.

The Elms was completed in late summer of 1901 at a reported cost of only $1.4 million for the 60,000-square-foot mansion. It was rumored that Berwind had kept down costs by bartering coal for building materials and that his father-in-law, who owned a quarry in Italy, gave his daughter and son-in-law a deal on the marble.

The couple threw an opening party on August 30 that Newporters still talk about more than a century later. More than 350 guests attended the ball, which was themed as an 18th-century French cotillion appropriate to d'Asnières. Two orchestras played, spelling each other so that the music could be nonstop in the ballroom. Mrs. Berwind also brought in monkeys to cavort about the gardens for the amusement of her guests. They were probably less amused when the beasts escaped and rampaged through the lawns and gardens of fashionable Newport for the rest of the season.

The Elms was a bit of a contradiction. Behind the scenes it was extremely modern. It was the first mansion in Newport built with electricity as well as gas and a very impressive fire suppression system that included full-fledged firehoses hidden in the servants' staircases on each level. The electricity was provided by a huge steam boiler system fired (of course) by coal. But the illusion of 18th-century decorum was always maintained. A tunnel was built beneath Bellevue Avenue so that the coal trucks could unload out of sight and workers could cart the coal underground into the subbasements of the Elms.

That decorum was established in no small part by the decorations of Julius Allard et Fils, who treated each room with a separate but related French historical style. (Allard was honored at the Elms by having his name cast in the oversized bronze of a lion slaying a crocodile that stands on the terrace.) While the Preservation Society is still trying to recover some of the furnishings sold at auction in 1962 after the death of Julius Berwind's sister Julia, a number of pieces original to the house have either come back or proved too cumbersome to ever remove.

The French Renaissance style library, for example, contains a handsome Henri IV–style Renaissance table that Allard manufactured in Paris, as well as an elaborately carved fireplace and a copy of a Renaissance-era painting of *Madonna and Child*. The bright, high-ceilinged Orangerie features two large statues—*Apollo* and *Aphrodite*—from Chateau d'Asnières. The grand ballroom—which occupies the central third of the first floor—was likewise modeled on d'Asnières and is decorated in the Louis XIV style. (The gilded Steinway piano is not original to the room, though it does come from the Berwind family.)

The dining room is almost entirely original, and it is a tour de force of Italian Renaissance style. The massive table seats up to 26 guests, and many of the paintings were rescued from the 18th-century palace Ca' Corner della Regina in Venice (now the museum of the Venice Biennale). They depict various stories in the life of Roman general Scipio Africanus, a purported ancestor. The elaborate coffered ceiling and intricate moldings are actually cast plaster that has been painted and gilded, but there is nothing faux about the bronze chandeliers with Baccarat crystal pendants.

Perhaps the most unusual room at the Elms is the Breakfast Room—something of a misnomer, as the Berwinds and their myriad of visiting nieces often used the room for all meals. Allard had rescued three large black lacquer Chinese panels that dated from about 1750 and manufactured a matching fourth to surround the room. A proper 18th-century French palace would have had a *chinoiserie* room in this style, and Allard thought it important to replicate at the Elms. It is one of the few remaining lacquer rooms in the world, and although some panels are warped, they were stabilized in a 2008 renovation that should preserve them for generations to come.

The seven bedrooms (with six baths) up the grand marble staircase are somewhat less dramatic than the rooms on the entry level, and the lack of original furnishings makes it slightly harder to imagine just how the Berwinds lived. A massive marble table does stand at the top of the stairs—one of the pieces auctioned off but never removed because, to everyone's surprise, it turned out to be carved of a single block and weighed more than a ton. The family sitting room on the second level, above the ballroom, is perhaps the most casual room in the house, and it is easy to imagine several of the nieces draped over the sofas and chairs reading magazines or sharing the latest society gossip.

The Berwinds never had children, and when Herminie died in 1922, Edward Julius invited his much younger sister Julia to be his hostess at the Elms and his New York house. He died in 1936, but Miss Julia continued to summer at the Elms until she died in 1961. The property was slated for the wrecking ball, but the Preservation Society of Newport County swiftly raised the money to buy it and open the house to the public.

Newport Casino and International Tennis Hall of Fame, Newport
194 Bellevue Avenue, Newport; 401-849-3990; tennisfame.com; open year-round; admission charged

If Newport's high society lived in the mansions on Bellevue Avenue, they played at the Newport Casino. Commissioned by *New York Herald* publisher James Gordon Bennett, Jr., as the "sporting mansion" for the resort's summertime elite, it was conceived, designed, and built in a single year by the architectural firm of McKim, Mead, and White. According to tradition, Bennett had made a bet with one of his polo buddies that he did not dare ride his pony onto the front porch of the Newport Reading Room, then the most prestigious men's club in town. His pal, Captain Henry Augustus "Sugar" Candy, did him one better by riding straight into the rooms of the club. Officers were not amused and revoked Bennett's membership. Miffed that they could not take a joke, he built his own club where he and his sporting companions would be welcome.

Perhaps almost by accident, Bennett commissioned a seminal piece of architecture. Charles McKim, who had become a part-time resident of Newport, created the Casino complex as an exemplar of the then-new Shingle style—an architectural response to the ornate excesses of the Queen Anne style that had become a self-parody in many homes of the wealthy. Driven by the country's revived interest in its colonial past, McKim drew on the traditional shingled buildings of New England and approached building design much as a shipwright would approach a hull—as an envelope containing space. The use of natural cedar shingles, which turned silvery gray in the New England weather, emphasized volume over surface ornamentation. It would become the signature style of McKim, Mead, and White during the firm's early years of creating informal, open-plan summer homes for the wealthy. The Casino's turreted towers, however, place it squarely in the Victorian period.

McKim's partner Stanford White created an interior with spacious open public areas and intimate, even secluded rooms. It was perfect for both showy displays of wealth and influence (like grand dinners) and for quiet discussions of less public business, such as the acquisition of railroads or the disposition of mines and factories. From the outset, the Casino contained meeting and reading rooms (intended to rival the Newport Reading Room), a billiards parlor, and rooms where members and their guests might stay while passing through Newport. Behind the three-story clubhouse, the grounds also held a court tennis facility and a theater with a ballroom.

The Newport Casino opened to its patrons in July 1880 as a sort of clubhouse for the wealthy. First opened to the public in August, it soon hosted concerts, dances, banquets, horse shows, tea parties, plays and skits, lawn bowling, archery, and both lawn and court tennis. Apart from some informal, friendly card games, it has never been a gambling casino.

The Casino's signature game was tennis, and it is treasured for the role it played in the development of the modern game. Although tennis had ancient antecedents in court games, lawn tennis dates from just a few years before the establishment of The Casino. It was patented in London in 1874, spread immediately to the United States, and within a year was played as far afield as India and China. When the Newport Casino opened, it had three lawn tennis courts—one for men's singles, one for doubles, and one for women's tennis. The US Lawn Tennis Association held its first national championship at the Newport Casino in 1881, and the sport soon became one of the facility's principal activities. National championships continued as an annual event in Newport through 1914.

As Newport wealth declined in the 20th century, the Newport Casino began to suffer. By midcentury, it was in serious financial straits and its prime property was eyed for retail expansion. One of Newport's own came to its rescue. James Henry "Jimmy" Van Alen II was born in Newport in 1902 as a scion of the Astor clan (his paternal grandmother was Emily Astor) and attended Cambridge University in England, where he became an avid tennis player. A national singles and doubles champion in court tennis, Van Alen helped found the International Tennis Hall of Fame at the Newport Casino in 1954. (He was inducted into the hall in 1965, in part for his scoring system that led to tie-breakers in tournament play.)

The Hall of Fame was sanctioned in 1954 by the US Tennis Association and was recognized in 1986 by the International Tennis Federation. The Hall's museum

maintains portions of the Casino building as it functioned in its days as a private club, but has devoted most club rooms to more than 1,900 artifacts of tennis history. The latest installation of the Hall of Fame includes video consoles where it's possible to see many of the greats from over the years perform at the top of their games. The Hall of Fame continues to host several tournaments, including the Hall of Fame Tennis Championships, the only grass court event of the ATP (Association of Tennis Professionals) World Tour held in the United States.

Visitors to the hall and museum can also explore the additional 7 acres of grounds. With a reservation, even nonmembers of the Hall of Fame Tennis Club can reserve a court to play a match at the Newport Casino.

Hunter House, Newport
54 Washington Street, Newport; 401-847-7516; newportmansions .org; open for guided tours late May through mid-October; admission charged

Before there was a Gilded Age in Newport, the city enjoyed its "golden age" in the middle of the 18th century. As one of the more cosmopolitan ports in the Northeast, Newport embodied a spirit of religious tolerance that attracted Quakers, Baptists, and Sephardic Jews to add a little diversity to the Congregationalists and Methodists common in the rest of New England. As the merchant families accumulated wealth and power, they built mansions on the harbor where they could look out on their ships. They also bought furniture and silver from Newport's burgeoning community of artisans and patronized such early portraitists as Long Island–born Robert Feke (c. 1705–c. 1752) and locally raised Gilbert Stuart (1755–1828) (see p. 43). Especially in the decades before the American Revolution, Newport boomed.

Many of these enclaves of historic homes remained in place, notably in the neighborhood known as the Point, the shoreline adjacent to the Goat Island causeway. Over time, the area became working class, and many of the large homes were broken up into tenements or boardinghouses. The district became the focus of conservation and preservation by Doris Duke's Newport Restoration Fund, which purchased more than two dozen buildings during the 1960s and 1970s. But it's not a stretch to say that preservation in Newport began with Hunter House. The story of this property is a chronicle of how a fine home is adapted to changing times.

The north wing of the house was built 1748–54 between Water Street and the shipping wharf for merchant and deputy governor Jonathon Nichols, Jr. After he died in 1756, another merchant and deputy governor, Colonel Joseph Wanton, Jr., bought the house and transformed the simple Colonial home into a central-hall Georgian mansion by adding a south wing and a second chimney. Records also show that Wanton commissioned decorative painting of the paneling in several rooms to make simple pine look more like exotic (and hence expensive) walnut and rosewood.

When the Revolution came, Wanton declared as a Loyalist and was ordered jailed by Continental Army General William West. He chose instead to flee, loading up his most precious possessions in one of his ships. As he was ashore bidding his wife farewell, the captain hauled anchor and sailed up Narragansett Bay to deliver

the ship and its cargo to the rebel cause. Wanton fled on foot and died penniless in New York City. When the French occupied Newport in 1780, the house became the headquarters for the commander of the French fleet, Admiral de Ternay.

When peace came, the house ended up in the hands of William Hunter (1774–1849), who would later become a US Senator and President Andrew Jackson's chargé d'affaires to Brazil. Around the time of Hunter's death, the wealthy of Newport began to move away from the harbor and out to Bellevue Avenue. The Hunter House lost some cachet because it was adjacent to the steamship landing, and shortly before the Civil War, it became a boardinghouse. A number of other architectural indignities were heaped on the 2½ story structure, among them the Victorian widow's walk atop the gambrel roof and a reorientation of the main entrance from the harbor side to the Washington Street (formerly Water Street) side.

But the house was known for its fine lines and for the carved woodwork in the front rooms and over the doorway (including a pineapple, traditional symbol for hospitality). The derelict building was scheduled to be demolished in 1945, when concerned citizens led by Katherine Warren stepped in. They formed the Preservation

Society of Newport County, raised $10,000 to purchase the Hunter House, and restored it to the period of Colonel Wanton (1757–79). Under Warren's leadership, the Preservation Society would also go on to become stewards of several Gilded Age mansions (see p. 57).

The initial restoration of Hunter House uncovered such treasures as an over-mantel painting of Newport harbor—the earliest known painting of the city—as well as 18th-century Delft tiles surrounding some of the fireplaces, pilasters with Corinthian capitals in the front rooms, and faux marble and wood-grain painting throughout the building. Interpretation of the house has changed over the decades, and it now presents highlights of the Preservation Society's extensive collection of Newport decorative arts and furniture from 1637 to about 1810. Several Newport cabinetmakers are represented, but some of the most exquisite pieces were crafted by the Goddard and Townsend families who worked in the immediate neighborhood. Among the paintings on display is a depiction of two spaniels that Gilbert Stuart painted when he was just 14 years old.

Herman Melville's Arrowhead, Pittsfield

780 Holmes Road, Pittsfield; 413-442-1793; mobydick.org; open late May through mid-October for guided tours; admission charged

In the landlocked Berkshire Hills, Herman Melville (1819–91) sat at his desk, gazed at Mount Greylock, imagined a white whale, and wrote America's great novel of the sea, *Moby-Dick*.

Melville's 18-month sojourn aboard the whaling ship *Acushnet* in the 1840s was well behind him, and he had begun to establish himself as a writer in Manhattan when he and his wife, Elizabeth Knapp Shaw, decided to move to the Berkshires. Melville had fond memories of spending boyhood summers on an uncle's farm and purchased a nearby 160-acre farm in Pittsfield in 1850. He shared the 1790s farmhouse with his wife, four children (three of whom were born here), mother, and sisters.

That was a lot of mouths to feed, and Melville and a farmhand grew squashes, pumpkins, turnips, corn, greens, and herbs, among other crops. He named the property, in fact, for the Native American artifacts that he dug up while working the land.

The children picked wild strawberries in the upland pasture in the early summer, and Melville made cider every fall from the apples in his orchard. He also added a chicken coop near the barn.

Melville never achieved his goal of tearing down the farmhouse and replacing it with a grander dwelling. But a year after the family moved in, he did add a piazza on the north side of the farmhouse. He was quite fond of covered porches, which combined, as he once wrote, "the coziness of in-doors with the freedom of out-doors." In addition, he wanted a place to sit in his rocking chair and take in the view across his meadow and all the way to Mount Greylock, the highest mountain in Massachusetts at 3,491 feet.

When Melville wanted a break from his household of women and children, he would retire to the barn. He and Nathaniel Hawthorne, who lived at nearby Tanglewood cottage in Lenox from 1850 to 1851, became close friends after an 1850 hike up Monument Mountain. Hawthorne often joined Melville in the barn where they could smoke, drink, and discuss their writing projects.

Melville had written the first draft of a book he called *The Whale* before he moved to Pittsfield. With Hawthorne's counsel to make the book more "serious," Melville sat at his desk, gazed at Mount Greylock, and revised his manuscript until it became *Moby-Dick*. In Melville's defense, it's not as great of a stretch as it might seem to imagine mountain as whale—especially when the summit is covered with snow in winter and fog rises from the peaks like sea spray. The novel was published in November 1851 to reviews that were tepid at best.

Melville also wrote three other novels, poetry, numerous magazine pieces, and a short story collection while living at Arrowhead. He was often inspired by the farm and the surrounding countryside, and many scholars consider that he was at the peak of his literary powers during the years that he spent in the Berkshires. He was not, however, earning enough money to support his family. In 1863, they sold Arrowhead to Melville's brother Allan and

returned to New York, where Melville worked as a customs inspector for the next 20 years. The property remained in the Melville family until 1927 and continued to be used as a private residence until it was purchased by the Berkshire Historical Society in 1975.

The Historical Society has taken many steps to restore the property to Melville's time. Part of the land is farmed as a Community Supported Agricultural Project, and heritage breeds of chickens and goats have been introduced. One of the first projects at the farmhouse was to rebuild Melville's beloved piazza, which had been removed. His study, which had been turned into a bedroom, was also restored.

Melville took all his furnishings with him when he left, but a few family pieces have found their way back and all other furniture is appropriate to the time period and the region. The sideboard in the dining room, for example, belonged to Melville's mother. Of even more interest is the inscription on the surround of the main fireplace. Allan Melville had text from the story "I and My Chimney" inscribed as a tribute to his brother, who would return for visits. The Melvilles entertained guests in the parlor, which was restored to its original hot pink and pale green color scheme. The surprisingly bright combination is perhaps the reflection of a home mostly filled with women.

Upstairs, the bed in the master bedroom may have belonged to Melville, but the room that most conjures up his presence is the study, furnished with a desk in one corner and a writing table and chair facing the window. Little clutters the surface except an inkwell, a few quill pens, a candle, a candlesnuffer, and a facsimile of a much-annotated manuscript. After he had fed his horse and cow, finished his other farmwork, and eaten breakfast, Melville would climb the stairs, close the door, and hole up here to work. His lunch was left at the door, and he would eat at a separate little table. When he had wrestled with his metaphoric angels long enough and the ink was dry on the page, he was ready to rejoin the family, perhaps for a stroll across the upper pastures, where the high whine of summer cicadas can be nearly deafening.

Or he might have just sat on his piazza, rocking into the gloaming as the great hump of Greylock closed in the horizon.

Hancock Shaker Village, Pittsfield
1843 West Housatonic Street, Pittsfield; 413-443-0188; hancockshakervillage.org; open mid-April through October; admission charged

The United Society of Believers in Christ's Second Appearing, more commonly known as the Shakers, called their Hancock community "City of Peace," and even today the tidy village, simple buildings, whitewashed fences, neat gardens, and rolling pastures embody a commanding sense of order and tranquility.

Established in the 1780s on land donated by local farmers drawn to the social and religious movement, Hancock was the third of the eventual 19 Shaker communities established in New York, throughout New England, and as far away as Kentucky, Ohio, and Indiana. It was also one of the most enduring, lasting into the 1950s, although numbers had severely dwindled from the peak of about 300 members in the 1830s. In 1960, the property became a museum that preserves about 750 of the original 4,000 acres that the Shakers once farmed, quarried, and lumbered. It also has about 6 miles of hiking trails.

Twenty buildings constructed between 1790 and 1916 have been preserved to form the compact core of the village, including the oldest, the Laundry and Machine Shop. As one of the largest and strongest of the communities, Hancock was one of the nerve centers of the Shaker network. Its architecture—especially the Round Barn—strongly influenced many non-Shaker buildings throughout New England.

All practical decisions regarding the community were guided by religious beliefs. Early Shakers considered their founder, British-born Mother Ann Lee, to be the female personification of God, so it followed logically that both the spiritual and

temporal leadership of Shaker communities should be in the hands of both men and women. The sexes, however, did not mix. The five-story 1830 Brick Dwelling exemplifies the separate but equal status that formed the core of Shaker life. About 100 brothers and sisters lived on separate sides of the buildings—each side a mirror image of the other, right down

to the entrance doors, staircases, and peg rails for hats and cloaks. Because the Hancock community was rich in land, it took in a large number of refugees from the outside world, especially widows and orphans. But it was not uncommon for older couples to join the sect, taking vows of celibacy and moving into the separate men's and women's quarters.

An early Shaker eldress declared, "There is no dirt in heaven," and the Shakers took her words to heart. Walking around the property, the phrase "neat as a pin" comes constantly to mind. Throughout the buildings, peg rails were attached to walls to hang clothing, tools, chairs, and mops. Tall cupboards were built into the walls so that no dust could accumulate beneath them. In the Shaker world, ingenuity was prized and they were generally quick to adopt innovations that would save time and effort. The Dwelling's kitchen was the epitome of modernity in its time—with running water, efficient ovens, and wood-fired appliances for boiling, steaming, deep-frying, and grilling.

Hancock Shaker Village boasts a major collection of about 22,000 Shaker artifacts that range from furniture and textiles to tools and drawings. Many are displayed in the buildings where interpreters are often available to talk about the lives of the people who made and used the objects. Throughout the day, there are also lectures and demonstrations of such crafts as spinning and weaving and making the signature Shaker oval boxes. There are also performances of Shaker music and dance, with observers encouraged to join in. Every building, it seems, holds a lesson, but it is also restorative to walk the property and partake of the sense of peace that the community so valued. In summer, a visitor can pause on a green lawn and actually smell the sweet clover and hear the gentle buzz of bees collecting nectar.

The Shakers worshipped in every aspect of their daily lives, but they also gathered for formal services in the gambrel-roofed Meetinghouse. The whitewashed, blue-trimmed interior is rimmed with built-in benches for visitors and possible converts who came to observe the Shakers sing and dance praises to God. The space provided a simple backdrop for the worship service, which was often characterized by ecstatic movement and dance—the actions that earned the sect the nickname "Shaking Quakers," or simply "Shakers" for short.

Museum staff farmers maintain specimen herb, flower, and vegetable gardens and raise livestock breeds common to western Massachusetts in the mid-19th century. Hancock's agricultural success is symbolized by the extraordinary Round Stone Barn that was built in 1826 at a cost of about $10,000. It replaced a wooden barn that burned down the year before and remains an ingenious and beautiful synthesis of form and function. It was designed to stable 50 cattle in stanchions radiating from a central haymow like spokes of a wheel. It was built into a hillside so hay wagons could drive up the slope and deposit their load in the haymow, where it dropped down to the cattle. The wagon then continued around in a circle on the upper level to exit where it had entered. (Oxen do not like to back up, so going forward was the most efficient way to move.)

The cattle stanchions had openings in the floor so that manure could be dropped to an even lower level, where it could be gathered to spread on the fields. This practical design make it easy to feed, milk, and clean up after the animals. Now long empty, the building has all the beauty of a Gothic cathedral. It is the exemplar of the Shaker act of worship through daily labor, which was, in the final analysis, the point of Shaker life.

The Mount, Lenox
2 Plunkett Street, Lenox; 413-551-5111; edithwharton.org; open May through October for guided and self-guided tours; admission charged

"We have to make things beautiful; they do not grow so themselves," Edith Wharton (1862–1937) proclaimed in her first book, *The Decoration of Houses*, written with architect Ogden Codman, Jr., and published in 1897.

Two decades before she would become the first woman to be awarded the Pulitzer Prize for Fiction (for *The Age of Innocence* in 1921), she established herself as an expert on designing and decorating with elegance and grace. And she almost immediately put her ideas into practice when she purchased 113 acres in Lenox in 1901

and enlisted architects Codman and Francis L. V. Hoppin to assist her in creating a house and gardens to suit her taste. The house was designed and built the following year at a cost of about $57,000 and boasted all the modern conveniences, including central heating, hot and cold running water, electricity, and a telephone.

Wharton drew on her extensive travels through Europe to create an English country estate with a French-style courtyard and Italianate terrace. She had been born Edith Newbold Jones into the wealthy and tradition-bound New York society family for whom the term "keeping up with the Joneses" was coined, but she dispensed with the Victorian style of her stodgy upbringing to create an estate full of grace and ease.

Wharton and her husband, Edward R. Wharton (more than a decade older and known to all as "Teddy"), lived here from May to October until 1911. At that point their marriage was beyond repair, and Wharton decided to sell the property and move permanently to France. But she always had a soft spot for what she called "her first real home." Although the rooms are filled with pieces on loan or from a designer showcase rather than with Wharton's own furniture, they nonetheless capture the spirit and lifestyle of the largely self-taught woman of independent spirit.

Wharton did not throw grand parties, but she did entertain friends such as writer Henry James, who loved to "motor" in Wharton's chauffeur-driven Pope-Hartford automobile and who once described the Mount as "a delicate French chateau reflected in a Massachusetts pond."

Given her preference for intimate gatherings, Wharton arranged her rooms to promote quiet conversation and relaxation. The dining room, for example, is flooded with light, which was believed to aid digestion. Wharton also preferred a round table so that all diners could easily engage in the undoubtedly lively discussions. Guests would adjourn to

the drawing room after dinner. Here, three separate seating areas allowed for more intimate chat. When the guests ran out of things to talk about, they could exit onto the terrace at the rear of the house for a game of Ping-Pong.

Also on the main floor, the library was Wharton's sanctuary and the one room in the house that nodded to her upbringing. Its carved wood panel walls and built-in bookcases were modeled after her father's library in her childhood home in Manhattan. Wharton, however, did not write in this cozy retreat. She wrote in her bedroom—in fact, in her bed—every morning from sunrise until 11 a.m. (Teddy had a separate bedroom.) Among the works that she completed here were her best-selling novel *The House of Mirth*, published in 1905, and *Ethan Frome*, published in 1911.

Wharton's bedroom windows looked out on some of her gardens, and she was as interested in landscape design as she was in architecture. She lavished great attention on her gardens and even once wrote to her lover, Morton Fullerton, that "decidedly I am a better landscape gardener than novelist, and this place, every line of which is my own work, far surpasses *The House of Mirth*."

In her 1904 book *Italian Villas and Their Gardens*, Wharton advised treating gardens as outdoor rooms, an approach that she embraced at the Mount. The property does include an Italian walled garden, but Wharton didn't stop there. She also created a formal French flower garden, an English-style meadow, terraced lawns, an allée of linden trees, and a kitchen garden. Some of Wharton's beloved dogs are buried in a graveyard on the property.

Restored at a cost of about $3 million, the gardens are once again some of the most extensive and lovely in New England. Although Wharton only spent a few months per year at the Mount, she was determined that the gardens would be of interest throughout the year, reflecting her conviction that a garden should display "a charm independent of the seasons."

Chesterwood, Stockbridge
4 Williamsville Road, Stockbridge; 413-298-3579; chesterwood.org;
open late May through October; admission charged

Daniel Chester French (1850–1931) left his mark on America with his masterful and evocative public sculptures that memorialized everyone from the Concord minuteman and Georgia colony founder James Oglethorpe to writer Washington Irving and Abraham Lincoln. But French also left his mark on the Berkshires, where he put his taste and talent to work to create a summer home and studio where he worked and lived with his family for more than three decades.

French purchased a working farm in Stockbridge in 1897 and laid out his estate to focus the best views toward 1,642-foot Monument Mountain. He turned his attention first to his studio, which was designed by architect Henry Bacon, with whom he also collaborated on public monuments. Completed in 1898, the Italianate style of the studio suited French's classical sensibilities, while the layout met his needs for a large, bright space. The 26-foot-high ceiling could accommodate equestrian statues too large for French's New York studio, and windows and a north-facing skylight provided plenty of light. Most ingenious, however, were the railroad tracks that ran from the studio to the outdoors. When French wanted to study a work in progress in the open air, he could throw open the barn doors at one end of the studio and use a railroad handcart to roll the piece outside.

Many of his monuments and memorials were designed or created here, and the studio still contains many of French's plaster sketches as well as a model of his most famous work, the seated Lincoln for the Lincoln Memorial in Washington, D.C. When he needed a break, French could relax on the wisteria-trimmed porch on the back of the studio and gaze over the property that he considered nothing short of "heaven."

By 1901, the original farmhouse had been replaced with a Colonial Revival–style home, also designed by Bacon to complement the studio. It is still furnished with French family pieces, including some from Margaret French Cresson, the only child of French and his wife, Mary Adams French. Although the Frenches enjoyed entertaining friends, their home was free of pretension. French, it seemed, never forgot the thrifty Yankee values of his upbringing in Concord, Massachusetts, and was said to enjoy growing grapes and even clipping hedges.

The property remained a working farm, but French also took an interest in every aspect of the landscape. He treasured the formal gardens and laid out the woodland paths where he enjoyed strolling. He would even occasionally exhibit his own work and that of some of his friends on the grounds. That delightful practice was revived when works by emerging and established sculptors were displayed during the summer of 1978. The now annual exhibitions are highly anticipated by the public and help maintain the artistic energy of the property. Chesterwood is one of the first places in the country to place large-scale abstract, conceptual, and figurative sculpture in outdoor settings carefully selected to complement each work. To date, more than 500 sculptors have been represented.

In 1911, French noted, "It is as beautiful as Fairyland here now. . . . I go about in an ecstasy of delight over the loveliness of things." He would have about two more decades to enjoy his idyllic retreat. He died at Chesterwood in 1931, and his funeral was held in the studio. French's wife, Mary, inherited the property, which passed to their daughter on Mary's death in 1939.

Also a sculptor, Margaret French Cresson had studied under her father as well as with other teachers. In 1955, she began opening the property to the public. In 1973, she died at Chesterwood—but not before she had preserved her father's legacy by conveying the property, now 122 acres, to the National Trust for Historic Preservation.

Jacob's Pillow Dance, Becket
358 George Carter Road, Becket; 413-243-9919; jacobspillow.org; season runs mid-June through August with free and ticketed events and performances

Jacob's Pillow Dance is a perfect balance of tradition and innovation. As visitors wander the grounds to admire the mountaintop view before a performance by flex dancers from the streets of Brooklyn, they can count on a bell to ring and summon them to the theater. It's been that way since the early days, and founder and pioneering modern dancer Ted Shawn (1891–1972) would approve.

Shawn was only 19 and bound for the ministry when a bout with diphtheria changed the course of his life—and of dance in America. Left partially paralyzed, he turned to dance, and his therapy soon became a passion. He explored ballet and ballroom dance but found his calling when he met Ruth St. Denis (1879–1968), who had already launched a career as a solo artist and choreographer. The two married in 1914 and founded the Denishawn Dance Company and School. They soon became the first couple of modern dance—then a radical form of expression that departed from European ballet to find inspiration in theatrical and ethnic dance traditions.

In 1930, Shawn purchased an old farm and former Underground Railroad stop on the crest of a mountain in Lee as a retreat. When he and St. Denis separated the following year, he set about realizing his dream of creating a troupe of men with such an athletic and muscular style that they would banish forever the effeminate labels often applied to male dancers. Company members constructed many of the buildings that still stand today and began offering "tea lecture demonstrations." The bold style and unconventional subject matter—Pawnee braves, African American sharecroppers, union machinists—struck a chord. Ted Shawn and His Men Dancers toured for seven years before the company dissolved and its members went to fight in World War II.

Other summer dance programming during the early war years proved that Shawn had succeeded in establishing a following for modern dance in the Berkshires. In 1942, a committee raised enough money to lift the property out of debt and installed Shawn as the director of the Jacob's Pillow Dance Festival, a position he held until his death in 1972.

The Ted Shawn Theatre— the first such facility designed exclusively for dance in the United States—was inaugurated

that year. Architect Joseph Franz (fresh from creating the Music Shed at Tangle-wood) sought to create a structure in complete harmony with its woodsy surroundings. The wooden building was utterly unadorned in keeping with both the spirit of Modernism and the tradition of Yankee frugality. Franz also created a bit of magic, as the back can be opened to the outdoors to give audience members a view of trees lit by floodlights. Still the chief performance venue at the Pillow, the theater also honors the Denishawn legacy with portraits flanking the stage—Shawn performing his Hopi Indian Eagle Dance and St. Denis as the Japanese goddess of mercy, Kwannon.

Early performers included Agnes de Mille, José Limon, the Alvin Ailey Dance Theatre, the Merce Cunningham Dance Company, Maria Tallchief, the Royal Danish Ballet, "Six American Indian Dancers from St. John's Indian School," and, often, Ruth St. Denis. That broad embrace of all forms of dance continues at the Pillow, where, in addition to modern dance, a summer season's performances might include ballet, street dance, tap, jazz, malambo, and flamenco featuring dancers from the United States, Argentina, South Korea, Germany, Algeria, and Burkina Faso.

The artistic lineup and the sylvan setting make a heady mix. The Pillow (as everyone in the Berkshires calls it) lies at the end of a twisting mountain road heavily overhung with branches. The complex sits at the top of the hill amid manicured lawns and wooded glens. On Wednesdays through Saturdays during the 10-week season, visitors might encounter free guided walking tours of the historic property or free discussions with choreographers, writers, filmmakers, and other cultural movers and shakers. Most popular are the Inside/Out series of free performances. That dancers take the stage in an outdoor amphitheater with stunning views simply adds to the allure. One almost expects dryads to spring from the trees and satyrs to emerge from the forest to stage their own kinetic poetry on the platform.

Old Deerfield
Historic Deerfield: 84B Old Main Street, Deerfield; 413-774-5581; historic-deerfield.org; open mid-April through December; admission charged

Memorial Hall Museum: 8 Memorial Street, Deerfield; 413-774-3768; deerfield-ma.org; open May through October; admission charged

English settlers first plowed the rich bottomland and built houses in what is now called Deerfield in 1669. Two years earlier, they had purchased 8,000 wilderness acres near the confluence of the Deerfield and Connecticut Rivers from the Pocumtucks, paying what the English thought was the magnanimous sum of 4 pence per acre. By 1673, 20 families were farming the land and had laid out the 1-mile thoroughfare still known as the Street (although mapping software refers to it as "Old Main Street").

The alluvial topsoil at Deerfield goes deeper than a man could dig, making it some of the richest and most productive farmland any of the settlers had ever seen. That land kept them at work, even though these pioneers at the edge of the frontier lived in constant fear of attack. That raid came in September 1675, when a confederation of Native American tribes tried to expel Europeans from New England in an uprising known as King Philip's War. Half the men of Deerfield were slain and the town was evacuated for the next seven years. But that fertile farmland called, and Deerfield soon had a population of about 200.

Tensions still simmered, as Deerfield represented the northern and western edge of the English colonies, which were engaged in off-and-on warfare with the French. In 1694, a well-fortified Deerfield beat off a surprise attack by Native Americans under French command. During Queen Anne's War, French and Native American warriors attacked Deerfield at dawn on February 29, 1704, killing 47 villagers and taking 112 captives whom they marched 300 miles to Canada.

"Not long before the break of day, the enemy came in like a flood upon us," the Reverend John Williams wrote in *The Redeemed Captive*, his account of the Deerfield Massacre that was published in 1707 and became hugely popular in the English colonies.

Very little else has happened in Deerfield since, but that moment in its history serves as a poignant reminder of what was gained and lost in the settlement of New England. To quote the overwrought but accurate observation of an anonymous government chronicler of the 1930s, Deerfield "is, and will probably always remain, the perfect and beautiful statement of the tragic and creative moment when one civilization is destroyed by another."

Precisely because so little changed, Deerfield was ripe for rediscovery as a perfect Colonial village when the Colonial Revival enthusiasm flared after the Civil War. The Pocumtuck Valley Memorial Association (PVMA) was founded in 1870 to preserve some of the historic houses along the Street. That broad 1-mile street looks a bit bare because its once-stately elms were felled by Dutch elm disease, but its solidly built houses, many of them nearly 300 years old, still stand sentinel along the road. They are maintained, at least on the exterior, in a style consistent with the early years of the 18th century as Deerfield rebuilt from frontier warfare.

Memorial Hall Museum, operated by PVMA, preserves many of the artifacts of 17th and 18th century Deerfield, including the nail-studded doorway of the 1698 John Sheldon House and Tavern, which sports some nasty tomahawk holes as graphic evidence of the ferocity of the Deerfield Massacre. Old Deerfield has long been a focus of research into colonial life, and Memorial Hall is an antiques-lovers museum of rustic furniture, pewter, pottery, and farm implements from the early settlement era.

Historic Deerfield, founded in 1952 to purchase and restore the old houses of the village, now owns several of them. It works closely with Memorial Hall Museum, and Historic Deerfield's Flynt Center of Early New England Life has open storage of the organization's permanent collection, along with two galleries showing selections from the textile and furniture collections.

At least a half dozen historic structures can be visited as part of Historic Deerfield, including the circa 1755 Sheldon House, which is furnished to show a typical farming family house 1780–1810, and the circa 1799 Asa Stebbins House, the first brick house in Deerfield. It showcases neoclassical decorative arts 1790–1820. It is also possible to stop at the Dwight House in the afternoon to see the apprentices' workshops with demonstrations of Colonial crafts of pottery, weaving, and woodworking.

Four houses are shown solely by guided tour. Most visitors elect to see the Wells-Thorn House, which gives an overview of Deerfield's heyday, 1725–1850. The Hinsdale and Anna Williams House highlights the Federal period, focusing on family life in the grand Federal mansion renovated in 1816. One of the more colorful homes is the 1734 Ashley House, which is shown as the minister's home with fine Colonial furniture and English ceramics.

The most personal home of all, however, is Frary House, which was constructed around 1750. In the 1890s, teacher, collector, and antiquarian C. Alice Baker made it a model of the Colonial Revival, filling it with Arts & Crafts basketry, ironware, and needlework and furnishing it with New England antiques.

Emily Dickinson Museum, Amherst
280 Main Street, Amherst; 413-542-8161; emilydickinsonmuseum .org; open for guided tours March through December; admission charged

Had she not left behind a trunk literally full of startling and wonderful poems, it would be tempting to dismiss Emily Dickinson (1830–86) as a unicorn of American letters—a quick flash of a white dress fluttering in an upstairs window. But she did leave behind those poems, and as further evidence of her existence, there is even one faint daguerreotype portrait made at Mount Holyoke Female Seminary when she was age 17—one of the rare occasions she left her father's house in Amherst. She had been encouraged to pursue studies at Mount Holyoke, but she found the separation from home and family to be unbearable. She returned home at the end of her first year, rarely to leave again. Like a domestic cat that rules each room of the house as a county within its realm, she made that 2½-story brick home her world in microcosm.

Little is known of Dickinson's personal life, but much has been speculated over the years. She did make one major trip outside Amherst in 1855, traveling to Philadelphia, where she met a minister named Charles Wadsworth. They corresponded extensively, and Dickinson fans and scholars have long linked them amorously. Others have suggested that she was far more infatuated with her friend Susan Gilbert, who married her brother Austin Dickinson and moved into the fancy Italianate house next door called the Evergreens. Still others have suggested that she was emotionally involved with Judge Otis Phillips Lord, a friend of her father's who was a frequent houseguest.

That house, which the family called the Homestead, was built for Emily's grandparents, Lucretia Gunn Dickinson and her lawyer husband, Samuel Fowler Dickinson, one of the principal founders of Amherst College. In 1830, their eldest son, Edward, moved with his wife, Emily Norcross Dickinson, and son, Austin, into the western half of the house. Later the same year, Emily Elizabeth Dickinson was born, to be joined three years later by her sister, Lavinia, who would be her lifelong friend and housemate.

The Dickinson clan did move out between 1848 and 1855, but ended up repurchasing the Homestead and expanding the property by adding a brick addition to the back for the kitchen and laundry, planting a decorative Italianate cupola on the house, and building a glassed-in conservatory for the younger Emily's plants. (The conservatory no longer exists.)

Now preserved (with the Evergreens) as the Emily Dickinson Museum, much of the Homestead has been painstakingly restored to its appearance as the poet knew it. The exterior had been stripped to bare brick in 1916 to fit the period tastes during the heyday of the Colonial Revival movement, but research showed that the brick house had been painted from the time it was built in 1813—originally red, then largely white. When Emily's father expanded the footprint and added the cupola, he also painted the house a vivid ochre, trimmed the details with white, and painted the shutters forest green. And so it appears today.

Emily's bedroom received similar attention during a two-year restoration that was completed in 2015. This was her sanctuary and the room where she wrote her letters and composed her poems. The second floor bedroom has windows that look south to the Holyoke Range and west to downtown Amherst. When Amherst College acquired the house in 1965, it removed the 20th-century wallpaper and floorboards from Emily's bedroom. Scraps of wallpaper uncovered at that time were used in the recent restoration to re-create the cheerful twining roses of the paper on the walls during Emily's years. Paint scrapings were used to re-create the trim colors.

The museum was also able to replicate some of the original furnishings. Using her personal writing stand and bureau from Harvard University's Houghton Library Emily Dickinson Collection as models, students at the North Bennet Street School in Boston made exact replicas.

Stepping into the room today is strangely disconcerting, for Emily Dickinson remains as elusive as ever. A dress form clad in a long white Victorian dress, as Emily was said to have always worn, stands posed at one of the windows. The narrow sleigh bed hints at a life alone, while the writing stand at another window—complete with facsimile manuscript—denotes the retreat of an author. Everything is prim and neat and very Victorian, right down to the portraits over her writing stand of her heroines, authors Elizabeth Barrett Browning and George Eliot.

Dickinson never published during her life, but after her death, her niece discovered a trunk containing more than 40 hand-bound manuscript books of her poems. Although she had shared a few verses with friends in letters over the years, she had largely kept the more than 1,800 poems to herself.

Lowell's Boat Shop, Amesbury
459 Main Street, Amesbury; 978-834-0050; lowellsboatshop.com; open year-round for guided and self-guided tours; admission charged

Wooden dories and skiffs may lack the grandeur of New England's historical tall ships, but they were critical working tools of the fishing trade and the Lifesaving Service and have been a mainstay of generations of recreational rowers. Few dories were quite so admired as those that came from Lowell's Boat Shop near the mouth of the Merrimack River in Amesbury. Over nearly two centuries, seven generations of Lowells built small craft here. Their family boat shop continues as a working museum where volunteers and apprentices make boats using designs that have stood the test of time.

Simeon Lowell had been building small craft farther up the Merrimack River when he bought land on a quiet bend in the river in Amesbury and set up his boat shop in 1793. The riverbank slope was perfect—just steep enough so that a workshop could be installed at street level, while the main boat loft where the vessels were assembled could sit downstairs at the water's edge.

In the early days of the shop, timber was shipped downriver from New Hampshire. The shop framed its boats in sturdy oak, then planked them in lighter and more flexible pine or sometimes cedar. (Later on, the shop got its wood from Maine via rail.)

The Lowell family knew better than to reinvent the wheel. They adapted the French-Canadian bateau (principally a river craft used in the fur trade) and the flat-bottomed English dory to build a hybrid vessel particularly suitable to the New England coast. With high sides, raked ends, and a wide, flat bottom, these small craft became known as "surf dories." They could be launched into and rowed through rough seas,

making them ideal for fishermen handlining for cod within sight of shore or tending lobster, crab, and fish traps.

Lowell's Boat Shop worked without drawn plans until the mid-20th century. Simeon and his grandson Hiram Lowell standardized construction by creating templates for each piece of the frame from the stems to ribs. Until the advent of steam-powered band saws in the late-19th century, almost all of the pieces were cut and finished using handsaws, planes, drawknives, slicks, and an adz.

In the mid-19th century, Hiram also modified the surf dory to create an iconic vessel of the American fishing trade. He made the dory bigger and straightened and raised the sides so it could hold more cargo. This design became known as a "Banks dory," as the Gloucester fishing schooners would carry as many dories as they could stack on deck to fish the nearby banks and also venture as far as the Grand Banks off Nova Scotia and Newfoundland. Each dory would carry one or two fishermen who would bait and haul handlines as they fished for such bottom fish as cod, haddock, and pollock.

Lowell's Boat Shop continues to build dories just as they did during the height of the Grand Banks fishing trade. The builders begin by assembling the flat bottom, to which they attach the bracket-like frames, the stem, and the stern. This phase of the construction, amply demonstrated in the exhibits at the boat shop, is called a "skillet" because it resembles an old-fashioned iron pan with legs for cooking over an open fire—the kind of pan known as a "spider skillet." The skillet is then clamped onto a construction bed for planks, seats, and rails to be added. These days, builders use some glue in the construction process, but planks are attached with "clinch nails," which are bent over by an iron form once they penetrate the planks. Traditionally, the skiffs and dories were caulked with oakum—fiber that's impregnated with tar or pine resin. The wood and the oakum would swell to make the boat watertight.

Painting of the boats was a simple matter as well. Every boat was painted the same, with a combination of white lead paint, red brick dust, and linseed oil. The mixture was dumped over the finished boats and spread around with a mop. More than a century of accumulated excess paint still covers the floors on the boat building level.

As the fishing trade slacked off at the end of the 19th century, Lowell's Boat Shop began to make an increasing number of surf dories for the US Lifesaving Service and invented another variant for recreational boaters. The "Amesbury rowing skiff" debuted in the 1860s to meet the needs of urban rusticators. The so-called "gentleman's skiff" was smaller in scale than a fishing dory. It also had shorter sides and the wide transom of a skiff (one of the chief features that distinguished a skiff from a dory). The lighter craft was much easier to row, especially on the placid waters of a lake or a protected cove.

Lowell's sold them by the hundreds to camps and resorts and especially to the Girl Scouts and Boy Scouts well into the middle of the 20th century. The boat shop even had its own peculiar way of keeping track of production. From 1897 through 1919, the operators branded the number of each year's boats onto one of the cross beams, noting that in 1911, Lowell's Boat Shop built an astonishing 2,029 boats.

The seventh generation of Lowells sold the shop in the 1980s, and a decade later it came under the Newburyport Maritime Society. Finally, the nonprofit Lowell's Maritime Foundation was formed in 2006 and operates the shop as a living museum of boatbuilding. In addition to tours, Lowell's Boat Shop offers rowing classes, boatbuilding instruction, and apprenticeship programs.

Cape Ann Light Station, Thacher Island, Rockport
Thacher Island, Rockport; 617-599-2590; thacherisland.org; launch from Rockport operates mid-June to Labor Day; island is accessible year-round by kayak or boat; launch fee and landing fee charged

The last light station established under British rule in Massachusetts, twin lighthouses on Thacher Island have served as aids to navigation in the rocky waters between Rockport and Gloucester since 1771. Even the island's name speaks of the need for the warning beacons. During the Great Storm of 1635 (as chroniclers of that period called it), Anthony Thacher and his wife were thrown up on the island as the sole survivors of a shipwreck that took the lives of 21 others, many of them

members of the Thacher family. In recompense, the General Court of Massachusetts gave the island to Thacher during its 1636–37 session. Although never excavated, a rock cairn on the beach is, according to tradition, the spot where Thacher interred the body of his daughter after it washed ashore.

The island sits in heavily trafficked waters about 1 mile from Rockport harbor and 2 miles from Gloucester harbor. In 1771, Massachusetts bought back the 50-acre rock and erected two 45-foot-tall wooden lighthouse towers. Their beacons were first lit on December 21, 1771, and in 1773 were officially designated as Cape Ann Light Station—the first light station on the American coast that did not mark the entrance to a harbor. In 1775, the lights went dark because local authorities felt that they were of more help to the British navy than to local fishermen, smugglers, and privateers. The lights were relit after the Revolution in 1784.

Nearly a century of Cape Ann weather took its toll, and in 1860 the original towers were torn down. A year later, the current pair of 124-foot conical stone lighthouses had been built and were operating. They were set 298 yards apart on a corrected north-south axis, allowing mariners to adjust their compasses for the declination from true north while sailing Cape Ann waters. The towers sit 53 feet above sea level, with the focal plane another 112 feet, 6 inches from the base. They were fitted with 10-foot-high first-order Fresnel lenses and oil-wick lamps. During the 20th century, north tower's Fresnel lens was disassembled and effectively destroyed,

while the south tower lens was moved to the Coast Guard Museum and is now displayed at the Cape Ann Museum.

Until the north tower was shut off in 1932, the Thacher Island lights were the last twin lights operating on the New England coast. The south tower was switched over to electric illumination, flashing a single white light five times at intervals of 20 seconds. The light was automated in 1979 with a 24-inch flashing red beacon visible for 19 miles. The last Coast Guard keeper left in 1980. In 1998, the Coast Guard changed the illumination of the south tower to an even larger, solar-powered rotating red beacon.

Federal oversight of the island has changed over the years. The north half of the island is owned by the US Fish & Wildlife Service but is overseen as a wildlife sanctuary by the town of Rockport. A new light was placed in the north tower in 1989 as a "private aid to navigation." Its 15-watt fluorescent bulb shines through a 10-inch amber beacon to replicate the original candle-powered light of 1771. The town owns the south half of the island, but the Coast Guard maintains the south light.

The nonprofit Thacher Island Association operates a small campground on the island and runs a summer launch service from Rockport, but many visitors opt to come by private boat or kayak. (A small landing fee is assessed, so bring cash.) The boat ramp is adjacent to a building marked "Cape Ann Light Station," which is the service building for both lights. It's the only sanctioned landing spot, as the north half of the island has literally gone to the birds as a National Wildlife Refuge. As a result, much of the grassy area behind the rack line on the shore is off-limits from late May into August, when giant black-backed and smaller herring gulls nest here. They are a protective lot, casting a baleful eye on human intruders. Fortunately, there's a trail system, which also helps visitors avoid the poison ivy that curls around amid the Virginia creeper, beach roses, honeysuckle, chokecherries, and staghorn sumac.

The north tower is open during the summer. The observation deck at the top of the 156 steps provides views southward to Boston (more than 30 miles away) and northwest to the high mountains of Maine. Visitors with sharp eyes might also see a rusty iron pole jutting out of the water to the southeast about ½-mile offshore. This pole marks the group of ledges called "Londoner," since they wrecked many a Boston-bound vessel from London in the early 1700s before the light station was built.

House of the Seven Gables Historic District, Salem
54 Turner Street, Salem; 978-744-0991; 7gables.org; open for guided tours year-round; admission charged

In the modern age of reality television, perhaps it's not surprising that people have trouble telling fact from fiction, but visitors shouldn't go looking for witches or ghosts at the House of the Seven Gables, whatever they might expect from Nathaniel Hawthorne's 1851 book by the same name. The author considered it a further examination of the moral questions posed in his first novel, *The Scarlet Letter*, but Hawthorne made a point of labeling *The House of the Seven Gables* as a romance because he would employ aspects of fantasy in his Gothic tale of the sins of the fathers being visited on each succeeding generation.

It was a subject that Hawthorne took personally. His great-great-grandfather, John Hathorne, was one of the most prominent judges at the Salem witch trials—an association the author tried to minimize by changing the spelling of his surname. In the romance, the wealthy Colonel Pyncheon of Salem covets the waterfront property of farmer Matthew Maule. When Maule is convicted of witchcraft, he curses Pyncheon from the gallows. Pyncheon chokes on his own blood at the inauguration of his waterfront mansion, and each generation of his descendants fares horribly until they flee the mansion, leaving it to decay in dark abandon.

Hawthorne based the setting for his moral fable on an actual waterfront mansion owned by his second cousin, Susanna Ingersoll. The house had a marvelously medieval cast to it, having been originally constructed in 1688 for Captain John Turner and enlarged several times. Hawthorne was a frequent guest, and he was

fascinated with the house's sense of history. His fascination might very well have saved the structure for posterity.

Three generations of Turners occupied the house until they sold it in 1782 to another merchant captain, Samuel Ingersoll. When he died at sea, the house passed to his daughter Susanna. As a result, the house is more broadly known among preservationists as the Turner-Ingersoll mansion. When philanthropist Caroline Emmerton purchased it in 1908, she worked with prominent Colonial Revival architect Joseph Everett Chandler to restore the building as a tourist attraction that would support her settlement house work assisting immigrant families to Salem. (More than a century later, it continues to support programs for immigrant youth.) Over the next two decades, she added other historic structures to the grounds, including the house where Nathaniel Hawthorne was born and where he lived until age 4, when his father died.

The original Turner mansion was quite the showpiece in its day. Founded in 1629, Salem made its first fortune in the cod trade and an even bigger fortune in international shipping. The merchant captains did not hide their lights under a bushel, and even at the end of the 17th century, nothing trumpeted one's wealth like a trophy house. In a peculiar interpretation of Calvinism, these Puritans saw wealth as evidence of goodness in the eyes of God. When Turner erected his mansion, most houses in Salem would not have been as large as his low-ceilinged kitchen, with its massive fireplace hung with iron pots.

Construction of Colonial houses typically began with the fireplace and chimney, and the other rooms were built around them. The original downstairs parlor of the Turner mansion eventually became the dining room, and John Turner II had it grandly remodeled to make it one of the earliest Georgian interiors in the country. Emmerton and Chandler kept the original Georgian wooden paneling of the room added by John Turner II in the early 18th century and placed the interpretation at the end of the Turner years. Hallmarks of Salem's merchant class include the blue and white Cantonese china and paintings of Chinese harbor scenes.

The original house was small—just two rooms stacked to 2½ stories. This portion represents the central core of the current house. By 1676, Turner had pushed it outwards in all directions, adding a kitchen lean-to and north kitchen ell and a spacious south wing with its own chimney. This wing accommodated the "new" parlor as well as the master bed chamber on the second level. When the Ingersolls bought the house from John Turner III, they remade the home to their own Federal-era upper-class taste.

The "new" parlor is interpreted as Susanna Ingersoll kept it. One of the most powerful businesswomen of 19th century Salem, she often entertained her author cousin in this spacious room with bold floral wallpaper and verdigris-green trim. The stories that passed between them over afternoon tea or evening brandy (from the hidden liquor cabinet) remain sealed, but she may have convinced him to set his new novel in the venerable manse.

Unlike most surviving early Colonial houses, the Turner-Ingersoll mansion remains where it was built. The merchant owners could keep an eye on their wharf and watch over their ships when they were in port. The Colonial Revival gardens on the property are probably not historical, but they lend a certain charm. The 1750 red Georgian house where Hawthone was born in 1804 was moved to the campus in 1958, and while it is less representative of the Colonial Revival restorations carried out a half century earlier by Emmerton and Chandler, it does evoke an atmosphere in which Hawthorne might have mulled over the original sins of his forebears. It contains one real prize: the Chippendale-style fall-top desk where the author wrote.

Locks and Canals Historic District, Lowell
67 Kirk Street, Lowell; 978-970-5000; nps.gov/lowe; open year-round; admission charged for Boott Cotton Mills Museum and for canal boat tours

European visitors to the United States in the 1840s had two attractions at the top of their itineraries: Niagara Falls and the city of Lowell. They represented, as one Scotsman observed, the wonders wrought by the hand of God and those by the

hand of man. As a planned industrial city, Lowell was a grand experiment to see if the industrial revolution could take root in America without the wretched social ills of English factory towns. It would take just under a century for the paternalistic system of the early textile mills to degenerate into the conditions that led to the Bread and Roses strike of 1912, but Lowell began with the proposition that great sums of money could be made while lifting up its workers to a better life.

When Thomas Jefferson's Embargo Act of 1807 cut off American access to English cloth, codfish aristocracy scion Francis Cabot Lowell saw an opportunity. He toured England in 1810, ostensibly for his health, and managed to visit the textile mills of Manchester. A quick study, he memorized the workings of the power looms, and when he came home, he and master mechanic Paul Moody managed to replicate them. Lowell set up a mill on the Charles River in Waltham in 1814 that was the first in North America to bring all the processes of manufacturing textiles under a single roof.

Lowell died in 1817, but his fellow investors, led by Nathan Appleton, looked to expand with a site that had greater water power. They settled on the mile-long Pawtucket Falls of East Chelmsford on the Merrimack River. A transportation canal had been built around the Pawtucket Falls in 1792 to connect the upper Merrimack River with Newburyport on the ocean, and in 1803 the Middlesex Canal linked the river directly to Boston. In 1821, Appleton and his associates quietly bought up all the farmland around the riverbanks and the majority of stock in the Proprietors of the Locks and Canals on Merrimack River, as the company was known.

They formed the Merrimack Manufacturing Company and began to build an industrial town on a scale never before seen. They called it Lowell in honor of the man who set it all in motion. Kirk Boott was charged with constructing the canal and lock system and building the mills. The Merrimack Mill on the canal of the same name started operation in 1823, and more canals and mills followed in short order—Hamilton in 1826, Lowell in 1828, the Western Canal in 1831–32 feeding the Tremont and Suffolk Mills, and the Eastern and Northern Canals as well as several feeders and penstocks.

Boott ran the city-building operation with an iron hand, transforming a farming village of a dozen homes into a model industrial community. The construction of the canal network made Lowell the "Venice of America," and much of the city still sits on islands surrounded by canals and the Merrimack River. A parallel network of waterside walkways connects the remaining mills and other historic sites, letting visitors walk down the same paths the workers took on their way to the spinning jennys and the looms. Lowell's ambitious municipal public art program has filled many of the plazas and squares along the route with heroic sculpture. For example, "The Worker," set where Market Street crosses the Merrimack Canal, memorializes the Irish laborers who dug the canals by hand in the 1820s and 1830s.

One of the greatest of the mill operations—and the best preserved by the Lowell National Historical Park—was the Boott Mills complex, inaugurated in 1835. Six mills were built here between 1835 and 1843. The production was staggering. By 1848, Boott was producing 10.5 million yards of cloth per year on 35,000 spindles. By 1884, Boott's six mills had swelled to 140,000 spindles and 3,875 looms. With its handsome 1864 clock tower, Boott Cotton Mills is the best surviving example of early mill architecture in Lowell, perhaps because Boott was able to hang on to the bitter end of New England textile manufacturing in the 1950s. Now converted into a museum, the historic structure maintains an operating 1920s weave room on the first floor while interpretive exhibits fill the second.

Park rangers hand out ear plugs before allowing visitors to enter for a paid tour of the Boott Cotton Mills Museum. The original textile mills were notoriously noisy, and the volume here is, at best, a dull roar as volunteers operate a few of the power looms to make souvenir dish towels (available in the gift shop). At any one time they run only a dozen or so of the 88 looms on the floor, but even so, the noise is so intense that it is possible to feel the air vibrate.

One of the more famous of the mill girls, Lucy Larcom, wrote in her 1889 memoir, *A New England Girlhood*, that "I discovered, too, that I could so accustom myself to the noise that it became like a silence to me. And I defied the machinery to make me its slave. Its incessant discords could not drown the music of my thoughts if I would let them fly high enough."

Just across Boardinghouse Park from the mill is the Mogan Cultural Center, where exhibits make the daily lives of the mill girls seem more tangible. (For a broader perspective, it also holds the Center for Lowell History.) While American industrialists were only too happy to adopt British textile technology, they sought to establish a more humane system of employment. English mills typically employed entire families at low wages, but the Lowell mills—at least initially—hired only young women from the surrounding countryside, providing them with clean boardinghouses, fair wages, and moral instruction. These farm daughters would work at the mills a year or two, make some money for a dowry or to pay the family mortgage, and return home. In practice, this system created the first class of working women in America.

Not only were the mill girls among America's first independent women, they were among the first workers to organize. The paternalistic system collapsed as soon as Lowell's mills had competition, and the mill girls staged strikes for better pay and working conditions as early as 1834 and petitioned the state legislature for relief from exploitation. The mill owners responded by cutting wages and speeding up machines—and by hiring immigrants to work the mills. If the farmers' daughters didn't like the new working conditions, longer hours, and lower wages, then refugees from the Irish famine were happy to have the jobs. The cycle continued into the early 20th century with successive waves of immigrants from Quebec, Italy, Greece, Baltic Europe, and the eastern Mediterranean.

Lowell National Historical Park maintains much of the original industrial architecture and infrastructure of Lowell's manufacturing heyday, along with extensive educational exhibits and activities. From Memorial Day to Columbus Day, it even has canal boat tours that last up to two hours. But modern Lowell has also made peace with its textile past, and several of the old brick mills have been transformed into apartments, condos, and live-work spaces for artists. America's first working city is still on the job.

Walden Pond, Concord

915 Walden Street, Concord; 978-369-3254; mass.gov/locations/walden-pond-state-reservation.html; open year-round for day use; parking fee charged

Brief as it was, Henry David Thoreau (1817–62) lived the life that his friend and mentor Ralph Waldo Emerson could only imagine. As a leading disciple of Emerson's Transcendentalist ideas, Thoreau hung handsome, down-to-earth clothes on his friend's abstract skeleton of ideas. Thoreau's two-year experiment of living in a cabin on the shores of Walden Pond (compressed to a single year in his 1854 book *Walden*) has made that 102-foot-deep, spring-fed glacial kettle pond and its surrounding woods into hallowed ground for conservationists. The pond and land around it now constitute the 335-acre Walden Pond Reservation under the Massachusetts state park system.

When Thoreau floated the idea of living in splendid isolation close to nature, Emerson had just the spot for him. He had purchased 11 acres on Walden Pond where the two of them would go on long walks in the woods. There's no formal record of Emerson offering encouragement, but Thoreau erected a rough cabin near the shore of the pond and moved there on July 4, 1845. As he famously wrote, "I went to the woods because I wished to live deliberately, to front only the essential facts of life, and see if I could not learn what it had to teach, and not, when I came to die, discover that I had not lived."

Although *Walden* is often presented as an unburnished account—almost a diary—of life at the pond, it is a carefully shaped book that omits a great deal and plays up small moments to fashion an essentially heroic account of plunging into Nature with a capital "N." Although he takes account of his isolation, the cabin was about a mile and a half along the railroad tracks from Concord village, and Thoreau was never quite as dependent on his bean patch (actually a 2½-acre garden!) as he would like readers to believe. He rarely missed Lidian Emerson's spread at Sunday dinner.

In some respects, the Concord-born and -raised Thoreau was more the scholar than Emerson. He was also educated at Harvard (where he balked at paying five dollars for his master's diploma, commenting, "Let every sheep keep its own skin"). Thoreau read widely in Greek mythology and philosophy, Eastern theology and philosophy, poetry,

and—in the habit that made him most American—in agriculture and science. It was this grounding in the physical world of phenomena, as opposed to the abstract world of phenomenology where Emerson dwelt, that distinguished him from the intellectuals of his age.

He lived at Walden Pond to see if he could reconcile the physical, spiritual, and symbolic worlds. Although his design might have lacked scientific rigor, Thoreau intentionally constructed the experience as an experiment. By the time he moved back to town in September 1847, he had proved (at least to his satisfaction) that living simply made him happier and put him more in tune with the natural world around him.

In 1922, the Emerson family donated the land surrounding the pond to the Commonwealth of Massachusetts with the stipulation that the state must preserve "the Walden of Emerson and Thoreau, its shores and nearby woodlands for the public who wish to enjoy the pond, the woods, and nature, including bathing, boating, fishing and picnicking."

Many visitors to Walden come seeking the enlightenment that Thoreau wrested from his months in the woods, almost as if they had climbed the mythic Himalayan peak to ask a hermit yogi the meaning of life. There are no signposts to nirvana here, but there is a replica of Thoreau's cabin with a rather bizarre sculpture of him out front, an entire network of hiking trails, and the site of the original cabin marked out with stones on the ground. More to the point for many who live in the area, there is a sandy beach with lifeguards in the summer. The Visitors Center, built 2015–16, provides trail maps, restroom facilities, and interpretative displays about Thoreau and his significant impact on such later conservationists as John Muir and Rachel Carson.

Although very crowded during summer weekends, at other times Walden Pond lives up to Thoreau's own summary, in terms he borrowed from Eastern philosophy. It was, he wrote, "lower heaven."

Ralph Waldo Emerson House, Concord
28 Cambridge Turnpike, Concord; 978-369-2236; nps.gov/nr/travel/ massachusetts_conservation/ralph_waldo_emerson_house.html; open late April to mid-October for guided tours; admission charged

Born in Boston in 1803, Ralph Waldo Emerson was the linchpin of a disparate group of mid-19th-century New England writers who were drawn to his home and his ideas. He studied at Boston Latin School from age 9 and then at Harvard College from age 14. Following a brief stint as a schoolmaster, he studied at Harvard Divinity School and was ordained as a Unitarian minister in 1829. He served as junior pastor at Second Church in Boston and as chaplain to the Massachusetts legislature.

In 1829, he married Ellen Louisa Tucker when she turned 18, but his young wife was already ill with tuberculosis. When she died in 1831, Emerson suffered a crisis of faith and began to move further and further away from the teachings of his church. During an 1833 trip to England, he became friends with the Scottish philosopher Thomas Carlyle and met William Wordsworth and Samuel Coleridge.

Although hardly bookish—he was an average student at Harvard—Emerson embraced thinking as a profession. He and Carlyle would be correspondents and close friends until the Scot's death in 1881. Taking Carlyle as inspiration, Emerson began giving public lectures on the Lyceum circuit. He gave his first of an estimated

1,500 lectures in November 1833 while still living with his mother. Finally possessing a means to earn a living, he moved to Concord in 1834 to the family home known as the Old Manse.

That first lecture, on "The Uses of Natural History," expanded on his experience in Europe visiting the Jardins des Plantes, the botanical gardens in Paris's fifth

arrondisement beautifully cataloged in the system developed by Antoine Laurent de Jussieu. His musings on seeking a scientific order in the natural world were the beginnings of what would become his influential work, *Nature*.

In January 1835, Emerson wrote a letter proposing marriage to Lydia Jackson, an intellectual woman who was deeply involved in social issues of the day, including the movement to abolish slavery. They had met when he lectured in her hometown of Plymouth, Massachusetts, and by all accounts, they were mutually smitten. They were both eager to marry—he was 32, she 33—and had only met twice before his proposal. In July, Emerson purchased the house on Cambridge Turnpike where they would live after their marriage in September.

Lidian, as Emerson called her, was loathe to leave Plymouth for what she saw as the wilds of Concord, but her husband-to-be acceded to the wishes she expressed in a letter that "it cannot be fine until trees and flowers give it a character of its own." He spent several hundred dollars adding two rooms and creating the landscaping that she would complete with her gardens. They ultimately had four children and lived in the house until his death in 1881 and hers in 1892.

The house became the intellectual nerve center of American letters, and Lidian Emerson became the hostess to the intellectual elite. Emerson's most productive period came shortly after they moved in. He began collecting his lectures as essays, and the publication of *Nature* in 1836 and the *American Scholar* in 1837 cemented his reputation both with the public and with his literary and philosophical peers.

He became the leading theorist and proponent of Transcendentalism—an American twist on the Romantic notion that the divine is to be found in Nature, not in a godhead.

Emerson's friend and protege, Henry David Thoreau, grounded Emerson's flights of metaphysical fancy in moral challenges of the social world. Thoreau often boarded with the Emersons and helped care for the children and fill the woodbox. When Thoreau was jailed on a matter of conscience and principle, as he recounts in "Civil Disobedience," Emerson paid to have him released. Even when Thoreau was ostensibly living the hermit's life at Walden Pond, he was usually at the Emerson table for Sunday dinner. Other regular visitors included Bronson Alcott (Louisa May's intellectual gadfly father), Margaret Fuller (groundbreaking journalist and social activist), and Elizabeth Peabody (radical educator and first American translator of Buddhist texts). The dining room table could seat up to 18 people.

Visiting the house feels a little like visiting one's scholar grandfather. The home is a simple center hall Federal house with two large rooms at either side of the entry. On the right is Emerson's study, where he did the majority of his writing sitting at a rocker pulled up to a round table in the middle of the room. The furnishings here are reproductions, as the original study is now at the Concord Museum across the street, and Emerson's private book collection is in the special collections of Harvard's Houghton Library. All other furniture is original to the house, as are such personal

touchstones as Emerson's walking sticks which he used on his jaunts to Walden Pond (see p. 107).

The family bedrooms are on the second floor. Guests would stay in the "Pilgrim's Chamber" on the first floor across the hall from the study. Writers from around the country would make the pilgrimage to Concord in hopes that Emerson would write something positive about their work.

Others simply wrote to him, and his response could make or break a career. Edgar Allen Poe he rejected as "the jingle man," and the Boston publishers wouldn't touch him. Walt Whitman, on the other hand, sent a first printing of *Leaves of Grass* and received in reply one of the most famous blurbs in American publishing: "I greet you at the beginning of a great career, which yet must have had a long foreground somewhere for such a start."

The house has remained in the Emerson family. Ellen Tucker Emerson, Ralph and Lidian's daughter, lived in it until her death in 1909, and other family members inhabited parts of the house until 1948. Since 1930, however, it has been a house museum open to the public on a seasonal basis.

Louisa May Alcott's Orchard House, Concord
399 Lexington Road, Concord; 978-369-4118; louisamayalcott.org; guided tours year-round; admission charged

Visitors to Orchard House are often surprised to learn that Louisa May Alcott was in her mid-twenties before she and her parents and two surviving sisters settled in Orchard House just outside Concord center and within walking distance of family friend Ralph Waldo Emerson (see p. 109). Her novel *Little Women* painted such a rich picture of four young girls growing up here that it is easy to assume that this is where the clan was born and raised.

But the family had lived in more than 20 other homes as father Bronson Alcott

struggled to earn a living as an educational reformer. When he purchased the 18th-century property in 1857, a friend of his wife, Abigail May Alcott, declared that it was only "fit for pigs." Bronson spent a year restoring the house and continued to tinker and make improvements for the unprecedented two decades that family

members spent here. Today about 80 percent of the furnishings are from the Alcotts and reflect the warmth of a settled family life and their rising fortunes as Louisa began to achieve literary success.

From a young age, Louisa wrote "theatricals" that she and her sisters would perform, as well as poems and short stories that appeared in popular magazines. She published her first book, *Flower Fables*, in 1854 but began to garner national attention after the publication of *Hospital Sketches* in 1863. It was based on her experiences as a Civil War nurse in Washington, D.C. Her service was cut short when she came down with typhoid fever and had to return to Orchard House for a long recuperation.

Her literary career received a big boost when her publisher asked her to write "a book for girls." Louisa was 35 years old but seemed to have little trouble reaching back to girlhood years. She certainly didn't lack for setting or subject matter. *Little Women* is based in Orchard House, and the March family members are only thinly disguised versions of Louisa, her sisters, her father, and the girls' beloved mother, "Marmee." Louisa wrote the novel between May and July 1868, and it was well received from the start. It has never gone out of print, and countless young girls, as seemingly diverse as Patti Smith and Hillary Clinton, found a role model in Jo March, Louisa's spunky fictional counterpart.

Many make their way to the home to see where Louisa sat to write and where family life unfolded. Tours begin in the kitchen and move quickly to the dining room

and parlor where the young women would perform their theatricals. The dining room table is set with an embroidered cloth and fine china and glassware. Bronson Alcott built a rather primitive china cabinet to hold his wife's lovely tableware, but of most interest is the melodion that belonged to Elizabeth (called Lizzie by the family, but appearing as Beth in the novel). She died shortly before the Alcotts moved into Orchard House, but Louisa's novel warmly memorialized her sweet personality and related the details of her tragic death from scarlet fever.

Anna Alcott (Meg in the novel) celebrated her 1860 marriage to John Bridge Pratt in the parlor. An aspiring actress, she met him when they performed in a play at the Concord Dramatic Union, which Louisa and Anna helped establish. The fictionalized account of the wedding ceremony has proven so romantic that men have been known to bring their girlfriends to Orchard House for surprise proposals. Orchard House often re-enacts Anna's wedding to John during the month of May.

May Alcott (Amy in the novel) was a talented artist whose career was furthered by her sister Louisa's support for her studies in Paris, London, and Rome. May's paintings hang throughout the house, including a series of masterful copies of European scenes by J. M. W. Turner. Although the family was in dire financial straits when they moved into Orchard House, all three daughters had the luxury of private bedrooms, and May even used the walls of her long, narrow room as a canvas. Restoration work has uncovered many of her images of Roman and Greek figures, chariots, mothers and children, and angels. Staff can't help but wonder what other treasures might someday come to light. Her room is furnished with lovely French Provincial furniture that Bronson purchased for her from a catalog. In one corner, an open trunk overflows with some of the costumes that the sisters used for their theatricals.

Bronson Alcott has a reputation as a rather strict father, but he and Abigail clearly encouraged their daughters to be true to their talents and never shrink from self-expression. Louisa occupied a big bedroom at the front of the house looking out onto Lexington Road. Between two windows, Bronson built a small semicircular desk so that his daughter would have a place to write. To cheer her sister as she spent hours in bed recuperating from her illness, May painted a likeness of an owl below the mantel on Louisa's fireplace. And to give her something pretty to gaze on as she wrote, May painted blooming flowers growing up a narrow wall beside the desk.

Gropius House, Lincoln
68 Baker Bridge Road, Lincoln; 781-259-8098; historicnewengland
.org; open June through mid-October for guided tours; admission
charged

In the world of historic preservation, 40 years is pretty much the blink of an eye. But Historic New England (then the Society for the Preservation of New England Antiquities) knew that it had a groundbreaking structure when it brought the Walter Gropius House under its wing in 1979—and thus became the first traditional preservation organization to accession a modern house.

Architect Walter Gropius (1883–1969) was the founder and first director of the Bauhaus school of modern design. He fled Nazi Germany and eventually moved to the United States in 1937 to become a professor and ultimately chairman of the Harvard Graduate School of Design. He brought with him his Bauhaus principles of simplicity, economy, functionality, and beauty derived from form rather than unnecessary decoration. Although he; his wife, Ise; and their daughter, Ati, left Europe with few material possessions, Gropius was soon able to once again put his principles into practice by building not just a family home, but the first example of Bauhaus domestic style in the United States.

Sympathetic to the disruption in the life of the Gropius family, philanthropist and arts patron Helen Storrow offered Gropius a 4-acre plot of land on her Lincoln estate and supplied him with the funds for construction. Soon a Modern house—costing about $20,000—began to take shape on a slight hill at the edge of an apple

orchard. Completed in 1938 and featuring a flat roof, glass brick wall, and exterior spiral staircase, the rather modest 2,300-square-foot house was nothing like its neighbors—until Marcel Breuer built his home nearby the next year. In fact, the Gropius house set off a mini-boom in Modern house construction in the immediate area.

Walter and Ise Gropius had spent months touring New England so that the architect could internalize the local building vocabulary. The flat roof of the home is something of a departure from local norms in the snowy climate, but like many New England homes, the Gropius House is constructed of white clapboards with black trim. The clapboards, however, run vertically and the black trim usually represents a metal frame for windows far larger than the Yankee norm. Despite its practicality and crisp appearance, glass brick never really caught on in New England.

Gropius embraced the use of new, often industrial materials, such as cork and linoleum flooring, acoustic plaster, welded steel, and chrome, both as a practical and aesthetic matter. But guided tours of the house nudge visitors past any misconceptions of Modern design as cold or sterile to emphasize the rich and warm lives lived within the iconic structure. The Gropiuses did manage to bring much of their Bauhaus-designed furniture with them, and the house contains the largest collection of such pieces on display outside Germany. The tubular steel chairs and end tables and the bentwood lounge chair are literally more comfortable in their new home than they had been in the Colonial-style house the family had rented when they first arrived.

On the ground level facing the street is the office where Walter and Ise worked side by side at a Bauhaus-designed double desk that elevates the door on file cabinets found in every student apartment. Light floods in through the glass brick wall that separates the office from the dining room. The L-shaped living room, with long vistas on one side and a forest view on another, is spacious and comfortable. Gropius's Bauhaus colleague Marcel Breuer designed most of the furniture, which would not look out of place in a Design Within Reach showroom. Gropius received an early example of an Eero Saarinen "Womb Chair" as a 70th birthday gift, and it claims pride of place in the room.

In the dining room, a round white Formica table (also designed by Breuer) is set with Prolon bowls and plates, a line of Modern-design melamine dinnerware originally made in Florence, Massachusetts. A virtual Who's Who of the great artists and architects of the time made their way to the Gropius house, including Breuer, Frank Lloyd Wright, Lyonel Feininger, Igor Stravinsky, Henry Moore, Joan Miró, Eero Saarinen, and Alexander Calder. The conversations around that table must have been riveting.

But ultimately, as daughter Ati Gropius Johansen wrote in a 2012 Historic New England publication, the structure "was not a 'demonstration' house. . . . It was a

happily functioning and livable house in which the Gropius family felt very much at home." A strong believer in collaboration, Gropius involved his wife and daughter in making design decisions.

By today's standards, the upstairs living quarters are strikingly modest. Contemporary home-buyers would be aghast at the limited closet and storage space, but pleased with the his-and-hers sinks in the master bathroom. Many intellectuals fleeing Europe in the years just before and during World War II were houseguests, and the guest bedroom is furnished with two single beds arranged end to end as daybeds. Teenager Ati's room opened onto a second-floor deck connected to that exterior staircase, which gave her a sense of privacy and independence but still allowed her parents to keep an eye on her.

Of all the features of New England architecture, the Gropiuses were most taken with the screened porch. But, once again, Gropius adapted the idea to his family's own particular needs. Rather than placing it on the front of the house where it might darken the interior and where the family would be distracted by street noise, he moved it to the rear of the house and placed it perpendicular to rather than parallel to the back wall. This private getaway became, in effect, a year-round living space. Breezes kept it cool in summer, and the south- and west-facing sun made it warm enough in winter for Gropius to enjoy a game of Ping-Pong or settle in to watch one of his beloved horse operas, such as *Bonanza*, on TV.

Revere Beach Reservation, Revere
Revere Boulevard, Revere; open year-round dawn to dusk. State monitors water quality from Memorial Day to Labor Day. Lifeguards are on duty from late June until early September.

"It was the grand and refreshing sight of the natural sea beach, with its long, simple curve, and its open view of the ocean," wrote pioneer landscape architect Charles Eliot in 1896. "Nothing in the world presents a more striking contrast to the jumbled, noisy scenery of a great town. . . ." He was surveying his work for the Metropolitan Park Commission at Revere Beach, and rather like the biblical Creator, at the end of each of the first six days, he pronounced it good.

Eliot was a Harvard graduate and son of Harvard president Charles W. Eliot. More conservationist than public health reformer—a designation his mentor Frederick Law Olmsted readily embraced—he was bent on halting development of natural lands around Boston. His grand projects for the infant Park Commission would include not only Revere Beach, but also the Charles River Basin, the Blue Hills, and the Middlesex Fells. Only Revere Beach would be largely completed before his untimely death in 1897 from spinal meningitis. Yet, arguably, the salvation of the great crescent-shaped barrier beach for public use was one of the greatest contributions of early conservationists to the quality of urban life.

Only 6 miles north of Boston, the 2.8-mile stretch of Revere Beach was irresistible to city dwellers, especially after the Boston, Revere Beach and Lynn Railway was built along the top of the dunes in 1875. Private bathhouses, restaurants, and amusements sprang up along the rail line as a jumble of environmentally reckless

construction that reached down to the high-tide line. At Eliot's behest, the Park Commission began acquiring the land in 1895, and by the end of that summer, Eliot's crews had wiped the shoreline clean. They moved the railbed 400 yards west (where it now serves the MBTA's Blue Line trains from Boston) and replaced the rails with a carriage road and a promenade—now Revere Beach Boule-

vard and the broad sidewalk beside it. When he wrote his initial report, he had a lot to crow about. Indeed, it *was* good.

It still is. Per Eliot's original design, eight open-air wrought iron and wood pavilions line the beach, and the modern addition of a short concrete seawall creates a bit of separation between beach and promenade. As a proper Victorian, Eliot could not have foreseen the youthful sunbathers who sprawl atop that wall, but it's nice to think that he would be pleased that modern beachgoers so thoroughly enjoy Revere. The beach is smokefree, but the promenade falls outside the reservation's jurisdiction. Power walkers, joggers, dog walkers, and cyclists on the sidewalk have to contend with beach chair road blocks, where clusters of older smokers puff away while they catch some rays. Yet the mood always stays light. Live and let live. It's always too nice a day to get into a beef.

The beach itself never gets as congested as the promenade or the boulevard. At the narrowest point, it stretches 100 yards from the seawall to the high-tide line, and at its widest, it sprawls a full 400 yards. Games of Frisbee, touch football, and even petanque don't begin to crowd the sands. Hundreds of families stake out their turf with blankets surrounded by a flotsam of beach chairs and plastic toys. Scantily clad sunbathers sprawl on beach towels. Small children prepare for civil engineering careers as they construct sand castles. Heavily oiled musclemen twitch beneath the solar glare, sending ripples from their delts to their glutes while hoping someone is watching.

Even after Eliot's design scoured the entertainments from the beach, Revere had a second honky-tonk era between the world wars. Time, weather, and changing property values have swept away the lures of yesteryear, so the infant incubator, the big band ballrooms, and such fearsomely named roller-coasters as Cyclone and Thunderbolt survive only in the fading postcards next to the order window at Revere Beach fixture Kelly's Roast Beef, a comparative newcomer established in 1951.

The beach, however, persists as Eliot envisioned it. Even he could never have imagined one of today's pastimes—watching big jets take off from nearby Logan Airport and make a long bank rightward over the Atlantic bound for faraway places.

Yet to escape the city, as Eliot observed, all you really need is the soft sand of Revere's luminous crescent.

Longfellow House, Cambridge
105 Brattle Street, Cambridge; 617-876-4491; nps.gov/long; open for guided tours late-May through October; admission charged

Given his patriotism and his fascination with American myth and history, it must have given Henry Wadsworth Longfellow (1807–82) considerable pleasure to know that George Washington had, indeed, slept in his house—even if it was decades earlier. The large Georgian manse known as the Longfellow House was constructed in 1759 for merchant John Vassall. Many of the Massachusetts Bay Colony's wealthiest merchants chose to live in Cambridge to enjoy the amenities of life in a college town. And many of them, like Vassall, were loyal subjects of the king. Like the others, Vassall built on "Tory Row," the stretch of Brattle Street that begins just behind Christ Church and extends about a mile out of Harvard Square. Surrounded by long, green lawns and Georgian gardens, these blocky mansions sit in removed majesty as models of proportion and order. As anti-crown tensions rose in the mid-1770s, most of their owners fled. The state auctioned off their homes after the Revolution.

When George Washington came to Cambridge in July 1775 to assume command of the Continental Army and continue to lay siege to the British who held Boston, he chose the vacant Vassall house as his headquarters. He would stay for nine months, welcoming Martha to their first wartime home, receiving diplomats, and plotting strategy. He left the house in April 1776 after the British withdrew all their forces from Boston on St. Patrick's Day.

The house was sold in 1791 to Andrew and Elizabeth Craigie, who enlarged and redecorated what was soon known as "Craigie Castle." It could have been called "Craigie's Folly," as the expansion plunged the couple into debt. When Andrew died, Elizabeth was forced to take in boarders to make ends meet. One of them was a young Harvard professor of modern languages, Henry Wadsworth Longfellow, who began renting two rooms in 1837, shortly after his return from Europe, where his first wife, Mary, had died of complications from a miscarriage.

On his grand tour before assuming his professorship, Longfellow had met Frances "Fanny" Appleton in Switzerland. Her father was one of the three founders of the Merrimack Manufacturing Company, which developed the mill system in Lowell and pioneered the American textile industry. Appleton was initially skeptical of a poet-scholar wooing his daughter, but the young widower was persistent, often walking from Cambridge to Beacon Hill to call on her. When they finally wed in 1843, her father presented them with Craigie Castle as a wedding gift. It remained in

the Longfellow family until the Longfellow House Trust donated it to the National Park Service in 1972.

The house is largely presented as it functioned during the years that Fanny and Henry lived here. In many ways, it is the house of a literary lion. Longfellow and Nathaniel Hawthorne had been classmates at Bowdoin College, and Hawthorne was a frequent visitor. Ralph Waldo Emerson usually stopped in when he deigned to visit Boston from his Transcendental dukedom of Concord. Anthony Trollope and Charles Dickens visited from England, and Julia Ward Howe often popped by from across the river in Boston. Although his wife's fortune and his immense popular success with such verse books as *Evangeline* and *Song of Hiawatha* had allowed Longfellow to resign from Harvard in 1854, the intelligentsia of the day beat a path to his door.

It was a boisterous and for many years happy household, and the tour of the house touches both on the public rooms, where Fanny and Henry entertained, and the private family quarters. The couple had six children, five of whom survived infancy. The eldest, Charley, became an adventurer and world traveler. His younger brother, Ernest, became a noted painter. The three girls so lovingly described in Longfellow's poem "The Children's Hour" as "grave Alice, and laughing Allegra, and Edith with golden hair" all went on to fulfilling lives. Born in 1850, Alice was the only one of the three never to marry. As a preservationist and philanthropist, she was behind the establishment of the Longfellow House Trust that opened the property to the public in 1930.

Tours of the house tend to focus on the Longfellow family life even more than on Longfellow's literary career, since his heavily cadenced and rhyming verse has gone out of fashion. Guides tend to brush over the capstone of his literary career—his deeply felt translation of Dante's *Divine Comedy*. The background to that work is sad. In 1861, Fanny was sealing locks of hair from the children into envelopes when the hot wax set her clothing on fire. Henry sought in vain to smother the flames, but she died and he was so badly burned that he grew a full beard to cover the most obvious scars. And then he undertook the translation, following Dante's journey through the three realms of the dead as he sought his beloved Beatrice in the afterlife.

One of the last famous writers to visit Longfellow was the poet Oscar Wilde, who paid his respects on his 1882 lecture tour of America. Wilde recalled that "Longfellow himself was a beautiful poem." The gray eminence of American letters died in the house later that year and was buried in the family plot of Mount Auburn Cemetery (see below).

Daughter Alice lived in the family home until her death in 1928. In 1917, she was joined by Edith's son, Henry Wadsworth Longfellow "Harry" Dana, who had lost his job at Columbia University for his pacifist activities and socialist proclivities. Harry and Alice began the massive task of archiving all the objects in the house—socks, spoons, letters, journals, recipes for apple pie, and anything else they could find. It would make the property one of the best-documented homes in American preservation. Harry was granted life tenancy in the house and lived in it until his death in 1950, working in later years as the curator when the house became a national monument.

Mount Auburn Cemetery, Cambridge and Watertown
580 Mount Auburn Street; Cambridge; 617-547-7105; mountauburn.org; open year-round; free admission

Supreme Court Justice Joseph Story spoke for a generation of Boston-area thinkers when he addressed those assembled for the consecration of Mount Auburn Cemetery on September 24, 1831. "All around there breathes a solemn calm, as if we were in the bosom of a wilderness," he reminded the crowd. "Ascend but a few steps, and what a change of scenery to surprise and delight us. We seem to pass from the confines of death to the bright and balmy regions of life."

It was as if the landscape itself echoed the biblical vale of sorrow and transcendent light of salvation. From the deepest dell of this new type of burial ground, one could walk to the summit of the Mount Auburn hillock and observe the blue curve of the Charles River and the busy industry of Boston a short distance downstream.

The establishment of Mount Auburn Cemetery marked the beginning of a new chapter in the American way of death. It was the first urban cemetery placed in the nearby countryside—a response both to overcrowding in the urban burial grounds and church graveyards, and growing public health concerns about burials in congested neighborhoods. Even more importantly, it marked a shift in public attitudes about death. Even the name of the place was new. "Cemetery" was a new coinage derived from Greek roots to describe a place where the dead repose. And the landscape design, in keeping with the concepts of Transcendentalism, was to express a certain kind of continuity.

Simply put, the beautiful garden landscape was intended both to console the bereaved and to inspire visitors to contemplate their own mortality. It was a place of sweet sadness—an expression of melancholy akin to the willow-by-the-water motif of mourning pictures, samplers, and other remembrances of the period. A progenitor of the rural cemetery movement, Mount Auburn helped establish the ideal of a cemetery as a tranquil retreat with flowers, grass, and trees. As families began to commemorate their loved ones with sculptural figures in this park-like setting, Mount Auburn began to attract visitors in large numbers, helping to launch the American park landscape movement. Nearly two centuries later, it remains both hallowed ground for remembrance and a landscape for aesthetic enjoyment.

The founders signaled their ambition to make a new place for the ages in the choice of architecture for the gate. The Egyptian Gateway was first erected in 1832 as a wooden structure dusted with sand, and when funds allowed, it was remade in Quincy granite in 1842–43. The designer, Dr. Jacob Bigelow, modeled the gate on renderings of the north and south portals of the Karnak Temple Complex in the

account of Napoleon's 1798–1801 expedition in Egypt, *Description de l'Égypte*. The stone version of his design, Bigelow said, would "entitle it to a stability of a thousand years."

Egyptian Revival architecture met Transcendental Romanticism to ignite a creative explosion of grave memorials at Mount Auburn Cemetery. More than 30,000 monuments fill the grounds, and they include major sculptural works by Augustus Saint-Gaudens (see p. 199), Thomas Crawford, and Edmonia Lewis, among others. The founders also encouraged the creation of monuments to civic heroes. One of the first was the obelisk erected to

commemorate the members of the 1840 US Naval Expedition who perished in the Fiji Islands. The massive Sphinx atop the hill opposite Bigelow Chapel marked the preservation of the Union in the Civil War.

The influences of John Ruskin and H. H. Richardson popularized Romanesque and Gothic architecture in Boston after the middle of the 19th century, and that trend was also reflected in the Gothic styling of sculptures and gravestones throughout the cemetery. Victorian sentimentalism also informed many of the grave sculptures of grieving women, guardian dogs, and—often on children's graves—sweet little lambs. Some of the plots were even fenced off and laid out like family parlors, with each member accorded her or his seat in the "room."

This extraordinary combination of park landscape and funerary art persists to the present. The original circulation system of the roadways has expanded in part to permit the passage of automobiles, but the original contours of the 1831 cemetery remain. Winding paths and roads create changing vistas at every turn. In accordance with the founders' interest in horticulture, most roads are named for plants and trees. The abundance of blooming plants and considerable forest canopy also make Mount Auburn Cemetery a natural island in an urban landscape. Migrating birds stop here for rest, water, and food, making the cemetery one of the most popular birding parks in Greater Boston.

More than 95,000 people are buried and memorialized at Mount Auburn Cemetery, including poets Amy Lowell and Robert Creeley, inventor Edwin Land, hospital reformer Dorothea Dix, painter Winslow Homer, architect Buckminster Fuller, author Bernard Malamud, cookbook author Fannie Farmer, and even Mary Baker Eddy, founder of Christian Science, whose tomb, contrary to urban legend, does not contain a telephone.

John Fitzgerald Kennedy Birthplace, Brookline
83 Beals Street, Brookline; 617-566-7937; nps.gov/jofi; open for guided tours late May through October; free admission

Fresh from their honeymoon, Joseph P. Kennedy and Rose Fitzgerald Kennedy moved into a seven-room Colonial Revival-style home at 83 Beals Street in Brookline in 1914. At the time, many young couples had to spend a few years in their parents' homes as they worked to establish themselves. But the Kennedys, both third-generation descendants of Irish immigrants with prominent fathers in Democratic politics, were a young couple on the rise. Boston's "streetcar suburb" of Brookline, home to many middle- and upper-middle-class Irish American families, was a perfect fit for them.

Four of the couple's nine children were born in their second-floor bedroom, including John Fitzgerald Kennedy on May 29, 1917. The family soon outgrew the house and moved to larger quarters nearby in September 1920. But Rose Kennedy fondly remembered the family's early days at Beals Street. Preferring to celebrate the birth of the 35th president rather than to only mourn his 1963 assassination, the Kennedy family repurchased the house in 1966.

"We were very happy here, and although we did not know about the days ahead, we were enthusiastic and optimistic about the future," Mrs. Kennedy recalled in 1969, when the home was dedicated as a National Historic Site.

She largely took on the task of restoring the Beals Street property to the joyful and busy days of her young family's life. Even with gaps in memory caused by the

passage of so many years, the specificity of Mrs. Kennedy's remembrances have helped to create an unusually personal experience for visitors.

By the time the couple married, Joseph Kennedy was already one of the youngest bank presidents in the country, and Rose Kennedy soon found her calling as manager of the household and

custodian of her children's education and moral upbringing. Whenever she took the children for walks to the grocery store in Coolidge Corner, she recalled, they would stop at Saint Aidan's Roman Catholic Church on the way home.

Some Kennedy family furnishings have been returned to the house, particularly in the dining room to the immediate left of the front door. The table set with fine china and glassware reflects a family that wanted to make a good impression on guests while also attending to the needs of young children. In addition to the formal table, a small table was set by a lace-curtained window. It holds the silver spoons and porringers for the couple's first two children, Joseph P. Kennedy, Jr., and John Fitzgerald Kennedy. Nearly two years older, Joe excelled at pleasing his parents while Jack sought attention by becoming the family clown.

Rose Kennedy was a firm believer that living rooms should indeed be for living and had fond memories of reading or sewing while her husband read the *Boston Transcript* and her children played in their pajamas before bedtime. The piano in the room was a wedding present from two of Rose's uncles. She had learned to play as a girl and had even accompanied her father, one-time Boston mayor John "Honey Fitz" Fitzgerald, on the piano when he sang at political rallies. In the privacy of their living room, the Kennedy family would gather around their piano to sing Irish songs and show tunes.

Rose and Joe's bedroom on the second floor was furnished with twin beds, a not uncommon practice at the time. Rose always gave birth in the bed closest to the window so that her doctor would have more light. A row of baby pictures of the four children born here hangs on the wall. One of the other bedrooms was used as the nursery, and displays include the christening gown worn by all nine children. A bookcase in the room reflects Rose's commitment to her children's education. Although Jack was considered rather lazy and undisciplined, he loved to read. He had been sickly as a child, and his mother had often read to him. A small chair displays copies of his two favorite books, *King Arthur and the Knights of the Round Table* and *Billy Whiskers*, a tale of a little goat that was always getting into trouble.

Rose found a quiet corner for a small desk where she would oversee the needs of the household, including the two servants who had living quarters on the third floor and handled the cleaning, cooking, laundry, and basics of childcare. But Rose missed no details on her children's growth and development, even keeping note cards for each child to record such things as illnesses and significant milestones.

Tours end in the first-floor kitchen at the back of the house, with its Glenwood stove, wooden icebox, and soapstone sink. Mrs. Kennedy had the most difficulty remembering this room since she didn't really spend much time there. She did however fondly recall that the family ate Boston baked beans for dinner on Saturday nights—and then again for breakfast on Sunday mornings.

African Meeting House, Boston
8 Smith Court, Boston, Museum of African American History; 617-720-2991; maah.org; open year-round; admission charged. Black Heritage Trail: 617-742-5415; nps.gov/boaf

In the years leading up to the Civil War, about half of Boston's 2,000 free blacks lived on the North Slope of Beacon Hill. As a group, they represented only about 3 percent of the city's population, but they had an outsized impact on both the city and the nation.

The heart of the community—and one of the stops on the Black Heritage Trail—was the red brick African Meeting House. Although blacks were allowed to worship in Boston's established churches, they were usually forced into segregated balcony seats and denied equal privileges. In August 1805, preacher Thomas Paul (1773–1831) and 20 of his followers formed the First African Baptist Church. By December 1806, the congregation was able to worship in the new African Meeting House. Both black and white Bostonians contributed to the $7,700 cost of the meeting house, and most of the labor was carried out by members of the black community.

Believed to be the oldest surviving black church building in the United States, the African Meeting House has an elegant simplicity in keeping with the Beacon Hill style developed by Charles Bulfinch and Asher Benjamin. Some scholars credit the design to Benjamin, but there is no written record to indicate that he drew the

plans. It is possible that some of the African American artisans he had hired to construct the Charles Street Meeting House two years earlier incorporated details from that structure.

The red brick exterior is unadorned, save by four graceful arched windows on the upper course. Surprisingly for the tight quarters on Beacon Hill, the interior is flooded with daylight, augmented by brass chandeliers. The ocher pews trimmed with mahogany rails curve gently like the interior of a clam shell facing the pulpit. A balcony level, reached by elegantly curving stairs, provides for an overflow crowd.

Paul was known as a spirited preacher, and the meeting house soon became the focal point of the black community. In addition to serving as a place of worship, one room was devoted to a school for black children until 1835, when the Abiel Smith School, now part of the Museum of African American History, opened next door to educate Boston's black children. The public schools were finally integrated in 1855, one of the victories in the community's struggle for equal rights.

In fact, the meeting house was a cradle of the civil rights movement on both local and national levels. In 1832, abolitionist William Lloyd Garrison founded the New England Anti-Slavery Society here. The following year Maria Stewart (1803–80), a former domestic servant who became a teacher, journalist, and abolitionist, used the African Meeting House as a forum to advocate for the rights of both African Americans and women.

Other prominent speakers to take to the pulpit at the meeting house included Harriet Tubman, Sojourner Truth, and Frederick Douglass. The black community also put their convictions into action. The meeting house functioned as a recruiting station for the 54th Massachusetts Regiment, the first volunteer regiment of black soldiers raised during the Civil War. The regiment left Boston in May 1863; within two months, nearly half of the soldiers had been killed or wounded during an attack on Fort Wagner in South Carolina. Their bravery and devotion to duty were lauded in the poem "For the Union Dead," by Robert Lowell and in the 1989 film *Glory*.

Perhaps most affecting is the *Robert Gould Shaw/54th Regiment Memorial* on Boston Common, a stunning high-relief sculpture that depicts the regiment marching to war. Struck by the lifelike renderings of "Colonel Shaw and his bell-cheeked Negro infantry," as he described them, Robert Lowell noted that "at the dedication, William James could almost hear the bronze Negroes breathe." Sculpted by Augustus Saint-Gaudens (see p. 199), the memorial was dedicated in 1897. It, too, is a stop on the Black Heritage Trail.

Boston's African American population grew after the Civil War and many people moved from Beacon Hill to more spacious homes in the South End and Roxbury. In the late 19th century, the meeting house was purchased by a Hasidic Jewish congregation from the North End to use as a synagogue. In 1972, the Museum of African American History purchased the meeting house. A $9.5 million restoration of the property, funded in part by the National Park Service, modernized the mechanical and electrical systems and restored the church to its 19th-century heyday, when it was ground zero for the movement to lift a people from bondage.

Arnold Arboretum, Boston

Hunnewell Visitor Center, 125 Arborway, Boston; 617-524-1718; arboretum.harvard.edu; Visitor Center and grounds open year-round, free guided tours mid-April through October; free admission

City dwellers need a place where they can mark the seasons through changes in a living landscape—a place to welcome the hopeful beginnings of spring with pussy willows and bright yellow forsythia and mark autumn with the blazing red foliage of maples. In Boston, that place is the Arnold Arboretum, the first public arboretum in North America and model for many around the world.

From the beginning, ambitions for the arboretum were high. In 1872, Harvard University received a bequest from the estate of New Bedford whaling merchant James Arnold (1781–1868) to establish what he envisioned as a plant collection "which shall contain, as far as practicable, all the trees [and] shrubs . . . either indigenous or exotic, which can be raised in the open air."

Harvard first set aside 137 acres of its Bussey estate in the Boston neighborhood of Jamaica Plain. The arboretum has since grown to 281 acres with 14,760 plants representing 3,800 taxa. Under the terms of a 1,000-year lease, the arboretum is owned by the city of Boston and managed by Harvard.

Charles Sprague Sargent (1841–1927), a Harvard graduate in biology, was appointed as the first director of the arboretum in 1873 and oversaw its growth and development until his death. Sprague enlisted Frederick Law Olmsted (1822–1903) to design the grounds. It was a challenge that the pioneer in American landscape design clearly relished since it fit neatly with his own theories about the importance

of natural space for the health of a city and its residents. "We want a ground to which people may easily go, where they shall, in effect, find the city put far away from them," Olmsted wrote. "We want depth of wood enough about it not only for comfort in hot weather, but to completely shut out the city from our landscapes."

The arboretum became one of the natural landscapes in Olmsted's Emerald Necklace, which stretches 7 miles through the city from the Boston Common and Public Garden to Franklin Park. With the Bussey property, Olmsted created a network of winding roads and pathways that follow the natural contours of the land with its ponds, meadows, and forest. Tree planting began in 1885, with naturalistic groupings of trees and shrubs by family and genus. Plant materials flowed in from all over the world, and the arboretum began to mount its own collecting efforts, most famously the early-20th-century expeditions under E. H. Wilson in western China. The arboretum continues to add to its collection, which emphasizes temperate zone woody species from North America and eastern Asia and is particularly rich in beech, honeysuckle, crab apple, oak, rhododendron, and lilac.

All that leafy beauty is a living laboratory for plant science. Research projects at the arboretum have included studying the evolution of the relationships among species using molecular genetics and the fine-tuning of our understanding of plant physiology and morphology. Caring for the collection has led to advancements in propagation of woody plants, understanding of plant diseases and other pathologies, and ways to use integrated pest management to reduce the use of chemical pesticides.

But the rigors of research are far from the minds of the joggers, dog walkers, and stroller-pushers who relish this woodsy paradise in the heart of the city. Most enter through the Main Gate from the Arborway and often stop first at the Hunnewell Visitor Center to check out the exhibitions and perhaps pick up a map.

Against a backdrop of rich green, the arboretum unfolds in a riot of color and scent from early spring through fall, with daffodils bursting into bloom in April and cherry, crab apple, and other fruit trees coming to life in early May. Mostly clustered around Bussey Hill Road, the arboretum's roughly 370 lilac plants of 170 species constitute one of the top collections in North America. They guarantee a joyful, fragrant series of blooms for about five weeks. So beloved is the collection in the hearts of Bostonians that the arboretum has celebrated it each year since the early 20th century with Lilac Sunday—a day of tours, family activities, and (in thoroughly 21st-century fashion) food trucks.

The blooms just keep coming with dogwoods and magnolias, azaleas and rhododendrons, hydrangeas and hibiscus. One 5-acre garden is devoted to plants in the rose family, including a new metal rose arbor that supports delicate white tea roses and blush pink hedgerow roses.

Although species are often bunched together, and most plants carry a small metal ID tag, the layout of the Arnold Arboretum is more broadly ecological than descriptive or even ornamental. Plantings flow one into another, and species are interplanted to provide a more natural environment both for the birds and insects and for the people who come to appreciate the displays. While it is true that the plantings might help homeowners visualize how a specific shrub or tree might look on their own property, the sheer natural beauty often undermines such rational intentions in favor of a romp through the landscapes of scent, color, and form.

The urban world does seem very far removed from this tranquil spot. But those who seek a reminder need only climb to the summit of 235-foot Peters Hill or 198-foot Bussey Hill for a view of the Boston city skyline floating in the distance above the canopy.

Boston Public Library
Copley Square; 617-536-5400; bpl.org; open year-round, check website for schedule of art and architecture tours and restaurant hours; free admission

"The main entrance to the Boston Public Library used to face Copley Square across Dartmouth Street. . . . It felt like a library and looked like a library, and even when I was going in there to look up Duke Snider's lifetime batting average, I used to feel like a scholar," wrote Robert Parker in his 1980 novel, *Looking for Rachel Wallace*. The late creator of the literate and sophisticated private detective Spenser neatly summed up the affection that many Bostonians hold for the so-called "palace for the people."

The Great and General Court of Massachusetts was ahead of its time when it established the Boston Public Library in 1848 and thus created the first large free municipal library in the United States. The city has always valued knowledge. Even original settler William Blaxton had a library. The Boston Public Library first opened in 1854 with 16,000 volumes housed in a former school building on Mason Street. From the start, the space was too small, and by the end of the year, plans were made to construct a new building on Boylston Street at Copley Square.

Designed by Charles Follen McKim (1847–1909), that building was completed in 1895 and received a modern addition by architect Philip Johnson (1906–2005) in 1972. It remains the main branch—and heart—of a library system that now boasts more than 23 million items and 24 branches throughout the city. In 1986, the McKim building was designated a National Historic Landmark, "as the first outstanding example of Renaissance Beaux-Arts Classicism in America."

Facing a challenge to equal but not overshadow Trinity Church on the opposite side of Copley Square (see p. 139), McKim drew inspiration from Renaissance palazzos and called on the skilled Italian construction workers and artisans who were building Boston's grand private homes to help bring his vision to life. The stately white marble building anchors its side of Copley Square with an air of quiet confidence. The horizontal façade is pierced with a row of 13 arched windows and 3 arched doorways. Symbolism abounds. Sculptor Bela Pratt's (1867–1917) bronze

figures of seated females representing *Art* and *Science* flank the entrance. A bust of Minerva, the Roman goddess of wisdom, is carved into the keystone above the middle door. But of all the exterior decoration, the words directly above Minerva are the simplest and most powerful: "FREE TO ALL."

Daniel Chester French's (see p. 85) sculpted bronze doors representing *Music and Poetry, Knowledge and Wisdom,* and *Truth and Romance* make a fitting ceremonial entry to the marble-laden interior. Many other noted artists of the day contributed to the rich interior decoration. Two sculptures of seated lions, the work of Louis Saint-Gaudens (brother of Augustus Saint-Gaudens, see p. 199), watch over patrons as they ascend and descend the main staircase, which was itself described by writer Henry James as "a high and luxurious beauty."

France's leading muralist, Puvis de Chavannes (1824–98), created the murals that wind up the staircase and along the second-floor corridor. The main panel, *The Muses,* captures the nine muses of Greek mythology and a nude youth representing the Spirit of Enlightenment amid an idyllic setting of olive and laurel groves on the Hill of Parnassus.

The McKim building is noted for the allegorical murals that grace its walls. Painter and illustrator Edwin Austin Abbey (1852–1911), who excelled at depicting literary and historical scenes in the Pre-Raphaelite style, created the sumptuous series of murals of the Arthurian legend of the *Quest for the Holy Grail* in the second-floor room now named for him. John Singer Sargent (1856–1925) spent almost

30 years working on his mural sequence, the *Triumph of Religion*, located on the third floor in a tall, narrow space of his own design. Sargent and his contemporaries viewed mural painting as the highest form of the painter's art. Known primarily for his society portraits, Sargent hoped to enhance his reputation and secure his legacy with this major project.

Robert Parker hit the nail on the head when he noted that simply being in this magnificent building could not fail to make any reader feel important. That's especially true in Bates Hall. The main reading room of the McKim building, it stretches the length of the Copley Square façade and features a beautifully detailed barrel vault ceiling, sandstone walls, terrazzo and marble floors, and 10-foot-tall English oak bookcases. Readers sit at long wooden tables illuminated by Arts & Crafts brass lamps with green glass shades.

The great surprise at the heart of the building is the central courtyard, which has always been an escape from the bustle of the Back Bay. The arcaded promenade, modeled on a Roman palace, protects readers from both sun and rain, and the fountain in the middle offers the cooling sound of water on even the hottest of days. The statue at the center, *Bacchante and Infant Faun* by Frederick MacMonnies (1863–1937), was a gift to the library from architect McKim. Fearing that the image of a nude dancing woman celebrated drinking and exposed her child to debauchery, proper Bostonians succeeded in getting it removed in 1897. Nearly a century passed before calmer heads prevailed and a copy cast from the original claimed its proper place in the courtyard.

Recent renovations to the McKim building carved out space for a casual cafe and the more elegant Courtyard Restaurant. Taking afternoon tea at a table overlooking the courtyard is one of the most gracious ways to spend an afternoon in Boston.

Ether Dome, Massachusetts General Hospital, Boston
Bulfinch Pavilion, Massachusetts General Hospital Campus; at the end of North Anderson Street, Boston; 617-724-9557; massgeneral .org/museum; open weekdays when not otherwise in use; call first for hours; free admission

Pain relief during surgery seemed an elusive goal as doctors tried everything from alcohol to hashish to opium to dull the pain but with little success. By the 1840s, some doctors and dentists were experimenting with nitrous oxide ("laughing gas") as well as ether as possible palliatives during surgery, since people who inhaled laughing gas or the volatile fumes of ether became intoxicated and lost consciousness.

In 1842, Dr. Crawford W. Long of Georgia observed that people felt no pain when intoxicated by ether, so he tried a minor operation on a patient who had been rendered unconscious by inhalation. It was successful, but Long kept the technique

quiet, not publishing his results until 1848. In 1844, dentist Dr. Horace Wells of Hartford, Connecticut, extracted a tooth from a patient under the influence of nitrous oxide and may have also experimented with ether.

Wells's former partner, William T. G. Morton, took the process a step further and finally caught the attention of the broader medical community. When his dental practice with Wells failed, Morton moved to Boston to set up shop while he also attended Harvard Medical School. His dental specialty was the making of false

teeth, but he needed to find a painless way to pull dead teeth. After purportedly experimenting on fish and a dog, he administered ether to himself on September 30, 1846, and later the same day pulled the tooth of a patient knocked out by the fumes. Convinced that he had stumbled on an original method of suspending sensation in patients, Morton approached Massachusetts General Hospital and asked to demonstrate his "preparation." The chief surgeon, Dr. John Collins Warren, invited him to participate in an operation scheduled for 10 a.m. on Friday, October 16, 1846.

At the time, Massachusetts General occupied a single building called the Bulfinch Pavilion. It was designed by Charles Bulfinch and was constructed in 1821–23 with oversight by Alexander Parris since Bulfinch was busy with the federal Capitol in Washington, D.C. The original structure was a model of the Greek Revival style, built in great slabs of local granite with tall pillars. The central section rose two stories above a raised basement and was capped with a square attic story with a saucer dome skylight. This was the operating amphitheater, modeled on those Bulfinch had observed in hospitals he had visited in New York, Philadelphia, and Baltimore in 1816. The pavilion was expanded in 1844–46, and the operating amphitheater took on its present form during that renovation.

The room's chief architectural feature is the skylit dome and the copper-lined vaulting on which it rests. Steeply raked seats rise in curved tiers on the south side of the room. The operating theater was directly below the oculus in the dome—now augmented by modern electrical lights. It served as an operating theater until 1867 and is currently used for lectures, classes, and meetings. The basic room design remains as it was in October 1846.

Many in the Boston medical community were skeptical of Morton's claims, so the observation gallery was packed with doctors and medical students that day. Morton was fussing with his equipment and showed up 15 minutes late. Fortunately for patient Gilbert Abbott, he arrived just before Warren proceeded with the operation without him. On entering the room, Morton took Abbott by the hand and assured him that the procedure would be painless. Morton produced his apparatus—a glass globe with both a narrow and a broad glass tube attached. In it, he placed a sponge saturated with ether. Abbott inhaled from the larger of the tubes and fell asleep within 5 minutes. Warren then removed the tumor on Abbott's neck and stitched him up. When the patient became conscious, he declared that he had not felt a thing. Warren announced to the assembled spectators, "Gentlemen, this is no humbug."

Word spread quickly of the success of ether to avoid sensation during surgery, and the operating theater has been known ever since as the Ether Dome. Boston physician and man of letters Oliver Wendell Holmes proposed to Morton that he call the state of dulled sensation "anaesthesia," correctly predicting that the term "will be repeated by the tongues of every civilized race."

As a brass plaque in the Ether Dome recounts, "Knowledge of this discovery spread from this room throughout the civilized world and a new era for surgery began." Morton himself saw little benefit, as his claim was contested by his former partner Wells and by Long.

Trinity Church, Boston
206 Clarendon Street, Boston; 617-536-0944; trinitychurchboston .org; open year-round for guided and self-guided tours; admission charged

Arguably the greatest work by architect Henry Hobson Richardson (1838–86), the 1877 Trinity Church on Copley Plaza is one of the most influential buildings in the United States. In 1885, it was selected as one of the 10 best buildings in America

by the American Institute of Architects; a century later, it was the only member of the original list still in the top 10. It epitomizes the Richardsonian Romanesque style that would be adopted across the country for libraries, churches, schools, and even railroad stations. Hallmarks of the style include a clay tile roof, roughly finished stone blocks, multiple colors of

stone, and weighty arches akin to the French Romanesque style. To Trinity, Richardson added a squat but massive bell tower, making the church a dignified yet joyous model of ecclesiastical architecture.

The congregation of Trinity Church, now an Episcopal congregation in the Anglican community, was first gathered in 1733. When the members decided they needed a new building, they purchased a block in the Back Bay where the church would be visible on four sides. But like most Back Bay real estate, it was little more than recently filled swamp. Working closely with his friend, Trinity rector Phillips Brooks (1835–93), Richardson came up with a Greek cross design with massive stone walls. It would be so heavy, Richardson calculated, that it would sink into the ooze below. So his workmen drove 2,000 wooden piles through the subterranean mud to support a network of granite pyramids. On those rocks he built his church, including that massive, 6,000-ton campanile.

Most American Episcopal churches of the mid- to late-19th century followed the English Gothic model with a long nave of three aisles. Looking at the lot and the way the church could stand in splendid isolation on all sides, Richardson opted for a Greek cross with equal-sized chancel, nave, and transepts radiating from a central square. The high but broad arches gave it a Byzantine volume, as if the building encapsulated a bit of soaring heaven. That voluminous construction with its inspirational dome left massive wall areas and broad supports between and under the windows to be covered in dramatic, large-scale murals in place of the immense mosaics of medieval Byzantine churches.

The murals by John La Farge (1835–1910) were his first major painting commission. Along with the other decorations for Trinity, they made his reputation as a leader in the American branch of the Arts & Crafts movement. Although the church construction was finished in November 1876, the murals and stained glass windows were not. La Farge had the entire interior covered with scaffolding, which was not removed until February 5, 1877, four days before the scheduled consecration.

Workers furiously cleaned up, finished the floors, laid the carpeting, and installed the pews. La Farge had painted the murals in just five months.

The center of Trinity Church was like an open theater, where rector Phillips Brooks could thunder out his sermons over the assembled faithful. One of the most charismatic and physically imposing preachers in 19th-century Boston, Brooks was a gifted orator. He could transport his parishioners on the wings of his words, which spewed out at a rate of 213 per minute, according to one awed listener who timed him.

Brooks had charged La Farge to give him something inspirational to look at when he preached, and La Farge obliged with the striking "Christ Preaching" windows, with an oversized Christ standing tall in blue and burgundy robes in the central pane flanked by aquamarine lancet windows. The La Farge windows were revolutionary because he layered opalescent glass to give them a translucent and milky appearance. That group was not installed, however, until 1883.

On the day of the consecration, only the Baptism stained glass in the chancel had been installed. The other spaces were filled with plain glass and were completed over the next few years, mainly by English workshops as donors stepped forward from the congregation to pay for them. While many of the workshops were traditional church window-makers, Brooks also managed to convince then avant-garde artists William Morris and Edward Burne-Jones to execute commissions.

Stained glass is placed at two levels—a series nearly at pew height of mostly smaller windows depicting a variety of biblical scenes and a far more triumphant series in the upper reaches of the church where they rain down a play of color on the matte walls and glisten off the walnut woodwork. Notably, the bell-like construction of the vaults gives Trinity stupendous acoustics where a preacher's voice, the joined chords of the choir, and the deep pipes of the organ all resonate in praise.

Union Oyster House, Boston
41 Union Street, Boston; 617-227-2750; unionoysterhouse.com; open year-round

Who first decided to eat an oyster is one of those gastronomic mysteries that will probably never be solved. But what is certain is that by the early 19th century Americans were in love with the bivalve mollusks. To help satisfy that craving, Atwood's Oyster House, as the Union Oyster House was first called, opened on Union Street in 1826 in a building that was already about a century old.

The Georgian-style row house near the edge of the harbor is one of the oldest brick buildings still standing in Boston. It had done duty as a dry goods store and as headquarters for the paymaster of the Continental Army during the Revolutionary War. The *Massachusetts Spy*, the newspaper of the Whig patriots, was published

here from 1771 to 1775. In exile after the French Revolution, the Duke of Chartres lived on the second floor from 1796 to 1800 and offered French lessons to fashionable Bostonians before returning to France and eventually becoming king as Louis Philippe I.

But the building's best use has been as a seafood eatery. The Union Oyster House has been in continuous operation since the doors first opened in 1826. It is undeniably the oldest restaurant in Boston and is considered by most scholars to be the oldest restaurant in continuous service in the United States. Although the Oyster House has grown over the years—especially in the last half century—the original central section still smacks of the 19th century.

The highlight of the venerable establishment is the horseshoe-shaped oak-trimmed oyster bar surrounded by nine ancient cast-iron stools bolted to the floor, each featuring a hard, flat, wooden seat on top. Oyster eaters barely sit anyway—they tend to lean on the bar with their elbows to avoid dripping the juices as they slurp oysters and cherrystone clams from their shells. The shucker works furiously at the soapstone shucking table (covered, alas, in epoxy to meet Boston's health code), digging out the Wellfleets, the Duxburys, the Damariscottas, and more from their piles of crushed ice. A few steps in from the street are the original white-painted, stall-style wooden booths. Each stall is lined with wooden benches built into the partition walls around a 4-foot-wide wooden table. Louvered half-doors used to be attached at the entrance to each booth to provide a modicum of privacy.

Early menus featured a limited selection of classic New England seafood. In addition to oysters raw or on the half-shell, diners could select stewed, roast, or fried oysters or stewed or fried scallops. Side dishes were simple—bread and butter, fried eggs, extra crackers—and dessert consisted of five flavors of pie. The current proprietors have barely changed the almost 200-year-old recipe for clam chowder.

One of the most well-documented early visitors was orator and politician Daniel Webster (1782–1852), who enjoyed a glass of brandy with each serving of a half dozen oysters. He was said to polish off at least six plates whenever he stopped in. Years later, John F. Kennedy (1921–63) also patronized the Union Oyster House, sitting upstairs in booth number 18 on Sundays to read the newspaper and eat lobster stew (now, alas, off the menu). What JFK chose to drink has not been recorded. But a plaque now marks the spot where he relished his peaceful Sundays.

No one spoke more eloquently of the establishment than *New York Herald Tribune* writer Lucius Beebe, who noted in 1931, "The Union Oyster House has been a cathedral, or more properly speaking a chapel, of seafood, its high altar the oyster bar, its acolytes and priests the white-coated experts who render available and edible its Cotuits [type of oyster] and Little Necks, its worshippers [sic] the patrons whose mouths water and whose nostrils quiver at the salt odor of lobster broiling on a coal fire in its kitchens."

For all its history, the Union Oyster House has only been owned by four families. The menu has certainly been expanded, but fresh local seafood—oysters especially—remain the backbone. The restaurant serves about 1.5 million a year.

Fort Warren, Georges Island, Boston
Boston Harbor Islands National & State Park; 617-223-8666; bostonharborislands.org; ferry service from Long Wharf early-May through Columbus Day

For the first two centuries after Boston was founded, 39-acre Georges Island enjoyed a peaceful existence as a farming community. But in 1825, the US government decided that its strategic location at the entrance to Boston Harbor made the island more valuable for coastal defense. Construction of Fort Warren began in 1833 and the fort was dedicated in 1847.

Named for Revolutionary War hero Dr. Joseph Warren, who was killed in the 1775 Battle of Bunker Hill, the handsome fort was built of granite from Quincy and Cape Ann and features 8-foot-thick walls designed to withstand cannon fire from enemy ships. Although its defensive system had become virtually obsolete by the time it was completed, Fort Warren still served the country well. It never was attacked by an enemy, but was most immediately put to use as a training camp. During the Civil War, it served as a notably humane prison for about 2,300 captives,

including Confederate soldiers and sailors, elected officials, and even northern political prisoners. Union soldiers stationed here are said to have composed the lyrics to the marching song "John Brown's Body."

The fort was modified during the Spanish-American War and for World Wars I and II and was finally decommissioned in 1947. A decade later, it was purchased by the regional park system of the Metropolitan District Commission. It is now a centerpiece of the Boston Harbor Islands National & State Park, which consists of 34 islands and mainland parks that offer natural areas of beauty and recreation for city dwellers.

From spring to fall, ferries from Long Wharf make the roughly half-hour journey to Georges Island. Passengers arrive at the wharf where granite for the fort's construction was once unloaded and walk past the guardhouse that would have stood as the first line of defense if enemies had ever come ashore. It now holds plaques detailing the fort's construction. A drawbridge used to provide another layer of protection to the sallyport, or entrance, to the fort. Now visitors cross a wooden bridge over a dry moat. If enemies had made it across the drawbridge, they would have been met with the heavy oak door affixed with iron rods to protect it from blows by an ax.

The roughly star-shaped fort encloses a grassy parade ground that seems a bit like a public park until visitors notice the large Gothic structure at one corner. Built in 1863, it was the largest of the fort's powder magazines and was once lined with wood to provide climate control for its inflammatory contents. The parade ground was used for infantry training, marching exercises, and inspections. During their downtime, soldiers might exercise, engage in races, or play baseball. Today's visitors often follow suit by tossing around a baseball or football. In addition to tours of the fort and island, summer ranger-led programs often include Civil War–era lawn games and vintage baseball. Visitors can also walk along the ramparts to inspect the concrete batteries where guns were once mounted and to take in the views of the Boston skyline and neighboring islands, including Little Brewster, where the 1783 Boston Light, also a National Historic Landmark, is the last staffed lighthouse in the country.

It's somewhat disconcerting to leave the open parade ground and the bright, breezy ramparts to enter the slightly dank interior of the fort. Visitors can follow long corridors and peek into such spaces as the living quarters for officers and enlisted men, the bakery, and the fort's original hospital.

Some believe that a Lady in Black haunts Fort Warren, and the dim, deserted hallways certainly give free rein to the imagination. According to legend, the wife of a Confederate prisoner dressed in men's clothing so that she could sneak into the fort and try to free her husband. The couple was discovered by guards, and, when the wife's gun misfired, she killed her husband instead of one of the captors. Already distraught, she was sentenced to death. Her only wish was to die in women's clothing, and the Union officers provided her with black robes that she wore to the gallows—and still wears as she wanders the fort alone.

Blue Hill Observatory, Milton
Great Blue Hill, Milton; 617-696-0562; bluehill.org; open year round, call for weekend hours; admission charged

New Englanders are fond of saying that if we don't like the weather, we only have to wait a few minutes for it to change. Probably no one enjoys those capricious skies more than the staff and volunteers at the Blue Hill Observatory, which is, after all,

the country's oldest meteorological observatory with continuous records. Founded in 1885, the observatory has stood witness to more than 130 years of thunderstorms, hurricanes, and blizzards—not to mention the clear blue skies that New Englanders long for.

Abbott Lawrence Rotch (1861–1912) was only 25 years

old when he founded his private scientific station for the study of weather and atmosphere. A member of a prominent Boston family with roots in whaling and shipping, Rotch earned a degree in engineering from the Massachusetts Institute of Technology but found himself increasingly fascinated by the emerging science of meteorology. He purchased a piece of land on the summit of Great Blue Hill, the highest peak on the East Coast from Boston to Miami where the Atlantic Ocean is visible, and spent $3,500 to construct a stone tower observatory. Rotch knew how to do things right. At midnight on January 31, 1885, he set off fireworks and then proceeded to make his first climatological observations.

Rotch continued to tinker with the facility, expanding it twice and even razing the original two-story tower in 1908. He replaced it with a three-story cylindrical mini-castle built of concrete—one of the first steel-reinforced-concrete buildings in the United States. It perches 635 feet above sea level, making it about a 1-mile trek from the parking lots at the foot of the hill. From the Route 138 north lot, it's also easy to walk up the paved maintenance road, which has limited vehicular traffic. From the Route 138 south lot, it's a moderate hike through the woods of the Blue Hills Reservation up the Red Dot Trail before intersecting with the road. The left fork of the trail is a somewhat easier climb with fewer clambers over boulders.

This little slice of American and scientific history is in many ways the cradle of meteorology. Working with his chief observers, Rotch gained a worldwide reputation and was named the first professor of meteorology at Harvard University. In addition to the unbroken log of each day's weather, the observatory made the first detailed record of cloud statistics in America. Those observations provided the first scientific description of types of clouds, their height, and the velocity of their movement in the western hemisphere. The observatory ingeniously launched kites to begin the worldwide soundings of pressure, temperature, humidity, and sometimes wind speed. Much later, in the 1930s, the Blue Hill Observatory sent balloons carrying weather instruments into the upper atmosphere, thus pioneering the practice of remote telemetry for direct atmospheric observations.

Rotch traveled to Europe frequently (he ballooned above Paris and reached the summit of Mont Blanc three times) and made a point of attending the meetings of the International Meteorological Organization (now World Meteorological Organization), which was founded in 1873 to encourage countries to exchange weather information. When he returned to Blue Hill, he brought back state-of-the-art recording instruments, amassing what many considered the best collection of such instrumentation in the New World.

Guided tours of Blue Hill Observatory begin in what is effectively a trophy room of these Victorian-era scientific instruments, many of which remain the best of their kind. The Campbell-Stokes recorder, for example, measures sunlight intensity from spots burned on paper charts when the sun's rays shine through a pure quartz sphere. Bound books on the shelves contain meticulously handwritten observations from across the decades. (The warmest temperature ever recorded was 101 degrees Fahrenheit on August 10, 1949, and on August 2, 1975. The lowest was -21 degrees Fahrenheit on February 9, 1934.) Because the measurements have been made from the same spot with the same kind of instruments every day, their consistency is unparalleled around the globe.

Old meets new on the next level up, where the oldest mercury barometer in continuous use (since January 1, 1888) shares space with a battery of computers and chart printers. The observers keep records using all the historic equipment at periodic observation times, but modern electronic equipment also makes continuous charts of such data as wind speed, gusts, and direction. They provide around-the-clock records. When the observatory started, its staff took readings every hour. Over time, it became obvious that conditions changed too slowly to require that frequency. Now human observers make their official notations three times a day at 7 a.m., 10 a.m., and 1 p.m.

Sun or rain, they climb onto the roof to record cloud types, optical phenomena such as rainbows or sun dogs, and visibility. From this elevation 671 feet above sea level (counting the tower's 36 feet), a clear day spells 90 miles of visibility, revealing portions of four states. But the observers relish pea-soup fog and clouds as much as sunshine. For weather buffs, even a soggy stratocumulus cloud has a silver lining.

John Adams and John Quincy Adams Birthplaces, Quincy
1250 Hancock Street, Quincy; 617-770-1175; nps.gov/adam; houses open for guided tours from third week of April through mid-November; admission charged

Before the Clintons, before the Bushes, before the Kennedys, even before the Harrisons, America's first political family dynasty was the Adams clan, which produced our second and sixth presidents, an influential congressman, and three ambassadors to the Court of St. James in the United Kingdom. The descendants of those early national leaders saw to it that the legacy of their forefathers was preserved and honored, so the modest farmhouses where John Adams was born in 1735 and John Quincy Adams was born in 1767 have improbably survived on their original foundations at the foot of Penn's Hill. The two houses and the Old House at Peacefield, the more expansive Adams family estate, constitute the Adams National Historical Park. As the city has grown up around the once-bucolic sites, tours begin at the park's headquarters in downtown Quincy, where visitors board a trolley to visit all three homes.

The John Adams birthplace was purchased along with 6 acres of farmland in 1720 by John Adams's father (also John Adams), a church deacon, a farmer, and—when farm chores permitted in the winter—a cordwainer. Covered in weathered cedar clapboards and sitting on a stone foundation, the house features 12-over-12 windows and a central entry. The original house consisted of four rooms—two upstairs bedrooms over the two principal downstairs rooms. A summer kitchen was added to the house at a later date.

In the Main Room, to the right of the entry, a large open-hearth fireplace provided the home's central heat. This was the room where the family carried on its daily business. The opposite side of the entry was the Best Room, which contained the more prized furniture and had a painted floor and woodwork. When John Adams first established his law practice, he was as yet unmarried and still lived with his parents. They gave him the Best Room to use as his first law office. The room is shown with a small harpsichord, an elaborate mirror, and more decorative chairs than the rest of the house. Both the John Adams and John Quincy Adams birthplaces have reproduction furnishings that show how simply the family lived.

When his father died in 1761, John Adams inherited the equally small house next door. He spent three years renovating and expanding it before moving in with his new bride, Abigail Smith (1744–1818), in 1764. The painted clapboard exterior and the interior's painted walls, floors, and woodwork combine with such touches as hooked rugs on the floors to depict a rather more prosperous existence. Two rooms are dedicated to the law offices. By the eve of the Revolution, John Adams was representing up to 60 clients per month. He and Abigail lived here for the first two decades of their marriage, and John Quincy Adams was born in an upstairs bedroom in 1767.

Destiny called, and when John Adams was selected as a delegate to the Continental Congress in 1774 and again in 1775–77, he left Abigail in charge of the farm and their four children. On June 17, 1775, Abigail took young John Quincy Adams with her to the top of Penn's Hill, where they could observe the British bombard-

ment of Charlestown in the Battle of Bunker Hill. Although he found time to pen the Massachusetts Constitution in his office in 1779, John would often be absent for the next decade as he negotiated the 1783 Treaty of Paris, which established American independence, and then served as America's first ambassador to the king of England. When John and Abigail returned home from London in 1788, they moved into the more comfortable farmhouse that the family came to call the Old House at Peacefield.

Like his father, John Quincy Adams was often away from home—first as minister to the Netherlands under President George Washington, minister to Prussia under his father's administration, minister to Russia under James Madison, and as Secretary of State under James Monroe. In 1824, he was elected president and served one term, losing a bid for re-election to Andrew Jackson. His father had died in 1826, but the younger Adams did not return to the Old House until he left office. But he resolved to keep all the family houses together and bought

out other interests in the properties so they might be preserved. The Old House is furnished with family pieces and must be maintained as the family left it in 1927. Always a man of public service, John Quincy Adams returned to the House of Representatives in 1831, where he served literally until his death at age 80 in 1848.

Succeeding generations of the Adams family—notably John Quincy's son Charles Francis Adams (1807–86) and his sons, Henry (1838–1918) and Brooks (1848–1927)—kept the family flame alive. Charles Francis served as ambassador to the Court of St. James, wrote a biography of his grandfather, and edited the letters of his grandmother, Abigail, thereby preserving her legacy of influence on her husband as one of the minds that shaped a young nation. Henry and Brooks wrote histories of their own, fulfilling the prophetic words of John Adams "I must study politics and war, that my sons may have the liberty to study mathematics and philosophy, geography, natural history, and naval architecture, navigation, commerce, and agriculture, in order to give their children a right to study painting, poetry, music, architecture, statuary, tapestry and porcelain."

Battleship Cove, Fall River
5 Water Street, Fall River; 508-678-1100; battleshipcove.org; open April through December; admission charged

It might sound counterintuitive, but Battleship Cove is as much about love as it is about warfare. This sheltered spot at the confluence of the Taunton River and Mount Hope Bay holds the largest collection of preserved US Navy vessels in the world, a largely floating testimony to the sweep of 20th-century history and the valor and sacrifice of individual seamen. But some of these craft would not have survived to tell their stories if it weren't for old sailors' affection for their ships.

USS *Massachusetts*
It all began in 1962, when the USS *Massachusetts* was stricken from the Navy Register and seemed destined for the scrap heap. For the men who had served aboard

the battleship affectionately called "Big Mamie," it seemed an undeserving end for a ship that had served her country with distinction.

Built at the Fore River Shipyard in Quincy, Massachusetts, the *Massachusetts* was launched in September

1941 and commissioned at the Boston Navy Yard in May 1942. She first saw action in late 1942 during the invasion of North Africa, but spent most of the wartime years in the Pacific participating in the invasions of the Gilbert Islands in November 1943, the Marshall Islands in January 1944, and the Palau Islands in September 1944. As the war drew to a close, her 16-inch guns were aimed at a number of strategic Japanese targets, including Iwo Jima and Okinawa, and strategic factories on Honshu, the largest of Japan's "home islands."

The *Massachusetts* remained part of the Pacific fleet until she was deactivated in 1946. About 2,200 men served aboard her at any time, and as early as 1945, former crew members had begun to hold annual reunions. Nearly two decades later, when they realized that their ship was in danger, they began to raise money to save her. Massachusetts schoolchildren gave a boost to the campaign, and the *Massachusetts* was settled in Battleship Cove in June 1965 and opened to the public in August.

USS *Lionfish*

In 1973, *Massachusetts* was joined by an entirely different kind of vessel: the USS *Lionfish*, a Balao-class submarine commissioned in November 1944. She spent the waning days of World War II on patrol in the Pacific, where she dodged Japanese torpedoes, destroyed a Japanese schooner, and fired on and most likely struck a surfaced Japanese submarine. She also transported B-29 survivors and patrolled off the coast of Japan so that she could rescue downed fliers.

It appeared that the active life of the *Lionfish* was over when she was decommissioned in January 1946, but she was called back to duty in January 1951 to participate in training cruises and NATO exercises. She was again decommissioned in December 1953—and recommissioned again in 1960 to serve as a training vessel. She was finally stricken from the Navy Register in 1971. By 1973, she was welcoming visitors at Battleship Cove.

Lionfish was one of the few submarines of her class not upgraded to a "GUPPY" configuration to improve battery capacity, underwater speed and maneuverability, and fire control. As a result, she represents the World War II submarine configuration—rather like having an antique that has never been refinished. Because she represents the vintage experience, *Lionfish* is a very popular exhibit for Battleship Cove visitors fascinated with life beneath the waves.

USS *Joseph P. Kennedy, Jr.*

The destroyer USS *Joseph P. Kennedy, Jr.*, joined the mini-fleet at Fall River in 1974. Like the *Massachusetts*, the "Joey P," as her crew called her, was built in the Fore River Shipyard. She was commissioned in December 1945 and was named for the oldest child of Joseph and Rose Kennedy (see p. 126), a navy pilot killed in a secret mission the previous year.

Destroyers, which typically hold a crew of close to 300, may not be as intimidating as massive battleships or as flashy as sleek submarines, but they are, as war correspondent John Steinbeck once wrote, the "busiest ships of a fleet," charged with defending battleships and aircraft carriers from torpedo boats.

Although she was completed in only eight months, the *Kennedy* did not serve during World War II. She did see active duty off the coast of North Korea, joined in NATO maneuvers, and served as one of the recovery vessels for the Gemini space program. In 1962, President and Mrs. Kennedy watched the America's Cup Races in Newport, Rhode Island, from her torpedo deck. A few months later, she was thrust onto the world stage during the Cuban Missile Crisis. As part of a naval blockade, she stopped and boarded a Greek freighter to search for missile components—a role she reprised in the docudrama *Thirteen Days*. By the time the movie was released in 2000, the "Joey P" had already enjoyed nearly 25 years of peaceful retirement at Battleship Cove.

PT 796 and PT 617

Few World War II Patrol Torpedo, or "PT" boats remain. The fast, easily maneuvered craft usually attacked enemy ships under cover of darkness and earned popular acclaim for their daring after the public learned of the bravery of Lieutenant John F. Kennedy and his crew when their boat was sunk by a Japanese destroyer off the Solomon Islands in August 1943.

Ironically, those PT boats that survived the war were often stripped of valuables and burned to avoid the cost of returning them to US waters. Thanks to the restoration efforts of a national organization of PT veterans (the boats generally had quarters for 12 to 17 men), two PT boats are on display at Battleship Cove.

The PT 796 was not active during World War II but did help to develop specialized equipment for river patrol boats in Vietnam while serving at a navy ordnance testing station in Panama City, Florida. Although not an exact replica of Kennedy's PT *109*, she was towed as a float in the president's 1961 inaugural parade and was finally decommissioned in July 1970.

PT *617* joined PT *796* at Battleship Cove more than a decade later. She is, in fact, the type of vessel that Kennedy commanded, though her active days were tamer. She served as a training vessel and a diving platform in Florida—activities that left her in such poor condition that it took about five years to complete her restoration.

In addition to the beautifully maintained but clearly well-used vessels, Battleship Cove is the site of the National Destroyermen's Museum and the National PT Museum and has a number of other displays that place the ships in the context of World War II and the Cold War. But the ships themselves give mute testimony to the seamen who answered the call to duty. The clang of steps on the steel decks, the high steps over compartment thresholds, the narrow little bunks stacked one atop another—each sight and experience tells a little more about what it was like to serve aboard these floating homes that were also platforms for warfare when the need arose.

New Bedford Whaling National Historic Park

Visitor Center at 33 William Street, New Bedford; 508-996-4095; nps.gov/nebe; open year-round; free admission

Seamen's Bethel: 15 Johnny Cake Hill, New Bedford; 508-992-3295; open mid-May through October; donation requested

New Bedford Whaling Museum: 18 Johnny Cake Hill, New Bedford; 508-997-0046; whalingmuseum.org; open year-round; admission charged

More than a century and a half ago, seaman Herman Melville probably tripped on the same uneven granite paving stones that visitors still tread carefully today. On January 3, 1841, he shipped out on the whaling bark *Acushnet* and would not see New England's shores again until 1845. Moreover, it would be a decade before his masterpiece based on that voyage would see print as *Moby-Dick* (see p. 77).

That greatest of American epics still defines New Bedford, which Melville himself described as "perhaps the dearest place to live in all New England." The city was, in fact, living high when Melville sang its praises. In the 1850s, it claimed the title as the world's whaling capital by launching more ships to search the oceans for the leviathans than all other ports in the world combined. It was said that the city's men fell into three categories: those away on a voyage, those returning, and those

preparing for the next trip. To that could be added a fourth group: the men who got rich from the whale oil that greased the machines of industry and lit the lamps and candles of the industrial world.

The rapid rise of petroleum in the years after the Civil War began to eclipse whale oil. Whaling went into steep decline by the 1880s, and the last whaling vessel sailed from New Bedford in 1925. (For the last American whaling vessel still afloat, see p. 28.) Although the city continues to make a living from the water (the commercial fishing fleet generally leads the country in the dollar value of its catch), the stately brick and granite buildings just uphill from the working waterfront had become so decrepit by the late 1960s that they were threatened by urban renewal. Thanks to the efforts of local preservationists, a 13-block district was saved and is now preserved as the New Bedford Whaling National Historical Park. It is no theme park; it remains a living part of the city where life goes on amid old warehouses and chandleries, stone banks, and candle factories that have survived the indignities of neglect to be reborn as antiques shops, restaurants, and art galleries.

The Greek Revival US Custom House at William and North Second Streets, however, has seen no need to reinvent itself. Completed in 1836, it remains the oldest continuously operating custom house in the country. The most impressive Greek Revival structure in the historic district is the so-called "Double Bank" at Water and William Streets in the heart of what was the financial capital of the whaling world. The eight-columned circa-1831 building held two different financial institutions that served New Bedford's 40-plus millionaires.

These days, the New Bedford Whaling Museum anchors the historical park. It was founded in 1903 to memorialize the achievements of whaling entrepreneur Jonathan Bourne, Jr. It deftly balances modern conservation issues that whalers could not have imagined with the story of the industry that made New Bedford's early fortunes. In fact, the museum excels at capturing the life of an ordinary seaman—perhaps like Melville—who stowed all his worldly possessions in an 18-by-18-by-42-inch trunk for three or four years at a time, spent his days suspended between long bouts of tedium and quick encounters with utter terror, and fitfully slept away his nights in cramped quarters below decks that a whaler once described as "a compound of foul air, tobacco smoke, sea chests, soap kegs, greasy pans, tainted meat, foreign ruffians and seasick Americans."

The centerpiece of the museum is the 89-foot, half-scale model of Bourne's most successful ship, the bark *Lagoda*, which earned the equivalent of $16 million in a dozen voyages over 48 years. The ship, displayed with her square-rigged sails open, is flanked by full-size examples of the small boats that were lowered over the side. From these open whale boats, little bigger than fishing dories and absolutely dwarfed by the humpback, blue, and right whale skeletons suspended from ceilings, men harpooned and rode the whale to its death on a "Nantucket sleigh ride."

The whale did not always lose these epic battles, as attested within the walls of the Seamen's Bethel across the street from the museum. It was built in 1832 by the New Bedford Port Society for the Moral Improvement of Seamen. It's unclear whether the bethel helped to curb sailor's impulses toward gambling, drinking, and womanizing as the proper Quaker citizenry of New Bedford had envisioned. Nonetheless, as Melville wrote, "Few are the moody fishermen, shortly bound for the Indian Ocean or Pacific, who fail to make a Sunday visit to the spot." The marble cenotaphs on the walls that memorialize New Bedford's sailors lost at sea could hardly have been comforting as they foretold every sailor's worst fears: "died of consumption at sea," "bitten by a shark while bathing near the ship," or "lost from a boat while in pursuit of a whale."

In an example of life following art, the bethel's bowsprit pulpit was installed in 1961 to resemble the one that Melville imagined in *Moby-Dick* and which John

Huston had replicated in Ireland for his 1956 movie based on the book. Visitors inspired by the movie to visit the bethel were so disappointed to discover a traditional box-style pulpit that the port society yielded to popular demand and constructed the bowsprit pulpit in 1961.

Flying Horses Carousel, Oak Bluffs, Martha's Vineyard
15 Oak Bluffs Avenue, Oak Bluffs; 508-693-9481; mvpreservation .org; open Friday of Memorial Day weekend through Columbus Day; admission charged

By the late 19th century, the town of Oak Bluffs on the island of Martha's Vineyard was a bustling summer resort community. Visitors would arrive by ferry and spend their days swimming in the ocean, strolling along the waterfront promenades, attending band concerts, frequenting dance halls and ice cream parlors, and even riding a narrow-gauge train to Edgartown, 5 miles away. But every self-respecting resort also needed a carousel. New Yorker F. O. Gordon came to the rescue in 1884, when he transplanted a beautiful model, most likely from Coney Island, to the Oak Bluffs harbor front.

At 36 feet in diameter, the Flying Horses Carousel features 20 prancing horses and 6 chariots and was produced by carousel maker Charles W. F. Dare around 1876. It is believed to be one of only two Dare carousels still in existence (the other is in Watch Hill, Rhode Island see p. 39) and the only platform carousel operating in the United States on which the horses do not go up and down as the platform revolves.

Almost as if to compensate for the horses' lack of movement, Dare and his artisans lavished extra attention on their appearance. According to an 1878 Dare catalog of "Constructions for Seaside and Summer Amusements, Carousels, Organ Figures, Fixtures &c," each horse was completed to a "perfection of finish and the near approach to life in effect." That included real horsehair tails and large glass eyes inset with tiny carved animals. The cost for such artistry was $25 to $35 per steed and $12 to $18 for each double-seated chariot.

In 1889, the town purchased the carousel and moved it to its current location in a red wooden building at the foot of Circuit Avenue, an area that also featured other amusements such as a bowling alley and a skating rink. The Flying Horses Carousel is the survivor—a reminder of simpler days and the thrill of a sweet, pretty ride.

At some point, it even inspired a rope-jumping rhyme: "There's a carousel in Oak Bluffs town / The horses don't go up or down / The horses just go 'round and 'round / On the carousel in Oak Bluffs town."

The town eventually relinquished control of the carousel, and, as it passed through private hands, it began to lose its luster. When plans were launched to dismantle the carousel and sell the horses to collectors, the Martha's Vineyard

Preservation Trust stepped in and purchased it in 1986. Rather than being destroyed, the carousel was restored to its 1870s appearance, including the decorative panel paintings of marine and equestrian scenes that had badly deteriorated. Each horse received the attention of an expert in carousel restoration and left the workshop with new horsehair manes and tails.

The carousel was originally powered by steam but was converted to electricity in 1900. These days, a 10-horsepower motor keeps things turning smoothly. The 1923 Wurlitzer Band Organ still uses original paper rolls to play old favorite tunes of the late 19th and early 20th centuries. And the children of summer still reach for the brass ring.

Martha's Vineyard Camp Meeting Association, Oak Bluffs
2 Trinity Park, Oak Bluffs; 508-693-0525; mvcma.org; open in summer, inquire about schedule of walking tours; museum admission

The small house movement may be gaining momentum these days, but in Oak Bluffs it's really nothing new. The town has been proving that small is beautiful—and colorful—for more than a century and a half. Unprepared visitors are forgiven if they think they have stumbled into a Brothers Grimm fairy tale.

Making an architectural statement, however, was the last thing on the mind of Jeremiah Pease when he established a Methodist camp meeting on a half-acre site in a "venerable grove of oaks" in 1835. The movement to seek salvation through an intense week of prayer and preaching had begun in Kentucky around 1820 and spread north fairly quickly. Originally called Wesleyan Grove, the first meeting featured nine tents for participating church members. By 1868, church groups and individual families seeking greater privacy had erected about 570 tents.

Participants also began to seek greater comfort as they extended their stays beyond the typical week or two so that they could be inspired by the Oak Bluffs

seaside setting as well as by the sermons of the ministers. At first, families improved upon their tents by adding wooden floors and uprights. It wasn't long before they took the next logical step and began to erect tiny wooden houses that would fit on their tent lots. Local carpenters created a unique version of Carpenter Gothic style, with houses constructed of vertical tongue-in-groove boards of yellow pine that served as both interior and exterior walls. A typical house might feature double doors that look a bit like tent flaps and are flanked by small windows. On the second floor, a door might open to a balcony that protects the front door from rain. Meeting-goers typically slept upstairs and used the main floor for eating and socializing.

Carpenters employed band saws—a relatively recent invention—to create the filigree trim that added a dash of whimsy to each cottage. To make their cottages stand out, homeowners painted them with cheerful, contrasting colors. Later, most added covered porches so that they would have a good place to sit and watch the comings and goings of the community.

The original cottages surround the Tabernacle, built of wrought iron in 1879 to replace a giant tent erected a decade earlier to protect worshipers from sun and rain. The circular structure does look a bit like it might house a carousel, but it is a rare surviving late-19th-century wrought iron structure. Church services are still held in the Tabernacle, but as the community has become increasingly interdenominational, it is also a lovely setting for all types of cultural events and for the graduation exercises for the Martha's Vineyard Regional High School.

From its modest beginnings, Wesleyan Grove grew somewhat organically and served as a model for other camp meeting sites around the country. The original central preaching area and tent sites were surrounded by a road now called Trinity Circle. From this outer ring, paths led to other smaller tent circles, which were in turn linked to each other by additional paths. The community now features more than 300 cottages on 34 acres. At its height in the 1880s, the campsite held about 500 cottages, but some have been relocated or joined together to make larger living quarters. Some have simply been torn down.

But the fascination with the tiny dwellings and the tight-knit community remains. All the cottages are privately owned and some are available for rental. The seasonal Cottage Museum, located in an original structure, also offers visitors a chance to see how people learned to live in these tight spaces. It features period furnishings as well as photos and other artifacts.

Jethro Coffin House, Nantucket
16 Sunset Hill, Nantucket; 508-228-1894; nha.org; open late May through mid-October for guided tours; admission charged

The so-called "Oldest House" on Nantucket is a good reminder that history and personalities are often intertwined. On the surface, the weathered gray shingled house appears to have been an incredibly generous wedding gift to a young couple just starting out. But dig a little deeper and Nantucket's own version of Romeo and Juliet—or the Hatfields and McCoys—comes to light.

The fortunate couple who received the house as a wedding gift in 1686 were Jethro Coffin and Mary Gardner, and they represented perhaps the extremes of the social circles on the small, lightly inhabited island. Coffin was the grandson of Tristram Coffin, one of the original 10 English proprietors who settled the island in 1659–60 as part of the New York colony. Lacking the practical skills to make a go of it on an island, the proprietors invited a number of skilled tradesmen to join them in the new settlement. Among them was Mary's father, fisherman John Gardner.

Not only was he a tradesman, but, to make matters worse, Gardner was one of the leaders in the "Half-Share Revolt." The proprietors had relegated the invitees to status as second-class citizens by granting each of them only half a vote in island government. Gardner led the appeal to the provincial authorities in New York; ultimately, the protest led to the establishment of town meeting governance where each property owner had an equal vote. Although the rebellion was accomplished without bloodshed, it left bad feelings all around.

So it's easy to imagine that neither family was particularly thrilled when Jethro and Mary fell in love. But the familial differences were somehow smoothed over, and the couple married in the house in 1686. John Gardner contributed the 1½-acre house plot, and Jethro's father, Peter Coffin, who had a thriving lumber business, contributed the lumber. Today, the house is the oldest house on Nantucket that was built as a dwelling and stands on its original site. It's also the only surviving structure from the 17th-century English settlement.

Located on the outskirts of Nantucket town on a small rise known as Sunset Hill, the house was about a 15-minute walk from the docks and an equal distance from the original Quaker meetinghouse at the end of Main Street. In all likelihood, the classic story-and-a-half saltbox with central brick chimney was one of the largest houses on the island at the time when most young married couples still lived with their parents. It was carefully sited to face south to take advantage of passive solar heat and to allow the north wind to glide over the steeply pitched roof. A formal parlor was reserved for Jethro's business dealings—and for town meetings, since it was one of the largest indoor spaces outside of the meetinghouse.

Daily life took place in a single room with a big fireplace for cooking. Life was not easy, even in one of the biggest houses in town. During the harsh Nantucket win-

ters, only that one room had heat, and firewood was soon in short supply as Nantucketers cleared the land. The family probably ate two meals a day, and during the winter, Mary would have to prepare dinner before dark descended around 4 p.m.

The family eventually moved to the mainland, where Jethro helped run

the family business. The house was sold in 1708 to weaver Nathaniel Paddack. He and his descendants lived there until the 1840s, when they sold the house to cooper George Turner, who ultimately abandoned the house in 1867. It had been so well built that it didn't fall into ruin. In 1881, descendants of Tristam Coffin purchased the property, and in 1923, they sold it to the Nantucket Historical Association. The house was restored at that time and again in 1987 after being severely damaged in a lightning strike. It's now protected by a state-of-the-art lightning diversion system.

Recent restoration efforts have focused on returning the grounds to the Coffin times. A small apple orchard of heirloom varieties was planted and a kitchen garden was added behind the house. It contains a few vegetables—carrots, onions, cabbages, and parsnips—and about 50 varieties of herbs that were used for flavoring or medicinal purposes or to strew in the house to dispel odors and deter insects. But even in hard times, there was beauty. The garden almost certainly was also planted with flowers.

Rokeby Museum, Ferrisburgh, p. 167

VERMONT

Calvin Coolidge Homestead District, Plymouth Notch
3780 Route 100A, Plymouth; 802-672-3773; historicsites.vermont
.gov/directory/Coolidge; open late May to mid-October; admission
charged

World leaders need places where they can go to earth like Antaeus to renew and
muster their strength. For the 30th president of the United States, John Calvin
Coolidge, that place was Plymouth Notch, Vermont. Coolidge—who always went
by Calvin to avoid confusion with his father, John—was born on the Fourth of July
in 1872 in the downstairs bedroom of the house attached to the rear of what is now
called the Florence Cilley General Store. He was four when the family moved across
the street to what is commonly called the Coolidge Homestead. Although he left
for boarding school at age 11 and went on to a political career in Massachusetts and
Washington, DC, Coolidge returned to Plymouth Notch with the regularity of a
homing pigeon. This small, rustic village in central Vermont was the wellspring of
his identity.

The village has changed little since Coolidge's day, and the National Historic
Landmark site encompasses more than a dozen structures that paint a picture of
rural Vermont during the time that Plymouth Notch served as the Summer White
House.

As the little seen and seldom heard vice president of the more outgoing Warren
G. Harding, Coolidge was thrust into the political spotlight when Harding died in
1923. Coolidge was visiting the family homestead when a messenger brought the
news that the president had passed away. (The house had no electricity, telephone,
or, for that matter, modern plumbing.) His father, a notary public, administered the
oath of office to his son by lantern light at 2:43 a.m. on August 3, 1923.

The Coolidge presidency is the principal focus of the President Calvin Coolidge
Museum & Education Center, the main nonhistoric structure at the site. A multi-
media exhibit uses Coolidge's own words, as well as historic artifacts, photographs,
and newsreels to relate the rise to power of the taciturn Vermonter who fervently
believed in small government and was of the opinion that "the chief business of the
American people is business."

The Coolidge Birthplace was the only structure in the village that had to be
restored to its original appearance. The Coolidge family (who as good Yankees never
threw anything away) donated all the original furnishings to bring the property back
to 1872—right down to the quilt on the narrow bed where Coolidge was born. Even

the attached general store, where John Coolidge was storekeeper when Calvin was born, remains much as Florence Cilley operated it from 1917 until 1945. In an age of faux old-time general stores, it's the real McCoy, right down to the rockers on the front porch, the pot-bellied stove, the penny candy, and the now-inactive post office that served the town until 1976.

Above the store, Coolidge Hall was used by the Grange for weekly dances and served as Coolidge's Summer White House office in 1924, when telephone and telegraph lines were brought in. Furnishings are original and include tables made for the president as well as a piano and snare drum from the "Plymouth Old-Time Dance Orchestra."

The homestead, where the family moved in 1876, is perhaps the best glimpse into Coolidge's childhood. The formal parlor is filled with heavy black walnut furniture with horsehair upholstery as well as an original rug, lace curtains, and cast-iron stove. Signage duly notes that one of Calvin's jobs as a boy was to bring in wood for the stoves.

The sitting room has the table, Bible, and kerosene lantern that figured in

Coolidge's oath of office. The upstairs, where Coolidge and his vivacious wife, Grace, would stay, is closed to the public, so the furnishings of their room are displayed in a downstairs bedroom.

Several other buildings figure in the family story, including the Plymouth Cheese Factory. Coolidge's father joined with four other men to create the factory in 1890 as a ready outlet for excess milk from their dairy herds. The cheese company went out of business in 1934, a year after Coolidge's death, but reopened under Calvin's son John in 1960. In 1998, the state took over the factory and brought the operation up to modern code.

Now operating as Plymouth Artisan Cheese, the small company uses some of the original 1890 equipment and allows visitors to observe the cheese-making process through big plate glass windows. Products include the traditional granular curd cheese of Plymouth as well as a range of flavored cheeses—all packaged in wax—and cave-aged wheels of mountain style, blue, and granular curd cheese. The cheeses are available to sample and purchase in the company store adjacent to the cheese-making facility.

Billings Farm & Museum, Woodstock
69 Old River Road, Woodstock; 802-457-2355; billingsfarm.org; open May through February; admission charged

Spreading its wings like an old sugar maple, the big brick Queen Anne house at the corner of River Road and Route 12 in Woodstock seems to cultivate *noblesse oblige* in its inhabitants—two families that played leading roles in natural resources conservation. It was built by Vermont lawyer and Congressman Charles Marsh in 1805 as a two-story, five-bay Federal house. His son, George Perkins Marsh (1801–82), was born elsewhere in town but grew up here until he was sent a few miles away to Dartmouth College at the age of 16.

The younger Marsh went on to an illustrious career in politics, science, and statecraft, serving as the minister resident to the Ottoman Empire under President Zachary Taylor and extricating an American missionary from imprisonment in Greece. Marsh returned to Vermont in the mid-1850s, but was soon on the road again when President Abraham Lincoln named him as minister to the king of Italy in 1861. He was to serve in Italy until his death in 1882.

But the acute observations of his Vermont boyhood stayed with him throughout his life. Early on, he made the connection that mud ran through the Woodstock streets after a heavy rain because Mount Tom, the gentle hill that rose behind his house, had been stripped of its trees. During his European travels, Marsh used that boyhood experience to understand the ravaged landscape of the Mediterranean. His 1864 book, *Man and Nature, or Physical Geography as Modified by Human Action*, argued that deforestation led to a ravaged, desert landscape and that stewardship of natural resources was a moral imperative. By providing a scientific and economic backbone to the spiritual and aesthetic arguments of Transcendentalism, Marsh effectively launched the conservation movement.

One man who was mightily persuaded was Frederick Billings (1823–90), who was born less than 20 miles north of Woodstock, made his first fortune as a land claims lawyer in the California Gold Rush, and cofounded the Northern Pacific Railroad (the railroad town Billings, Montana, was named after him). He moved back from California to Woodstock in 1864 and, impressed with Marsh's ideas, bought the author's boyhood home in 1869.

The conservation movement had not yet adopted the idea of leaving only a modest footprint. Billings quickly added a wing and mansard roof to the house, then engaged architect Henry Hudson Holley to enlarge the home into the full-blown Queen Anne mansion it is today. The interior is furnished with fine carved woodwork, including handsome bookcases forming a fireplace surround in the library, and many examples of fine Victorian furniture. The house was designated as a National Historic Landmark in 1967.

In 1871, Billings also set up a model farm on the property, now part of the Billings Farm & Museum, which is in turn part of the Marsh-Billings National Historic

Park. He stocked the dairy farm with Jersey cattle imported directly from the Isle of Jersey and set up a stock breeding program to build Jersey herds in Vermont. The farm has remained an active producer of milk and butter over the years and still keeps more than 60 head of Jerseys. It operates as a museum of Vermont's rural past, where visitors can tour the barns and calf nursery and even watch the afternoon milking.

Until his death in 1890, Billings spent his time perfecting an estate that would be a model of progressive farming and forestry. He ordered the reforestation of Mount Tom through the planting of native species as well as such exotics as Scotch pine, European larch, and Norway spruce. He also set up a 14-mile-long network of carriage roads and footpaths on the slopes of Mount Tom. Open to the public, they lead to the manmade lake at the summit called the Pogue.

Billings and his descendants maintained the parklands as stewards, all the time summering in the ornate red brick mansion. His granddaughter, Mary French Rockefeller, and her second husband, conservationist Laurance Rockefeller, established the Billings Farm & Museum in 1982, and in 1998 donated the 555 acres of the remaining Billings estate to form Marsh-Billings National Historic Park. The park now uses the mansion as its headquarters, but the family living quarters—still decorated in full-on Victorian frou-frou—and the creamery, where they made butter, are shown as they were in Frederick Billings's day.

Rokeby Museum, Ferrisburgh
4334 Route 7, Ferrisburgh; 802-877-3406; rokeby.org; open for guided tours mid-May to late October; admission charged

The Robinson family farm located on the east side of Route 7 in Ferrisburgh is as notable for its guests and visitors as for the four generations of the remarkable clan that made it their home for nearly 200 years. Tucked up in the northwest corner of Vermont, where the international border with Canada is close at hand, the farm became a significant stop on the Underground Railroad for fugitive slaves in the 1830s and 1840s. A century later, the Robinsons were pioneers in welcoming auto tourists to rural Vermont with accommodations in the farmhouse or in a small cabin for just $1 per night.

The property became a museum in 1961, and its landscape and artifacts tell vivid stories

of life in agricultural Vermont. Thomas and Jemima Robinson, who hailed from well-to-do Quaker families in Rhode Island, acquired the property in 1793 from Preserved and Deborah Dakin, who had cleared the land just a few years earlier and built the Cape Cod portion of the existing farmhouse. Tours begin in the kitchen with its big fireplace and south-facing windows to let in the light. The Robinsons added the Federal style front block in 1814 and began calling their farm "Rokeby" after Sir Walter Scott's book-length epic melodrama. All the furniture in the house comes from the Robinson family.

Although he was a city boy from Newport, Thomas Robinson displayed a knack for rusticity. He established a sawmill, a gristmill, and a fulling mill on nearby Lewis Creek and set Rokeby on the path to becoming one of the most successful sheep farms in Vermont. In 1810, he purchased some of the first Merino sheep to be exported from Spain and eventually kept a flock of about 1,500 head.

But it was Thomas and Jemima's son, Rowland Thomas, who would make a name for the farm by becoming one of the country's most ardent abolitionists. Born in 1796, he attended a New York boarding school, where he met his wife and soul mate, Rachel Gilpin. They married in 1820 and returned to Rokeby, where Rowland tended the flocks and ran his father's mills. The couple believed that their Quaker theology required them to stand up to the institution of slavery. Not only did they write and speak for the Abolitionist cause, they opened their home to dozens of fugitive slaves who stayed in the upstairs bedroom in the old portion of the house.

Rokeby Museum encompasses many original farm buildings as well as an interpretive center that relates the Underground Railroad segment of the farm's history. The Robinson family seemed never to throw anything away, so the museum has more than 15,000 pieces of correspondence from the 1790s through 1961, when Elizabeth Donoway Robinson created the museum in her will.

Letters from Rowland Thomas Robinson and Rachel Gilpin Robinson make this property one of the best-documented Abolitionist sites in northern New England and provide the basis for exhibits that explain Abolitionist practices during the period. Although the Robinsons made no secret of harboring fugitive slaves, their land was so close to Canada and so far from the South that slave-catchers rarely came looking for escapees.

The next generation of Robinsons was less confrontational. The most famous of them was the illustrator and author Rowland Evans Robinson, born in 1833. Although he studied illustration and engraving in New York City in his twenties, he returned to run the farm with his brother George. Rowland's illustrations of farm life form a poignant exhibit in the modern museum building, and examples of the magazines and books he illustrated are displayed in the farmhouse. He began to go blind in late middle age, but with the encouragement of his wife, artist Ann Stevens Robinson, he turned to storytelling, inventing a fictional village of Danvis, Vermont, as the setting for his celebrations of farm life. As a folksy writer, he helped establish some of the popular images of Vermont as a land of high mountains, great natural beauty, and taciturn (but wise) inhabitants—a Green Mountain mythos that has never quite dissipated.

Their son, Rowland Thomas Robinson, married schoolteacher Elizabeth Donoway and maintained the family farm, which was beginning to fall on hard times. They began taking in tourists in the 1920s to make ends meet—playing to some extent on the quaint and colorful image that Rowland's blind father had cultivated.

The museum maintains that tradition, offering an unusually detailed trail guide to the 90-acre property. The guide helps hikers discern the traces of past usages, including hay fields, pasturage for sheep and dairy cattle, and extensive mid-19th-century apple orchards. The farm buildings bear mute witness to generations of hard work with a smokehouse, a chicken coop, a creamery where the Robinsons made butter, and even a granary and slaughterhouse.

Shelburne Farms, Shelburne
1611 Harbor Road, Shelburne; 802-985-8686; shelburnefarms .org; open year-round, barns and house mid-May through mid-October; admission charged

The historic dairy farm and elegant estate at Shelburne Farms embody the potential for "green" living in the modern environmental movement. Drivers enter through a stone gate and follow a winding gravel road past sheep grazing contentedly in green pastures. As the hour of the late-afternoon milking approaches, Brown Swiss cows

file down the hill toward the barn. Even from the bucket seats of a mini-van, it's easy to picture the property a century ago, when teams of horses clopped along the roads and Shelburne Farms was a model of agricultural innovation. Today, the National Historic Land-mark property is devoted to conservation education while maintaining an active dairy farm and cheese-making operation in the heart of Vermont dairy country.

Don't expect to see the classic New England tableau of white farmhouse and red wooden barn on a rolling hillside. The "farmhouse" is a 111-room red brick mansion perched on Lake Champlain to maximize views of the Adirondack Mountains on the far shore. Shelburne Farms is not your average farm. For one thing, there's a great love story at its heart.

When young Lila Vanderbilt—granddaughter of railroad magnate Cornelius Vanderbilt—fell in love with one of her father's employees, her parents whisked her off to Paris to dampen her infatuation. But absence made her heart grow fonder, and when Lila returned from exile, she promptly married William Seward Webb.

In 1886, the couple began buying Vermont farmland and eventually amassed about 3,800 acres. (The current property is down to about 1,400 acres of woods and farmland.) They hired landscape architect Frederick Law Olmsted to design the grounds and New York architect Robert H. Robertson to design the mansion and farm buildings in a synthesis of Queen Anne, Shingle, and Romanesque Revival styles. When the Webbs were in residence at their model farm, they lived like country squires and entertained their friends in style.

For a full immersion into the Webbs' privileged world, book one of the mansion's 24 guest rooms, take afternoon tea with cucumber sandwiches and scones in the Tea Room, and wander among the rose gardens by the lake. Or simply take a guided tour that highlights the operations of the working farm and offers enough details about the lifestyles of last century's rich and famous to keep it interesting.

Tours begin in the Welcome Center, where you can buy the farm's own maple syrup, cheddar cheese, and yarn spun from the wool of the farm's flock of sheep. After an introductory video outlines the history of the estate, guests climb into a truck-drawn jitney to follow along the S-curves in the road, which was laid out by Olmsted to mimic nature. The road was originally lined with stately American elms, but Dutch elm disease killed them off. The estate has been replanting, in time-honored New England fashion, with hardy maple trees.

You can smell the barn even before you see it by the pungent aroma that some Vermonters jokingly call "essence of cow." The 5-story red brick barn with clock tower and bell serves as the base for cheese-making. The farm switched its herd over entirely to Brown Swiss in the 1960s, in part because their milk is slightly higher in butterfat and protein than milk from some other breeds, making it perfect for cheese production. Each of the 110 milking head produces more than 5 gallons of milk per day, which goes into the farm's well-regarded cheddar. Depending on time of day, visitors may catch the cheesemakers raking the curd or pressing the cheese. Samples of some of the aged cheddars are almost always available.

Kids gravitate to the farmyard, where they can sometimes try milking. Staff will usually guide them to a particularly patient cow while explaining that hand-milking takes about 20 minutes—twice as long as milking by machine. As kids await their turns, they can pet penned pigs, goats, and sheep.

Cute animals notwithstanding, the adults of a family are usually most impressed with the architectural detail and fine furnishings of the mansion, where about 75 percent of the furnishings are from the Webb family. (Some were originally in the family's hunting lodge or their home on Manhattan's Fifth Avenue rather than the Shelburne house.) In the dining room, a portrait of Lila Vanderbilt stands out against a red wall. It was painted while she was in Paris, and she defiantly wears a brooch that William Seward Webb had secretly given her. The headstrong young woman could not have imagined the life—and legacy—that they would create together.

As well as serving as the business offices for Shelburne Farms, their home also functions as the inn. Even if you don't plan to spend the night, it's worth booking ahead for lunch or dinner at the restaurant, which is literally a farm-to-table operation with most of the meat, vegetables, and fruit coming either from the farm's own gardens or from nearby growers.

Ticonderoga at the Shelburne Museum, Shelburne

6000 Shelburne Road, Shelburne; 802-985-3346; shelburnemuseum.org; open year-round; *Ticonderoga* May through October; admission charged

The last vertical-beam side-paddle-wheel steamboat in the country sits in a little valley on the rolling campus of Shelburne Museum on the eastern shore of Lake Champlain. The perch might not be quite as dramatic as the peak of Mount Ararat, where Noah's ark was said to have come to rest, but the ship in a field is a marvel for the modern age and testament to the will (and wealth) of the museum's founder, Electra Havemeyer Webb (1888-1960).

At age 18, Electra Havemeyer hit the Powerball of her day when she inherited a massive fortune built on the sugar industry. Throughout her life, she used her wealth to assemble beautiful, astonishing, innovative, and amusing things. Her parents had collected European and Asian art, but their daughter's tastes were more patriotic. She bought fine art by American painters (including Mary Cassatt and Winslow Homer)

and amassed some of the country's leading collections of American pieced quilts, circus memorabilia, scrimshaw, duck decoys, cigar store Indians—and buildings. Of the 38 exhibition buildings on the Shelburne Museum's 45-acre campus, about two dozen were moved from elsewhere, including a blacksmith's shop, a schoolhouse, a Shaker shed, a general store, and a jail.

But the most remarkable structure Webb added to her collections is the *Ticonderoga*, a Lake Champlain steamboat that had been built in Shelburne in 1906 and operated between ports in Vermont and New York. In her early days, the

boat served the urban getaway crowd. She would meet the evening train from Manhattan at Westport, New York, then sail overnight to St. Albans, Vermont. By the late 1930s, more modern ferries had made the glamorous but plodding steamship something of a relic. She continued to operate as an excursion vessel until 1953, when Vermont preservationist and author Ralph Nading Hill convinced Webb that she really needed to own a lake steamer. Webb tried to keep the *Ticonderoga* operating on Lake Champlain, but the age of steam had passed, and it was impossible to assemble a crew competent to maintain and operate the ship.

So at the end of the 1954 excursion season, the *Ticonderoga* was slated to be moved overland to her current berth on the museum grounds. The task of moving a 220-foot vessel that measured 59 feet across the beam was daunting. For one thing, the ship weighed 892 tons. Workmen dug a basin on the Shelburne shoreline, pumped it dry, put in temporary rail lines, and placed a railroad carriage inside. The basin was then opened to Lake Champlain so the vessel could sail in. Once she was in place, the basin was pumped dry and the ship settled onto her supports. Across the winter, the *Ticonderoga* was slowly hauled over highways, through the woods, and along the Rutland Railroad tracks to the museum grounds. The heroic effort is still considered a landmark in marine preservation.

Restoration of the vessel has also provided a benchmark for preservation of a ship. The *Ticonderoga* is shown as she operated in her heyday of 1923, and visitors to the museum can go aboard to explore from May through October. The contrast between the relatively small and simple staterooms and the grand public spaces is instructive. The dining room and the hallways gleam with carved woodwork and polished butternut and cherry panels, while the ceilings have had their gold stenciling completely restored. By contrast, the staterooms have simple white-painted wood panel walls, a chair, and a narrow bed. One wonders if the dandies of the day simply stayed up all night playing cards in the public areas rather than retire.

Furnishings in the promenade deck, dining room, captain's quarters, and barbershop are either original to the *Ticonderoga* or to other Lake Champlain steamers. In all, visitors can tour the grand staircase and four levels of decks and go behind the scenes to view the ship's huge, hand-built steam engine and coal-fired boilers, as well as the galley, the crew's quarters, and the pilot house.

Webb reportedly spent the winter that the ship was moved fussing with a model of the landscape where she wanted to display it. And just to complete the tableau (since she couldn't guarantee a dove with an olive twig in its beak), she also purchased the Colchester Reef Lighthouse and installed it nearby.

St. Johnsbury Athenaeum, St. Johnsbury
1171 Main Street, St. Johnsbury; 802-748-8291; stjathenaeum.org; open year-round; free admission

With a quick and responsive website and online access to ebooks, the public library of St. Johnsbury keeps pace with the ongoing revolution in information technology. But its very name, the St. Johnsbury Athenaeum (complete with the letter "ash"

composed of an "a" and "e" run together), speaks of an earlier era and lofty ideals. Boston, Salem, and Providence all boasted athenaeums early in the 19th century. These private membership institutions of books and art were named for classic Greek and Roman academies of learning, and they were intended to serve as repositories of all things bright and beautiful.

Horace Fairbanks (1820–88) had a rather more egalitarian view of an athenaeum. Born in Barnet, Vermont, just south of St. Johnsbury, Fairbanks was just 10 years old when his uncle and father invented the first practical platform scale and established E. & T. Fairbanks Company. Horace joined the company as a clerk at age 20 and rose to become president at a time when the Fairbanks scale manufacturer became one of the most successful companies in 19th-century America.

The Fairbanks family gave generously to St. Johnsbury. The founders of the scale company created St. Johnsbury Academy in 1842, and Horace's brother Franklin founded the Fairbanks Museum and Planetarium in 1889. Horace gave a public library—a center of culture for the shire town of Caledonia County. He donated the building and books for the library, which was christened the St. Johnsbury Athenaeum in 1871, and added an art gallery in 1873.

With its granite foundation and architectural trim, handsome brick walls, and high mansard roof, the building is the epitome of French Second Empire style adapted to Victorian New England. It has weathered well in nearly a century and a half in the challenging climate of the Northeast Kingdom. The original collection of 9,000 handsomely bound books was selected by William F. Poole, a pioneer in the public library movement and a founder of the American Library Association. They were placed in handsome wooden bookcases. Even today, the collection has the look and feel of a fine library, and the stacks smell ever so faintly of fine rag paper and bookbinder's glue.

Many 19th-century athenaeums have deaccessioned their art collections by transferring them to museums or selling them to support the library services. But the St. Johnsbury Athenaeum art collection remains intact within the striking Victorian gallery flooded with natural light. The paintings hang in heavy gilt frames on painted board-and-batten walls with black walnut wainscoting and floors.

When Fairbanks, then governor of Vermont, donated the gallery in 1873, it included about 50 paintings and some marble sculptures, all selected by Fairbanks himself. Further donations from Fairbanks's private collection and from members of his family have swelled the collection to more than a hundred paintings.

Horace Fairbanks had both artistic good taste and the money to indulge it. He purchased several striking paintings by Hudson River School landscape artists, including the 1859 *American Landscape with Rocks* by Asher Durand and the luminous 1876 *American Autumn on the Ramapo River—Erie Railway* by Jasper F. Cropsey. His greatest collecting coup, however, was the purchase at auction of Albert Bierstadt's *The Domes of Yosemite*.

Roughly 10 feet high by 15 feet wide, *Domes* is a gigantic painting of an equally larger-than-life landscape. The wilderness of the American West was just being fully surveyed in the mid-19th century, and Bierstadt traveled with the surveying parties, carrying along a primitive stereoscopic camera to document the sights. He first visited the Yosemite Valley in 1863 on his second trip west. Painted from a vantage point about halfway up Yosemite Falls, *Domes* was one of several Bierstadt landscapes of the American West that are often credited with inspiring the American conservation movement.

Financier Legrand Lockwood originally commissioned the work and paid Bierstadt the princely sum of $25,000 for it in 1867. Lockwood, however, lost his fortune when gold suddenly depreciated in 1869, and the painting was sold at auction after his death in 1872. Fairbanks snatched it up for the bargain price of $5,100, intending it all along as the centerpiece of the art collection he was planning for the Athenaeum. The gallery was even designed with a large space on the western wall to hang the work, and a viewing gallery was constructed on the opposite wall in 1882. The painting was removed in fall 2017. At the time of publication, it was scheduled for re-installation in July 2018.

A heroic vision of the country designed to inspire all who see it, *The Domes of Yosemite* still commands pride of place in the gallery as the crown jewel of the Athenaeum and the prized treasure of a small Vermont town.

Harrisville Historic District, p. 191

NEW HAMPSHIRE

USS *Albacore*, Portsmouth
Albacore Park, 600 Market Street, Portsmouth; 603-436-3680; ussalbacore.org; open March through November; admission charged

Named for one of the smaller but speedier members of the tuna family, the USS *Albacore* was created as a research vessel to help convert the US Navy's fleet of submarines from lumbering undersea turtles into greyhounds of the deep. As such, she was one of the most specialized vessels ever constructed in the Portsmouth Naval Shipyard, which has built US Navy ships since 1800.

The key role of submarines in World War II had convinced both the US and the USSR that undersea vessels could control the balance of power on as well as under the waves. Both superpowers also recognized the severe limitations of World War II–era subs. They relied on diesel power plants that needed constant refueling, and while fast enough when cruising on the surface, they were sluggish beneath the waves.

A crash program to develop a nuclear-powered submarine proceeded in the General Dynamic Electric Boat Division in Groton, Connecticut, resulting in the

USS *Nautilus* (see p. 25) and her successors. With no need for oxygen to burn diesel fuel, such subs did not need to come up for air—or fuel—for months on end. But the *Nautilus* was hampered by some of the design disadvantages of older subs.

As the nautical analog to a Formula 1 race car, the *Albacore* would change all that. From the outset, she was designed for optimal underwater performance. Engineers conducted extensive hydrodynamic and wind-tunnel testing to develop the teardrop shape of her hull before her keel was laid on March 15, 1952. She was launched in August 1953, commissioned in December of that year, and began her career as a test vessel in April 1954.

Over the next two years, the *Albacore* underwent tests under different sea conditions, frequently returning to the shipyard for tweaks to her hull design and auxiliary systems. In 1956, a major modification placed her single propeller aft of the rudder and stern plane controls. She was ready for her closeup. In May 1956, she had an underwater television camera strapped to her forecastle, and *Wide, Wide World* made the first live broadcast of a submarine dive on the NBC television network.

The teardrop hull was no longer a secret, and the US Navy quickly adopted the design for the Skipjack class of nuclear submarines that entered service in 1959–62. Soviet, British, and French submarines swiftly followed suit, as have most underwater vessels built ever since.

The *Albacore* kept shifting shape over her working lifetime, ultimately getting an X-shaped tail to improve maneuverability as well as a pair of contrarotating

propellers. She also tested new control systems, dive brakes, escape mechanisms, and approaches to sound-dampening. In 1966, she is said to have set a submerged speed record that remains unsurpassed. We have to take the navy's word for that, since the actual speed remains classified. During her 19-year active career without ever carrying a weapon aboard, the *Albacore* truly lived up to her motto, *Praenuntius Futuri*, or "forerunner of the future."

She lay in limbo for more than a decade after she was decommissioned in 1972 and stored in Philadelphia. She was stricken from the Naval Vessel Register in 1980 and was towed back to Portsmouth in late April 1984. Finally, on May 4, 1985, the *Albacore* made her last voyage, when she was towed up the Piscataqua River from the Portsmouth Naval Shipyard. That October, she was floated onto a concrete cradle in Albacore Park, where she has been landlocked ever since as a museum.

Many of the approximately 35,000 visitors per year are former crew members, other veterans, and former workers from the Portsmouth Naval Shipyard. But the research sub is also popular with a younger generation, in part because visitors are encouraged to put themselves in the place of the crew. She still stirs submariner dreams because she evokes both the can-do era of postwar naval research and the romance of sailing beneath the waves.

Visitors are welcome to take the controls, peer through the periscope, and (if they are agile enough) slide into one of the bunks stacked three and four high with 18 inches or less between the bottom of one mattress and the top of another. The *Albacore* may have been the technological cutting edge of its day, but a manual typewriter in the ship's office and a rotary phone on the bridge are reminders that "that day" was more than a half century ago.

Moffatt-Ladd House & Garden, Portsmouth
154 Market Street, Portsmouth; 603-430-8221; moffattladd .org; open for guided tours June through Columbus Day weekend; admission charged

Grand houses tend to have larger-than-life characters living in them, and the Moffatt-Ladd House in Portsmouth is by no means an exception. If you are the kind of sightseer whose eyes glaze over at the first mention of genealogy, you might want to bring toothpicks to prop them open. The story of this house is the tale of its quirky inhabitants.

Merchant John Moffatt was one of the wealthiest men in the New Hampshire colony, and he didn't mind showing it. In 1763, he ordered this striking Georgian mansion—one of the finest in the colonies—constructed on a bluff above a tidal landing on the Piscataqua River. The first three-story house erected in Portsmouth,

it was to be a wedding gift to his only son, Samuel, and his young bride, Sarah Catherine.

The Great Hall that ran three-quarters the length of the ground floor was the perfect place for a young man on the make to entertain. The Moffatts threw lavish parties those first few years, assuming a role at the center of Portsmouth society. But Samuel was not half as astute a businessman as his father. Among his many ventures was a partnership to fetch a ship full of slaves from Africa—a favorite get-rich-quick scheme in certain quarters in the mid-18th century. Most of the enslaved Africans died in the Atlantic crossing, and the voyage proved a financial debacle that saw Samuel fleeing Portsmouth for St. Eustatius in the West Indies to avoid debtor's prison. His wife and one of their children followed in 1769, a year after Sarah Catherine had planted a famous damask rose, whose offshoots continue to bloom in the garden.

As part of the complicated legal and financial maneuvers of John Moffatt to save his son's possessions, the elder Moffatt moved back into the house in 1769 with his daughter (and Samuel's sister) Katharine. About a year later, Katharine married William Whipple, a successful ship's captain and merchant. Because Whipple was both her cousin and the captain who had spirited her brother beyond the reach of the law, the marriage was kept secret until Katharine was obviously with child. At that point, Whipple joined the household, bringing along with him his enslaved servant, Prince, as well as an outstanding collection of fine Portsmouth furniture, some of which remains with the house.

The Whipples took charge of raising two of Samuel Moffatt's children, and William rose within revolutionary politics. He was one of three representatives from New Hampshire to sign the Declaration of Independence and became brigadier general of the New Hampshire Militia. Family legend long held that Whipple brought a fistful of horse chestnuts back from Philadelphia and planted one in the garden to commemorate the signing of the Declaration. The enormous tree, which still stands, was designated the Millennium Landmark Tree for the State of New Hampshire in 2000.

Inheritance of the mansion became complicated by the terms of old John Moffatt's will. After several years of litigation between branches of the family, the winners of the lawsuits simply sold the house to their lawyer, who in turn gave it to his daughter, Maria. She was the wife of up-and-coming merchant Alexander Ladd. In 1819, when the Ladds moved in, they promptly redecorated.

Decorators always stress making a good first impression. That's certainly what the Ladds did when they covered the walls of the Great Hall in an elegant gray wallpaper in the "views of Italy" pattern by DuFour of Paris. It was a bold statement of wealth and social standing. The Ladds had a long and happy tenancy, and when Maria died in 1861, she left the house to her daughters. Her son, Alexander Hamilton Ladd, bought the house from his sisters.

As cofounder of Portsmouth's only whale oil refinery and part owner of an extremely successful whaling ship, he could well afford a showcase manse. When he retired from his various ventures (including cotton cloth manufacturing and a Texas cotton brokerage) in 1875, he devoted himself to modernizing the house and building its signature terraced garden—to this day a favorite spot for Portsmouth society weddings. He lived in the house until his death in 1900, and his heirs donated it in 1911 to the National Society of the Colonial Dames of America in the State of New Hampshire to be preserved as a museum and to serve as the society's headquarters.

Apart from the creature comforts installed by A. H. Ladd (modern plumbing and heating, mostly), the interior of the house is a memorial to the early generations who lived here. Because the home contains artifacts from all eras of its occupants, it is a vivid illustration of how the Yankee aristocracy lived from the late colonial period through the Civil War. The many pieces of family furniture represent some of the finest extant examples of 18th- and early-19th-century Portsmouth

cabinetmakers. Other examples show the workmanship of furniture makers of northeastern Massachusetts.

The beautiful gardens, though, were A. H. Ladd's personal legacy. His design kept William Whipple's chestnut tree and Sarah Catherine Moffatt's rambling damask roses, but the rest represented his own passion for order, offering different vistas on the house throughout the blooming season. Each year the Colonial Dames even have a garden sale of plants from the garden and sometimes seedlings from the chestnut tree.

Warner House, Portsmouth
150 Daniel Street, Portsmouth; 603-436-5909; warnerhouse.org; open for guided tours June to mid-October; admission charged

Three centuries have passed since Ulster-born sea captain Archibald Macpheadris had a stylish 2½-story Georgian brick mansion constructed for him where Daniel Street led from Portsmouth's North Parish meeting house to the Piscataqua River waterfront. Macpheadris was a successful trader and married into the Wentworth

clan, who were themselves successful traders and deeply involved in colonial government. Finished in 1716 by English immigrant master builder John Drew, the house boasted 15-inch-thick brick walls laid in Flemish bond of locally made bricks. It would be Portsmouth's grandest home for the next half century.

Notable as the structure of the house may be, it is best known for the interior decoration that Captain Macpheadris ordered. Shortly after the house was finished, he commissioned a series of six murals for the central hall and main stairwell. Their extraordinary survival makes them the oldest Anglo-American murals in the country.

The identity of the artist is uncertain, although art historian Mary Black nominated Nehemiah Partridge (1683–c.1737), a New York artist who had been born in Portsmouth and whose father was an associate of Captain Macpheadris. Other historians have suggested that stylistic differences point to more than one painter. Some of the scenes are equally mysterious. It is easy to identify the sacrifice of Abraham, for example, and the Mohawk sachems who flank the window at the top of the staircase are likely two of the four Mohawks presented to Queen Anne in London in 1710. Far stranger, however, is a scene of a woman outdoors at a spinning wheel who is interrupted by an eagle swooping down to snatch a chicken while a dog barks. It is possible that the figures are somehow symbolic in a manner known only to Macpheadris and the painter—or that it is merely a fanciful scene.

Likewise, scholars have speculated widely on the image of a boy riding. The child is pictured with a crown and the letter "P" hanging from the pommel on his saddle. The most recent theory suggests that the boy was William, Duke of Gloucester, who would have restored the Stuart Scottish line to the throne had he lived. Macpheadris was well connected on both sides of the Atlantic and might well have been expressing Scots pride.

One bit of evidence that the murals had specific meaning to Macpheadris and no one else is that, when the captain died in 1729, his heirs papered over all but the paintings of the Mohawks. The captain's daughter, already once widowed, married Portsmouth merchant Jonathan Warner in 1760, and the Warner descendants occupied the house until 1932. The old murals were rediscovered around 1850, when a child playing on the stairwell peeled back a corner of wallpaper to reveal a horse's hoof!

The Warner House Association was formed in 1931 to buy the house and save it from being torn down and replaced by a gas station. In 1932, the house opened as a museum. In 1988, artisans who had worked on the Sistine Chapel restoration went to work on the Warner House murals, restoring them to their 18th century heyday.

Family belongings have come back to the house over the years, some by gift and others by loan. (The Metropolitan Museum of Art in New York, for example, has loaned some furniture.) The house is shown as a historic succession from the early 18th century through late Victorian times. (The Warner family only used it as a summer home after 1880.) Some of the most telling pieces are a series of five 1761 portraits of the extended Warner family by society portraitist Joseph Blackburn. The sixth painting of the group was the portrait of Jonathan Warner, sold to the Museum of Fine Arts, Boston. The Warner House displays a copy. Some striking examples of Queen Anne period Portsmouth furniture are also on display, including the library bookcase in the Setting Room attributed to important Portsmouth cabinetmaker Robert Harrold and a Sherburne high chest inscribed with the date 1733, making it the earliest dated example of Queen Anne furniture made in the colonies. Look for the angel face on the central drawer pull.

Governor John Langdon House, Portsmouth
143 Pleasant Street, Portsmouth; 603-436-3205;
historicnewengland.org; open for guided tours June to mid-October;
admission charged

George Washington never slept here, but he was entertained in the double parlor and wrote of the grand home that it was "esteemed the first in Portsmouth." That's exactly what John Langdon was aiming for when he had the Georgian-style mansion erected in 1784.

Like his brother Woodbury, John Langdon had opted out of his father's shipyard business in favor of learning the sea trade and becoming a ship owner. By the late 1760s, he owned a small fleet of vessels engaged in trade between the Caribbean, Portsmouth, and London and was one of the wealthiest men in Portsmouth.

But British control over the shipping lanes hampered his style, and he became an avid supporter of independence, even helping to confiscate British munitions from New Castle in 1774—one of the precipitating acts of rebellion that led to the American Revolution. He served in the Second Continental Congress but resigned to oversee the construction of the *Raleigh*, the *America*, and the *Ranger*—the first fighting vessels of the Continental Navy. During the Revolution, his vessels operated as privateers, seizing British shipping at considerable profit. When the war ended in 1783, John Langdon was flush. He wanted a house that would befit the grand poobah on the Piscataqua.

And he got it.

Impressive from the street with its symmetry and ample proportions, the mansion is a striking example of full-blown Georgian style. It is even more impressive inside, where the grand reception rooms that flank the front entry have high ceilings, large windows to flood them with light, and spectacular carved woodwork overseen by Michael Whidden III, who had also worked a generation earlier at the Moffatt-Ladd House (p. 181). Based on records of payment, the carvings in the two

front parlors—including the striking work around the showcase fireplaces—are attributed to the father and son team of Ebenezer and William Dearing of Kittery, Maine. Although most of the carvings are based on drawings in books by British architect Abraham Swan, the execution by Whidden

and the Dearings became a standard for the American Rococo style of decoration.

The double parlor to the left of the front entrance shows the classic Georgian signatures of thick crown molding, wainscoting, carved medallions, and window seats. The room was the largest in a private dwelling in Portsmouth, and it is easy to imagine a string quartet playing in the corner when Washington was entertained here at least twice. The parlor on the other side of the entry holds, among other pieces, an English harpsichord that Langdon bought for his daughter Eliza shortly after the house was built and Langdon's personal desk and bookcase.

Langdon's skill as a host and his social position in Portsmouth served him well. As a member of the Constitutional Convention, he was among the signers of the US Constitution and later served both in the US House and Senate. His political career continued once he returned home from the national capital, as he served in the New Hampshire legislature and three terms as governor. In 1812, he even declined an offer to be James Madison's vice president.

The master bedroom, on the second floor, serves today as a gallery of Portsmouth furniture—one of the main attractions of the house after its extraordinary woodwork. Only Boston and Philadelphia surpassed Portsmouth as a furniture-making center in the Colonial and early Federal periods, and the Langdon House has striking examples.

Following Langdon's death in 1819, the house passed to Eliza, who ultimately sold the property in 1833. It passed through two other families before being repurchased in 1877 by Woodbury Langdon (a descendant of John Langdon's brother) for his mother. Upon her death, Woodbury moved in with his wife, Astor heiress Elizabeth Elwyn Langdon. As avid followers of the Colonial Revival movement, they tore out most of the Victorian décor installed in the 1850s after a fire and restored the 18th-century appearance. They also engaged the firm of McKim, Mead, and White to replace the kitchen ell with a 20-room addition.

Elizabeth Langdon continued to live in the house at least part-time until 1946. By acquiring many of the abutting properties, she was able to extend the grounds and establish striking gardens, including a 100-foot arbor with climbing roses and grapes. In 1947, she deeded the property to Historic New England with the provision that her sister, Helen Kremer, had life rights to the house. When Kremer died in 1957, the house became a museum.

Guided tours focus on the original structure. The double parlor is also used for social events, and the gardens are a popular venue for weddings.

Robert Frost Farm, Derry
122 Rockingham Road, Derry; 603-432-3091; robertfrostfarm .org; open for guided tours early May through Columbus Day; admission charged

Fortunately for American literature, the young man who moved into the Magoon Place about 2 miles south of Derry village, New Hampshire, in 1900 didn't have much of an aptitude for chicken farming. The 26-year-old college dropout with a wife and one surviving child had never had a job that he could tolerate, and try as he might, raising chickens didn't engage him for very long. But the years he worked this hardscrabble southern New Hampshire farm forged the harried family man into one of the giants of American letters.

Robert Frost went on to win the Pulitzer Prize four times and became the white-thatched eminence whose poems were as widely read as they were widely praised. But this property would haunt his verse for the rest of his life, as he transmuted the

base metal of his agrarian struggles into the golden lines for which he will always be remembered.

"Something there is that doesn't love a wall . .," he wrote in the very first poem in *North of Boston*, his second book, published in 1914, that launched his career. And there behind the farmhouse, at the edge of the apple orchard just as he described it, the old stone wall remains, its topmost stones tumbled this way and that by the frost heaves. It is no stretch to imagine young Rob Frost the farmer and sometimes school-teacher walking the wall in spring-time with his neighbor Napoleon Guay, mending the tumbledown gaps. "Good fences make good neighbors," Guay insisted. Frost was never clear if he agreed.

In a sense, the farm and Frost are one. The big white 1880s farmhouse with its attached woodshed, two-hole privy, and spacious barn conjures up the family man and chicken farmer. Frost's oldest child, Lesley Frost Ballantine, directed the resto-ration of the farmhouse to the Frost era when the state acquired it in 1965 from a private owner who was using the property as an automotive junkyard. After a decade of restoration, the homestead opened as a New Hampshire state park and historic home.

Ballantine's remembrance of her childhood—augmented by her own journals of the period—brought about a restoration so vivid it almost seems taken from a painting. Even the wallpaper patterns were re-created, and the wooden floors were repainted the same color red as they had been in Frost's time. At times, the rooms almost look like settings for a portrait where the sitter and the painter have just stepped out.

A peculiar Blickensderfer typewriter sits on the kitchen table next to a kerosene lamp. It's not much of a stretch to imagine Frost at the table, gazing out on the farm pond and composing his poems by longhand, then typing them up on the machine. Steps from the soapstone sink with its knife-sharpening grooves is the entry to the small birthing room where three Frost children were born.

Although the farm had neither electricity nor running water (unless you count the water running from the hand pump), it did possess one technological marvel of the early 20th century. The Frosts had a telephone. They shared a party line with seven other homes. Frost could not resist listening in on his neighbors' conversations. His excuse was that he was only studying the flat Yankee pattern of their speech to ape it accurately in his verse.

The front parlor, appropriately enough, has a bookcase stuffed with books that Ballantine recalls from her childhood. They show the educated tastes of the era—the complete works of Ralph Waldo Emerson, the poems of Robert Burns—and a weakness for popular entertainment (Lew Wallace's novel *Ben-Hur*). Frost's wife, Elinor, homeschooled the children here, but the poet taught them astronomy from the windows of an upstairs bedroom. Each child had a star that was his or her own. Frost told them that for all their lives, wherever they might be, they could look to the night sky to find their family. That was Frost's secret—to make fixtures in the natural world touchstones to recover past thoughts and emotions. The Hyla Brook Nature/Poetry Trail crosses behind the orchard, hopscotching the brook of its name and following the Mending Wall. Walking the trail is almost like traipsing through the pages of *A Boy's Will* and *North of Boston*.

Frost would repeatedly return to the New England countryside, but when he sold the Derry farm in 1911 and moved to England the next year, he had farmed enough to last him a lifetime. And that was what he made it do. The land stayed with him long after he relinquished it. The poet himself observed many decades later, "I might say the core of all my writing was probably the five free years I had on the farm down the road a mile or two from Derry Village."

Harrisville Historic District
603-827-3722; historicharrisville.org; downloadable village walking tour available on website. Printed walking tour brochure available at Town Library.

Harrisville, the prettiest mill town in New England, is a nearly perfectly preserved example of a vanished way of life. Located on a southwestern New Hampshire ridge that divides the Connecticut and Merrimack river basins, the village comes as a surprise to travelers, as if a 19th-century brick mill town had passed through a time warp into the Granite State woods.

The layout of the community is dictated by the fall of the land—most notably the drainage from a chain of three ponds into a rocky ravine

where the Goose Brook outlet falls 100 feet in a quarter mile. In 1774, first settler Abel Twitchell erected a water-powered grist- and sawmill at the outlet. In the early 1800s, Twitchell and his son-in-law, Bethuel Harris, eased into wool carding and fulling and, by 1813, full-fledged production of woolen cloth.

Throughout the 19th century, cloth production boomed. The handsome brick and stone mills that straddle the ravine whirred with activity. As work opportunities expanded, the village swelled with new laborers, and Bethuel Harris and his sons, Cyrus, Aldon, and Milan, made sure that the temporal and spiritual needs of the community were addressed. What is now the Town Library was built at the edge of the mill pond by Bethuel Harris in 1839 as the original Congregational Church, and when the much larger "new" church was constructed nearby a year later, the smaller brick structure with its abbreviated belfry became the vestry. At the opposite end of the mill pond, the handsome brick storehouse held the finished goods from the mills.

The Harris clan built for posterity. Although this region of New Hampshire was thick with timber, most of the structures raised by the mill owners were made from Connecticut River Valley red brick. And they built with considerable aesthetic flair. The Harrisville General Store, built in 1838, probably by Cyrus Harris, demonstrates a Yankee adaptation of a Greek temple with a gabled front, granite lintels, and a porch supported by columns.

As new workers flocked into the village, the mill owners constructed brick boardinghouses. The 1851 Cheshire Mills Boarding House was the closest Harrisville ever got to the style seen in larger manufacturing cities. Three bays wide and nine bays long, it had the proportions of a factory itself—except that Cyrus Harris built it with maximum windows to let in the light, including seven dormers that jut out on each side of the slate roof. For more than a century, the boardinghouse was home to single male mill workers.

The Harrises built a few freestanding cottages, mainly for midlevel workers, such as foremen. When the Colony family took over the Harris assets in the 1850s and 1860s, they built wood-framed workers' cottages. Five of these 1½-story Greek Revival homes stand cheek by jowl in the upper end of the village along a street aptly called Peanut Row for the diminutive scale of the houses.

Other New England textile operations faded in the 20th century, but the mills at Harrisville continued making cloth until the craze for double-knit fabrics finally made it too expensive to retool. Cheshire Mills, the final survivor in the line of Harrisville mills, ceased operation in 1970.

As a community that continued to do what it was good at for more than 150 years, Harrisville survived with both its identity and its historic buildings intact into an era that suddenly valued preserving an authentic past. As early as 1957, influential architecture critic Ada Louise Huxtable wrote in the journal *Progressive Architecture in America* that New England mill villages "represent a trend-setting level of social and industrial planning seldom equalled since." Praising both their neat organization and unregimented uniformity, she noted that Harrisville "represents this planning logic and design facility to an exceptional degree." Architecture historian William Pierson noted in *American Buildings and Their Architects* (1972), "Harrisville is the only industrial community of the early nineteenth century in America that still survives in its original form."

When Cheshire Mills closed, townspeople and preservationists formed Historic Harrisville, Inc., to seek National Historic Landmark status for the village and to renovate the old mills and mill-related buildings to attract new businesses. Buildings owned by HHI now provide affordable housing as well as space for a daycare center, the post office, several artists and writers, a digital media company, and Harrisville Designs. HHI also owns and operates the Harrisville General Store—still the place in town to get coffee, snacks, and hot breakfast or lunch.

The textile legacy lives on through Harrisville Designs, founded in 1971 by John Colony III, scion of the same family that had owned Cheshire Mills since the mid-

19th century. Harrisville Designs spins all-natural 100 percent wool into knitting and weaving yarns and produces carded fleece for spinning and felting. It also offers an extensive array of three-day workshops throughout the year, with optional lodging in the 1853 Cheshire Mills Boarding House.

Franklin Pierce Homestead, Hillsborough

301 2nd NH Turnpike, Hillsborough; 603-478-3165;
hillsboroughhistory.org; open for guided tours Memorial Day
through Columbus Day; admission charged

Although New Hampshire exerts an influence on presidential politics dispropor-
tionate to its small and demographically unrepresentative population, the Granite
State has produced but a single US president. That son of New Hampshire, Franklin
Pierce, might have actually preferred the media sideshow of the modern presidential
primary system. Not until the forty-ninth vote of the 1852 Democratic National
Convention did he become his party's nominee.

Pierce was a compromise candidate. He had a fine if undistinguished record in
both houses of Congress, had served as US attorney for New Hampshire, and had
risen to the rank of brigadier general in the US Army during the Mexican-American
War. As a northern Democrat who opposed the Abolitionist movement as a threat
to national unity, he garnered considerable support from slave-holding states. In the
general election, Pierce went on to thrash Winfield Scott, the Whig Party's candidate and his former commander during the Mexican-American War. He became the
youngest president elected by popular vote.

Preserved and interpreted by the Hillsborough Historical Society, the house
where Pierce grew up (his family moved into it shortly after his birth on November
23, 1804) shows the milieu from which the fourteenth US president sprang. The

house was built by Pierce's father, Benjamin, who had been drawn to Hillsborough by the innate beauty of the countryside—and by the fact that, though poor, he could afford a log cabin with 50 acres of land. The elder Pierce entered public service, and by the time he built the house that would become the Franklin Pierce Homestead, Benjamin Pierce had risen to prominence and prosperity. He operated the building as a tavern until 1810, then converted it to a gracious private home where he entertained the celebrities of the day, including Daniel Webster.

The house is shown during its 19th-century heyday, around the time that Franklin left to attend Bowdoin College in Maine. It is a stately Federal-era house with just a hint of Greek Revival embellishment in the style of the front door—which, it appears, like good New Hampshire Yankees, the Pierces rarely used. (These days, a discreet sign at the base of the front gate directs visitors around to the side of the house for the entrance.)

Inside, the house has unusually high ceilings and spacious rooms. Tours enter through the dining room, located where the original tavern kitchen had been, with its black and orange painted floorcloth and vivid orange painted walls with stenciled edges. The large dining table, original to the Pierce family, seated the family, tavern guests, and the hired help.

The next room is shown as a tavern room. Originally unpainted, it too sports orange walls, a table with cards spread out, and a desk. Two of the chairs in the room are believed to be part of a set given to Benjamin Pierce by John Quincy Adams. The space was redecorated in 1818 to become the family's sitting room. On the opposite side of the front hall is the parlor, where women would eat, socialize, and even sleep (if they were guests). In 1824, the walls were covered with French wallpaper depicting the Bay of Naples. The Pierces paid $50 for the paper—enough to have purchased a small farm at the time.

Benjamin Pierce spent 57 years in public service in one form or another and threw frequent parties, which accounts for the second-floor ballroom with a sprung floor for dancing. (It was often partitioned into sleeping quarters during the tavern years.) In fact, the house seems to chronicle the life and times of Benjamin Pierce even more than the career of his famous son.

Franklin Pierce returned infrequently to his childhood home, partly because his chronically depressed wife, Jane, made no secret of her distaste for Hillsborough. She also hated Washington, perhaps because when the president-elect and his family were heading by train from Boston to Washington in 1853, the train derailed and their car rolled down an embankment. Their 12-year-old son, Benjamin, their only living child, was the sole fatality.

The small rooms on the third level of the homestead, which served as bedrooms for Franklin and his brothers, now contain memorabilia of the president's political life. The campaign posters and trophies of life in the White House touch largely on patriotic themes. Pierce is remembered by historians for professionalizing the federal civil service and rescuing thousands of jobs from political patronage. Ironically, he is also remembered for appointing a Bowdoin College friend to a sinecure at the Custom House in Salem, Massachusetts, giving Nathaniel Hawthorne the financial security to write some of his best works.

Those more positive aspects of Pierce's legacy were ultimately overshadowed by his continued support of slavery. As president, he vigorously enforced the Fugitive Slave Act and pushed the Kansas-Nebraska Act to open the new western territories to slavery. When Pierce sought re-election in 1856, his party instead chose the less controversial James Buchanan as its nominee.

Posterity may have judged Franklin Pierce as a president on the wrong side of history. The Franklin Pierce Homestead, however, recalls a happier time when country life seemed simple and the Pierces—Benjamin and Franklin alike—represented a self-made country-squire aristocracy of merit.

Canterbury Shaker Village, Canterbury
288 Shaker Road, Canterbury; (603) 783-9511; shakers.org; open mid-May through November; admission charged

The glacial hills of central New Hampshire sometimes seem fixed in reverie for an agrarian past. The back roads twist and turn as they follow the contours of the land, and the sturdy stone walls that once marked the property lines are frost-tumbled and nearly obscured by resurgent roadside trees. The forest has encroached on most of the long-ago meadows, and a riot of alders, birches, beeches, and Norway maples compete for light where farmers once grew alfalfa and timothy.

Canterbury Shaker Village appears as if it were a mirage. The road suddenly straightens and ancient sugar maples stand sentinel on each side of the pavement. A long green field behind a white rail fence rises up a hillside, and where the land flattens out, there stands the village: a cluster of sturdy buildings as straight-backed as any Shaker chair. For 200 years, this was one of the most vibrant communities of the United Society of Believers in Christ's Second Coming—more widely known as Shakers.

In 1782, Canterbury began the process of becoming a Shaker community when the farmer who owned the property invited the

Shakers to share the farm. In 1792, a covenant was signed, and the Shaker brothers and sisters systematically replaced all the buildings with Shaker structures, which typically had separate entrances for men and women. At its height around the time of the Civil War, Canterbury Shaker Village had a population of about 300 people and 100 buildings, including several mill buildings on the seven large, hand-dug ponds at the rear of the property.

A celibate sect, Canterbury, like the other Shaker communities, began to dwindle by the early 20th century. Ever practical, the Shakers took down buildings as the community shrank. When only 13 sisters remained, they made provisions to incorporate as a museum with a clause that allowed them to live out their days at the village. The last sister died in 1992. The present museum property is down from 4,000 to 694 acres and 24 buildings.

Several showcase buildings from the earliest years of the community still stand. The Meeting House, built in 1792, is the last intact first-generation 18th-century Shaker meeting house in the US. It epitomizes Shaker simplicity. The interior is one large, open room with pegs all around to hang clothing and chairs during the worship service, for the Shakers sang and danced their prayers. Iron and copper markers embedded in the floorboards are "stops" to indicate where everyone would stand during a dance. Guides will sometimes sing a verse or two of "Simple Gifts," the best-known Shaker song ("'Tis a gift to be simple, 'tis a gift to be free ..."), pointing out that the words contain dance directions like calls in a square dance.

Perhaps the most impressive structure is the Dwelling House, built in 1793 and expanded several times until it reached its current proportions in 1837. It is the largest building in the village. Several rooms are set up as they would have been used by the Shakers, including the larger and more private rooms of the elders. There are, of course, separate staircases for men and women, who lived in different wings.

The schoolhouse began as a one-story, one-room structure in 1823, but so many children were in Shaker care by the Civil War that it was enlarged to its present size. The nearby Carpenters' Shop, originally built as housing for visitors, often has artisans demonstrating the craft of making Shaker flat brooms, a reminder that Shakers invented the flat broom and manufactured them by the thousands.

While the Canterbury Shakers were rooted in a farming tradition, they were hardly Luddites. The village had its own electric lights before the rest of New Hampshire and its own telephone system. The Shakers owned (communally, of course) some of the first automobiles in the area and generally used the most up-to-date technology available. In 1858, Brother David Parker invented an industrial washing machine to use in Canterbury. It worked so well that the community then manufactured and sold the machines to resort hotels from Mount Washington south to Florida. Canterbury was also known for its textiles, particularly the woolen "Dorothy cloaks" that became fashionable as opera cloaks for women. They would take orders at resort hotels and make each one to a customer's specifications. The Canterbury sisters also operated knitting machines to make varsity sweaters for Dartmouth, Harvard, and Yale.

Like other Shaker communities, Canterbury began selling herb and garden seeds in the 19th century—after the Mount Vernon, New York, Shakers invented the paper seed packet. The gift shop at Canterbury, like those at Hancock Shaker Village (see p. 80) and Sabbathday Lake (see p. 223), still sells old-fashioned open-pollinated flower, herb, and vegetable seeds.

Shaker founder Mother Ann Lee instructed her followers, "Put your hands to work, and your hearts to God." Looking out across the broad green fields stretching to the treeline, it is easy to imagine a line of Shaker brothers shouldering their 10-foot-long seeding trays. They seem to march in time to a hymn, seeding the field as a form of prayer.

Saint-Gaudens National Historic Site, Cornish
139 Saint Gaudens Road, Cornish; 603-675-2175; nps.gov/saga; grounds open all year, exhibit buildings open Memorial Day through October; admission charged

Augustus and Augusta Saint-Gaudens were the power couple of the Cornish Colony, the bohemian assemblage of American artists, sculptors, intellectuals, and writers at the end of the 19th century. Augustus Saint-Gaudens was the lion among them—one of the most celebrated sculptors of his age and the craftsman of powerful imagery that endures in large-scale public monuments and even in current American gold bullion coinage.

Born in Dublin, Ireland, in 1848 to a French shoemaker father and Irish mother, Augustus Saint-Gaudens came with his parents to New York at the age of 6 months. He was apprenticed at age 13 to a cameo cutter and took art classes after work through his teens. At 19, he sailed to Paris to study at the legendary École des Beaux-Arts, then spent five years in Rome studying classical art and architecture. He clearly absorbed every lesson. When he received his first major commission in 1876—a monument to Civil War admiral David Farragut—he burst on the American art scene as if he had sprung fully formed from the head of Zeus.

From the outset, Saint-Gaudens was a master who exhibited keen psychological insight and empathy matched by impeccable artistic technique. Unveiled in 1881, the Farragut statue made his career in a time when America was hungry for public

monuments that celebrated its heroes and created an air of imperial permanence. For anyone who wanted a top-notch public monument during the Gilded Age, Augustus Saint-Gaudens was the go-to guy.

Flush with commissions, by 1885 Saint-Gaudens was looking for a summer place to escape the heat and hubbub of Manhattan. His childhood friend and lawyer Charles Beaman offered him a former country inn in Cornish, New Hampshire. Saint-Gaudens thought the building ugly and declined. His wife, known to all as "Gussie," had the better eye for landscape, and her vision prevailed. They rented for a few years, converting a hay barn into a studio and modifying the house to suit their needs. In 1892, the couple bought the property.

Saint-Gaudens transformed the Cornish land the way he transformed American public sculpture, imbuing a plain vernacular with a heroic classicism. "Aspet," as he named the house after his father's birthplace in Gascony, evolved into an estate with studios, formal gardens, a lawn bowling green, a toboggan run, nature trails, a 9-hole golf course, and a pervasive and romantic sense of well-being. It served as the Saint-Gaudens family summer home from 1885 to 1897. Once the sculptor was diagnosed with cancer in 1900, it became their permanent home until his death in 1907.

The Visitor Center at this National Park Service site has an excellent video that recounts all the official highlights of the life of Augustus Saint-Gaudens. It was a dazzling career that, by the video account, moved from triumph to triumph, such as the General William T. Sherman Monument in New York's Central Park, where a winged Victory leads the general on his resolute march to the sea, and the moving and powerful Shaw Memorial in Boston, with its ramrod-straight Colonel Robert Gould Shaw on horseback leading the doomed African American soldiers of the Massachusetts 54th Regiment into battle at Fort Wagner in Charleston, South Carolina.

But Saint-Gaudens was more than a sculptor of public bombast and military heroics. A modern casting of the Farragut statue may be the first piece most visitors see, but the New Gallery across the reflecting pool contains some of the sculptor's more intimate works, notably some of his early cameos, a few of his exquisite portrait reliefs (one of his contemporaries called him the greatest master of bas-relief since the 15th century), and the designs he created for the 1907 eagle and double eagle gold coins. The stunningly beautiful Standing Liberty of the double eagle is still struck as US Mint gold bullion coinage.

On the grounds, shrubbery surrounds a few of Saint-Gaudens's greatest works. They include the final version of the Shaw Memorial—even later than the one on Boston Common—and the Adams Memorial, a 1974 recasting of the haunting 1891 funerary sculpture commissioned by historian Henry Adams after the suicide of his wife, Clover. Adams called the hooded, androgynous figure *The Peace of God.* Saint-Gaudens called it *The Mystery of the Hereafter . . . beyond pain and beyond joy.*

A happier Saint-Gaudens seems to inhabit the 1904 Little Studio, where a ripely proportioned bronze nude of the goddess Diana with her bow drawn dominates the space. She was a model for the figure at the top of Madison Square Garden in New York. Along the walls and in the side rooms are other examples of bas-relief works by Saint-Gaudens. This was his private space, where he made drawings and models that were later enlarged and executed by his assistants in a much bigger studio, which burned down in 1944.

Saint-Gaudens made sure that the Little Studio afforded a maximum of aesthetic pleasure. After a trip to Italy, in 1889 he redesigned the building with a pergola supported by Doric columns and plenty of room to sit beneath the grapevines and let his eyes wander through the hollyhocks to the mountain vistas in the distance.

He did much the same with the circa-1800 Federal-style brick house, to which he added dormers and a west-facing porch propped up with Ionic columns. The upper floors of the structure now serve as offices for the US Park Service, but the rest of the house gives a feel for both Augustus's practical turn of mind (his desk on the stairway landing gives a clear view of visitors at the front door) and Augusta's Victorian sensibility (the sitting room filled with ruffles and doilies). The house contains the original furnishings and decorative objects that the sculptor picked up on his travels. But more than any objects, it is the view from that broad front porch, shaded by a honey locust tree Saint-Gaudens planted in 1896, that makes the domestic life seem suddenly vivid. Thanks to the National Park Service, every visitor can do as the Saint-Gaudens did: lounge on the broad porch in contented rustic splendor and watch the day march down the hill.

The Epic of American Civilization Murals, Hanover
Baker-Berry Library Orozco Room, 25 North Main Street, Hanover; 603-646-1110; dartmouth.edu; open year-round

How do Dartmouth College students focus on their studies when the eyes of history are always staring down at them? As they sit at massive wooden tables in the basement reading room of Baker-Berry Library on the Hanover campus, they are surrounded by art on a heroic scale.

Mural painting is art's equivalent of public oratory. It is loud, forceful, and vibrant and typically fills broad expanses of blank wall with grand subjects and universal ideas. Mexican painter José Clemente Orozco (1883–1949) was a master of the form, harnessing his own dynamic style of Expressionism to a revolutionary ideology. Whether a viewer agrees or disagrees with Orozco's point of view, it is impossible to look away.

Orozco was one of three central figures in the Mexican *muralismo* movement that arose in the 1920s after the end of the Mexican revolution. Along with Diego Rivera and David Alfaro Siqueiros, Orozco used his art as a political weapon. His paintings, like theirs, were graphic manifestos aimed at a broad, popular audience. All three muralists were great artists, and often supported themselves with commissions in the US as well as in Mexico. While living in the US between 1927 and 1934, Orozco painted murals at Pomona College in California and at the New School for

Social Research in New York City. His masterpiece of the period, however, was *The Epic of American Civilization* at Dartmouth College—arguably Orozco's most ambitious public work in the US.

Orozco painted the mural cycle between fall 1932 and winter 1934 while he was an artist in residence. Hiring him was a bold move for Dartmouth at a time when few colleges studied the work of living artists. A social critic whose revolutionary ideology championed the powerless indigenous peoples of Mexico, Orozco was attracted to Dartmouth in part because the college was founded shortly before the American Revolution explicitly to educate the Native American population and English colonists side by side.

Orozco first came to Dartmouth in May 1932 to demonstrate fresco technique on a corridor wall between the art building and Baker Library (now the Baker-Berry Library). He and members of the art department were immediately excited about the possibility of a much more ambitious mural cycle on the walls of the cavernous reserve reading room on the lower level of the library, which had opened in 1928. This tract of blank wall space was a field on which he could realize his grand vision of the sweep of history in the Americas.

When he signed the finished work on February 13, 1934, Orozco had covered 2,200 square feet with 24 different compositions. He worked in true fresco—painting on wet plaster so that the colors bonded chemically with the plaster and became part of the wall. Unlike many muralists, who work from full-scale cartoons transferred to the wall surface, Orozco drew only horizontal, vertical, and diagonal compositional guidelines on the walls. He usually completed a few square feet per day and would often spend an entire day painting a detailed face.

Wrapping around three walls of the room, the mural is divided architecturally, thematically, and historically into two sections. One represents life in the Americas before the arrival of the Europeans; the other shows history since the conquest of Mexico and projects a utopian vision of the future.

The mural has been the subject of controversy from the outset. Some American artists objected to the choice of a Mexican for a project at the height of the Depression. Other people were offended by Orozco's politics, especially his clear-eyed condemnation of political, religious, and academic institutions. The *Epic of American Civilization* presents Orozco's interpretation of history as a cycle of repression and rebirth—the enslavement of the human spirit and release from bondage, repeated again and again as various cultures dominated the Americas.

Beginning with the arrival of the Aztecs in the Valley of Mexico, Orozco sketches a vision of barbarous human sacrifice overcome by the deity Quetzalcoatl, who ushers in a Golden Age but then departs as the Aztecs revert to superstition and greed for power. The Aztec world goes up in flames with the arrival of the conquistador Hernán Cortés. Succeeding panels demonstrate dehumanization through the proliferation of crushing machinery. In perhaps the most controversial panel, "Gods of the Modern World," Orozco shows skeletal figures in European and American academic robes presiding over the stillbirth of useless knowledge—an audacious criticism on the walls of one of the country's preeminent colleges.

Orozco's climax of modern horrors, "Modern Migration of the Spirit," was similarly condemned for its unorthodox depiction of Christ leading an apocalyptic destruction of the symbols of militarism, religion, and authoritarian culture. But in Orozco's vision, destruction holds the seeds of rebirth. He projects a utopian future in which machines serve humankind and workers put down their tools to nourish their spirits.

The grand scope of the project—its sheer physical size and the complex integration of subject matter—marked a maturity in Orozco's work. He masterfully unified the themes of several disparate panels into a grand statement while solving the technical problems of creating form and color that would read consistently throughout such a major work. Many critics consider the *Epic of American Civilization* to be the greatest mural cycle in the United States.

In a 1990 interview with *Américas* magazine on the occasion of the mural's restoration, professor emeritus of art history Churchill P. Lathrop—one of the two professors who had been instrumental in bringing Orozco to Dartmouth—expressed his continued amazement. "We knew we'd get a good painting," he said. "We had no idea we'd get a masterpiece."

Omni Mount Washington Resort, Bretton Woods
310 Mount Washington Road, Bretton Woods; (603) 278-1000; omnihotels.com

In the White Mountains of New Hampshire, the view is everything. The ceremonial mile-long drive from Route 302 to the Mount Washington Hotel affords guests ample opportunity to appreciate the massive white stucco building with red roof against the backdrop of the Presidential Range. Just as its namesake mountain is first among equals at 6,288 feet, so too is the Omni Mount Washington Resort (as it is now known) first among survivors from the era of White Mountains grand hotels.

The Mount Washington was also the last grand hotel constructed in the New Hampshire mountains. Industrialist Joseph Stickney conceived of the resort in 1900 and brought in 250 Italian craftsmen to execute the stone masonry and stucco work that architect Charles Ailing Gifford's design required. Gifford also specified a steel superstructure that would speed the construction of the complex, rambling building. It was completed in slightly more than two years and was one of the first resort hotels in New England with electricity, modern plumbing, and central heating. To this day the hotel has its own private telephone system and post office.

Modern conveniences aside, it was also one of the most opulent hotels of its day, decked out with crystal chandeliers, Tiffany stained glass, and gilded mirrors. Its unusual octagonal dining room was designed to provide spectacular views of the

Presidential Range. At its opening on July 28, 1902, the hotel had a staff of 350. Although Stickney died a year later, his widow, Carolyn, continued to spend summers at the Mount Washington and added onto her husband's hotel with a second dining room and fourth-floor guest rooms.

The Mount Washington catered to a wealthy clientele from Boston, New York, and Philadelphia. At the peak of activity just before World War I, up to 50 trains per day stopped at the three Bretton Woods stations. (One station building is now a restaurant of the resort complex.) Well-off rusticators would bring the entire family for a month or even a full summer season. The men of the family would come and go by train to tend to business. They were acting on the Gilded Age maxim that enjoying the wilderness need not come at the expense of creature comforts. Few travelers of today have the time or the means for such an extended stay at the Omni Mount Washington Resort, but even a few days permit the contemplation of the majesty of the mountains from the hotel's elegant cocoon.

The ratification of the 16th Amendment in 1913 ushered in the era of the modern income tax and curbed even the appetite of the wealthy for resort extravagance. The Mount Washington adjusted to shorter stays and kept the doors open through the Great Depression. Although it closed in 1942 for World War II, the hotel hosted the Bretton Woods International Monetary Conference in 1944. Seven hundred thirty delegates from 44 Allied countries convened at the hotel for three weeks in July to hammer out a new post–World War II economic system. Although not all of the accords would go into effect until 1958, the conference established the World Bank and the International Monetary Fund and set the gold standard for currencies at $35 per ounce. The documents were formally signed in the Gold Room just off the main lobby. It is preserved as a historic site.

The resort continued slow expansion over the last quarter of the 20th century and has been an all-season property since 1999. When the Mount Washington first opened, guests prided themselves on hardly lifting a finger for their entire stay. Modern expectations of a resort emphasize a more active lifestyle. The Mount Washington absorbed two surrounding golf courses and even restored the Mount Washington Golf Course to its pioneering original 1915 Donald Ross design. It added the Bretton Woods downhill ski area and a Nordic ski-touring area to its holdings. The modern resort also has riding stables and clay tennis courts. But at the end of the day, the original rusticators may have had the right idea after all. Nothing beats sitting on the long front porch that extends the length of the building with a drink in hand, watching the sun go down on another day in the mountains.

MAINE

Old Gaol, York

6 Lindsay Road, York; 207-363-1756; oldyork.org; open for tours Memorial Day through Columbus Day; admission charged

Tourists driving from the outlet malls in Kittery to Perkins Cove in Ogunquit may not even lift their eyes from the line of bumpers straight ahead to take a detour into gracious York Village sandwiched between the two vacation destinations. But York, first settled as a fishing camp in 1624, was once the most important town in the region. It was the capital of the Province of Maine and the seat of the only law east of the Piscataqua. And it has the historic buildings to prove it.

In a familiar New England pattern, they cluster around the old town green. They include the 1747 First Parish Congregational Church, the 1754 Jefferds Tavern (now a tourist information center), the old graveyard, and on a hill above the tombstones, the Old Gaol. A jailhouse is atypical among preserved buildings—most preservationists gravitate to elegant homes, soaring churches, and other such uplifting structures. But the Old Gaol is unique.

Built in 1719 as the King's Prison for the Province of Maine, Commonwealth of Massachusetts, the jail is the oldest public building in Maine and quite possibly the oldest British Colonial building in America still standing where it was built. Now a half-clapboard, half-stone structure with a gambrel roof, the jail began as a simple stone structure of rough-cut granite walls nearly three feet thick containing just two cells. Wide oak planks covered the interior walls and floor, and each cell was lit through a chink window so small that even the most emaciated prisoner could not squeeze out to freedom.

For all intents and purposes, it was a dank dungeon where seven to nine prisoners might be held at any one time as they awaited the circuit judge who came to town four times a year to dispense justice. Until shortly before the American Revolution, it was the sole British Colonial jail in Maine, housing all prisoners apprehended between the Piscataqua and the Saint John Rivers—the southern and northern borders of Maine, respectively.

Prisoners made do with straw as both bedding and bathroom, and by the time a prisoner was released (an average of 28 days for women, 30 days for men), he or she was in no mood to return. The trials were often summary affairs resulting in some form of corporal punishment or public humiliation for the criminal—whipping at the post or being locked in the stocks for all to taunt. Some miscreants were punished for drunkenness, public displays of affection, or taking the Lord's name in vain. A few were convicted of murder and were hanged.

A circa-1736 addition to the jail added kitchen, dining, and parlor areas to the ground level. The parlor served both as booking center, where the prisoner's charges were read before he or she was incarcerated, and the judgment chamber, where the legal proceedings took place. The kitchen and dining room of the jail are shown as if the jailer and his family lived there, though recent scholarship suggests that at least some jailers might have lived in a separate house nearby.

In theory, debtors were confined in one cell and law-breakers in the other, but there was little difference between their conditions. Debtors' families argued that while criminals might be treated like dogs, debtors deserved better. When a second story was added in 1763, the dungeon cells were relegated to storage and the upstairs cells—much brighter and airier—were segregated by type of prisoner, with debtors in the more spacious accommodations. In 1799, an even larger debtor's cell—really more like a debtor's apartment—was added to the second story rear. Debtors were allowed to bring in their own furniture and were expected to work to pay off their debts. It is something of a surprise to see a fine bed with brocade canopy and a spinning wheel on display, but they represent actual artifacts from the early 19th century of the jail. Some debtors were even allowed to go to their place of work, if it was nearby, and return to jail for the night. When the Embargo Act of 1807 bankrupted many of York's merchants, the debtor's cell was busy.

The museum interpretation of the Old Gaol focuses on conditions in 1789, when William Emerson was the jailer. The front room of the structure is shown as the Emersons' parlor, and it includes period pastel portraits of the jailer and his wife, Eunice, by Benjamin Blythe, a noted artist from Salem, Massachusetts. Vanity was clearly not a crime by the time these portraits were painted. William Emerson poses with quill pen and book, proving that he was a literate man, while Eunice is draped with her most precious possession, an ermine shawl. Perhaps they were showing, in living color, their superiority to their charges.

As other communities grew and surpassed York, the jail had less regional significance, although it did serve as the York County Jail until 1860. At the end of the 19th century, it served briefly as a school and storage building, then as tenement housing. Although it had grown derelict, the structure was saved by the flowering of preservationism in York at the end of the 19th century. Restored by the Old York Historical and Improvement Society (an antecedent to Museums of Old York, which operates several other historic buildings near the green), the jail opened on July 1, 1900, as the Museum of Colonial Relics.

Sarah Orne Jewett House, South Berwick
5 Portland Street, South Berwick; 207-384-2454;
historicnewengland.org; open year-round for guided tours
(very limited in winter); admission charged

Most seventh-graders in Maine public schools are still required to read *The Country of Pointed Firs*, Sarah Orne Jewett's stories about life in a rural small town in Maine. The book was published to great critical acclaim in 1896 and remains relevant because Jewett's writings created a mythological Maine that persists in public imagination. (See the television series *Murder She Wrote* for a particularly cringe-worthy version.) It is not just a country of pointed fir trees. It is also a country of rocky harbors, billowing sails, and hayseed savants who hide their wisdom behind accents as thick as pea-soup fog.

Sarah Orne Jewett (1849–1909) was born and raised in South Berwick, a small town just 13 miles up the Piscataqua River from Kittery, Maine, and Portsmouth, New Hampshire, and the two adjacent family homes where she lived her entire life

are house museums of Historic New England. Jewett is so well remembered as a "regionalist" author that visitors half-expect to see a woodshed, washboard, and open-hearth kitchen fireplace rather than the home of a proudly cosmopolitan woman of the world. Jewett was a successful author and self-made woman at the end of the 19th century, and the home reflects her taste and interests.

Jewett was born in the 1774 Georgian house that her grandfather had purchased in 1819, but moved with her father, pregnant mother, and older sister, Mary, to a Greek Revival home next door in 1854. (That home houses Historic New England's reception center and museum exhibits.) Jewett would return to live in the Georgian home in 1877, when she and her sisters inherited it.

The Georgian house is an archetypal sea captain's home. The two-story clapboard structure has a hip roof that sprouts three gabled dormers. Inside, visitors step into the front entry hall by passing beneath a keystone arch supported by fluted pilasters. Rooms radiate from this spacious hall, but the most striking detail is the gorgeously carved staircase that took two carvers a hundred days to complete. The public rooms throughout the ground level also contain finely carved panels. The house seems an archetype because Jewett made it so by modeling the Brandon house in her first novel, *Deephaven* (1877), on the home.

Sarah and Mary, neither of whom ever married, moved into the house with their frail mother, Caroline, while their younger sister, Caroline Augusta, stayed in the Greek Revival house next door with her husband, Edwin Eastman. The sisters appreciated the fine 18th-century architecture and the Federal-era family furniture, but within about a year, Sarah and Mary redecorated the house to make it their own. They had attended the Centennial Exposition in Philadelphia in 1876 and had picked up a strong appreciation for the latest decorative rage, the Arts & Crafts style.

The front entry hall shows how well the eras fit together. The stair runner is a William Morris "Wreath" design, which the Jewett sisters complemented with an Arts & Crafts wallpaper featuring a bold pattern of tulips. A fine carved-back chair sits on the stairwell landing, while more utilitarian rush-seated chairs are lined up against the hall wall beneath the piece of art that seems de rigeur in every old Maine house: a painting of a tall ship in full sail.

To the right of the front door, the family library was Sarah's higher education, as she did not attend college after receiving a diploma from Berwick Academy. The handsome glass-fronted bookcases are filled with the family books, while some examples of her own volumes (she published more than 20 books and innumerable pieces of short fiction, sketches, and children's stories) are displayed on a table. Their covers, many of which were designed by a friend, the Boston stained glass artist Sarah Wyman Whitman, are striking examples of Arts & Crafts design principles extended to mass-produced books.

To the left of the hall in the rear of the house stands the dining room. It is most notable for the huge family heirloom sideboard, which served as the model for one in *Deephaven*. "From the little closets in the sideboard came a most significant odor of cake and wine whenever one opened the doors," Jewett wrote of the piece.

Both Mary and Sarah slept upstairs. Mary's bedroom was on the front of the house, where she could overlook the comings and goings on the main square of South Berwick. Sarah had a similar view from the desk at the top of the stairs, where she did most of her writing—in longhand, of course.

The sisters, however, spent less and less time together after 1881. That was the year when James T. Fields, Sarah's publisher at the *Atlantic Monthly*, died quite suddenly. Sarah had been a favorite of Fields and his wife, Annie Adams Fields, who became Sarah's close companion for the rest of the writer's life. Sarah would spend winters in Boston, where she and Annie entertained the cream of American and British literary society, summers in Maine, and spring and fall often traveling.

Jewett's fame hit its peak with the publication of *The Country of Pointed Firs* in 1896 and *The Tory Lover* in 1901, but injuries from a fluke carriage accident in 1902 left her barely able to write. She suffered two strokes in 1909 and left Boston to die at home in her beloved Maine. Mary lived in the house until 1930. Edwin Eastman, widower of the youngest sister, Caroline Augusta, donated both South Berwick homes to the forerunner of Historic New England.

Winslow Homer Studio, Scarborough
5 Winslow Homer Road, Scarborough; 207-775-6148;
portlandmuseum.org/homer; open for guided tours April through
December, arranged through Portland Museum of Art; admission
charged

"The rare thing is to find a painter who knows a good thing when he sees it," Winslow
Homer (1836–1910) once remarked to John W. Beatty, director of fine arts of the
Carnegie Institute, Philadelphia. Homer definitely knew a good thing or, more specifically, a good place. Like Claude Monet at Giverny, the artist spent the last quarter
century of his life at his studio on Prouts Neck in Scarborough. This rocky knob
jutting into Saco Bay just north of Old Orchard Beach is surrounded by a slate ledge
shoreline of heroic proportions. Homer would paint it again and again, usually in
stormy weather. The resulting seascapes are the definitive, archetypal images of the
rockbound coast of Maine.

It took Homer decades to find his home ground. Born in Boston, he grew up
across the river in Cambridge and apprenticed from 1854 to 1857 in the lithography
shop of John H. Bufford in Boston. Homer hated taking orders and immediately
launched a career as a freelance illustrator. In 1859, he moved to New York. where
he became a regular contributor at *Harper's Weekly*. When the Civil War broke out,
Harper's dispatched the young illustrator to the Virginia front. For the next four
years, Homer made illustrations of camp life and battles. But he also created his
first professional oil painting, *Sharpshooter*, in 1863. Its combination of fluid realism
and literal life-and-death subject matter foreshadowed both the style and the moral
compass of his mature work.

After the war, Homer spent a year in Paris, and on his return to the United States,
he flourished as an illustrator of rural New England scenes. But he was drawn to
landscape and sporting scenes in his personal work. In 1873, he began painting seri-

ously in watercolor, a medium
previously considered fit only
for field sketches, and became
one of the acknowledged
masters. Two years later, at
age 39, he gave up illustration
to pursue painting full time.
Homer spent 1881–82 in
Cullercoats, a fishing village
in northeast England, where
he concentrated on painting
seascapes and the fishermen

and their wives. The mature Homer, with his command of shadow, form, and marine subject matter, was beginning to take shape.

The Homer family first visited Prouts Neck in 1875, and the painter's brother, Charles, and their father ultimately bought most of the peninsula to develop as a summer community. They commissioned Portland architect John Calvin Stevens to construct 18 Shingle-style houses. And they built their own massive house, known in the family as the Ark. In 1883, they gave Winslow the carriage house for his own residence. Stevens helped transform it into a cottage, and the artist lived there the rest of his life. In 1890, Charles also gave Winslow the gift of a painting studio addition in the back—a room that the painter referred to jokingly as the Factory.

Since 2012, the Winslow Homer Studio has been open for tours. They are arranged through the Portland Museum of Art, which bought the property from descendants of the Homer family in 2004 and restored it as closely as possible to the painter's era. Weather permitting, tours begin with the view, which seems entirely in Homer's spirit. Below the studio, the slate ledges of the shore—twisted and broken by tectonic events—are pounded by the surf. This is the hard shore of Homer's masterpiece, *Weatherbeaten,* which is owned by the Portland Museum of Art. In all, 22 Homer oil paintings, 7 watercolors, and a few etchings can be traced to Prouts Neck subjects. From his studio, the artist had access to a marginal way—a public right of way that follows the mile-long circumference of Prouts Neck.

Architect Stevens adapted the carriage house to a 1,500-foot studio with only the most modest changes, even leaving the framing of the original box stalls. Homer lived here without electricity or running water, heating the structure with only the fireplace and a cast-iron stove. The main room of the first floor focuses on the hearth fireplace and a few personal Homer belongings—the bamboo and cane day-bed where he died and some mounted fish skins from an Adirondacks fishing trip. The hand-lettered sign he used to discourage visitors ("Snakes! Snakes! & Mice!") is propped over the mantel.

The two rooms where he painted—the 1890 addition and the upstairs loft—call on the visitor to imagine the painter, as the former has seating for a slideshow about the artist and the latter a number of panels about his career and thoughts about painting. But the loft's best feature is the balcony overlooking the ocean. Homer himself spent many an hour here. His brother, Charles, is said to have accused him of "wearing out the view." But what a view it is—straight out to sea and southward along the coast to Wood Island Light. And for just a moment, it almost feels like Winslow Homer is there himself, squaring up a vision with his hands.

Victoria Mansion, Portland
109 Danforth Street, Portland; 207-772-4841; victoriamansion.org; open for guided tours May through October and late November until early January; admission charged

To step inside Victoria Mansion is to conjure the ghost of one of the great luxury hoteliers of the 19th century. Ruggles Sylvester Morse was born in Leeds, Maine, in 1817 but left to make his fortune in the hotel business. He began at the Tremont in Boston, moved on to the Astor House on Broadway in New York, and finally owned a series of luxury hotels in New Orleans. The former farmboy returned to Maine in 1858 intent on building a summer residence for his homesick, Maine-born wife, Olivia. He charged architect Henry Austin, designer of Yale University's first grand library, to create a home that would rival the mansions of the Vanderbilts and Astors on Fifth Avenue in New York.

Austin heard him loud and clear and mined Morse's deep pockets to pull out all the stops in both construction and decoration. He started erecting the Italianate brick structure in 1859 and faced the front with brownstone and the sides with stucco. The house is

asymmetrical in shape, with varying rooflines to each side of the central four-story tower (itself vaguely suggestive of a campanile). Ornate windows, overhanging eaves, and a pair of two-story porches break up the straight lines of the façade.

Since Morse had to stay in New Orleans for the duration of the Civil War, Austin had all the time he needed to fashion the most modern, opulent, and luxurious domicile in the country. Per Morse's wishes, the house contained every amenity that his guests enjoyed at his hotels. It boasted gas lights, central heating, flush toilets, and hot and cold running water that used a rooftop rainwater collection system and a huge holding tank on the third floor. Each room also had a servant call bell. Reports at the time placed the cost of the house between $70,000 and $100,000—or $1.9 million to $2.8 million in today's currency.

Morse was among the first in the country to engage Gustave Herter, who would become known as a leading fine furniture maker and interior designer of the late 19th century, as decorator. The furniture was largely custom-made, and Herter oversaw all other manner of decoration. Morse demanded wall-to-wall carpeting in the front hall, for example, because that is what he placed in the lobbies of his luxury hotels. Rather than use wallpaper, Herter hired artist and decorator Giuseppe Guidicini, famed for his opera scenery, to paint frescoes and *trompe l'oeil* wall decorations. In the ground-level public rooms, almost anything that could be gilded was—all the better to reflect the gas lights.

Victoria Mansion was not only Herter's earliest known commission, it is the only one to remain intact. Following Ruggles Morse's death in 1893, his widow, Olivia, sold the house with all its furnishings to local merchant Joseph R. Libby. The Libbys occupied it until 1928 without making any significant changes, but they removed most of the contents when they left. However, about 90 percent of the items on the household inventory of 1894 have returned to the house museum, thanks to generous donations from the Libby family and descendants. As a result, Victoria Mansion is widely considered the best-preserved example of an Italianate mansion in the country. The stained glass, porcelain, silver, glassware, art, and Herter furniture are all original as are the finishes on the woodwork.

The house stood vacant after 1929 and suffered significant water damage when the hurricane of 1938 sent a tree crashing down on one corner. The city took over the property in 1940 and put it up for sale. Just as the mansion was about to be razed to build a gas station, William H. Holmes, a retired local educator, bought the property and opened it as a house museum in 1941. It has been open to the public ever since.

The soaring, three-story entry hall extends from the front to the back of the house. It feels very much like a hotel lobby with indirect light flooding down from the gigantic stained-glass skylight. The flying staircase in the center of the hall is lit by double gas globes suspended on chains from the third-floor ceiling.

The front parlor, to the left on entering the house, is a whimsical fantasy of gilt-encrusted mirrors, pastel-colored panels of singing cherubs, ornate vases and faux classical statues, and an Italian white marble fireplace surround carved with dancing figures. The theme is love, in all its allegorical manifestations. On the opposite side of the hall, the dining room displays a Herter table and chairs, and the rich American chestnut–paneled walls are carved with fruit, vegetables, fish, and wild game. Crystal wine glasses on the table signal that, unlike many of their neighbors at the time, the Morses did not subscribe to the temperance doctrine.

The upstairs bedrooms also have gorgeously carved Italian marble fireplaces as well as handsome double washstands. The walls are painted to look as if they are covered in damask silk, and the ceilings feature decorative frescoes. Painted walls and ceilings in the style of Pompeii decorate the second-floor bathroom and water closet (possibly the first flush toilet in Portland). Also on the second floor, the "Turkish room" was constructed as the men's smoking room since it was considered impolite to smoke in front of a woman at the time. Decorated in Islamic-style geometric wall and ceiling paintings, patterned Oriental rugs, damask window treatments, and hanging silks, it was cleaned and restored in 2007–2009 and emerged from the decades of haze to shine brightly again.

Portland Observatory, Portland
138 Congress Street, Portland; 207-253-1800; portlandlandmarks
.org; open for guided tours late May through mid-October;
admission charged

It's no stretch to say that Lemuel Moody was something of a visionary. In the early 19th century, communications were so rudimentary that important messages were delivered either by mail or messenger. The telegraph was but a glint in Samuel F. B. Morse's eye, and wireless communication was still a century away. As they had since antiquity, seacoast towns always kept a watchful eye on the ocean. A watchtower was as important then as a cell tower is today. So in 1807, Moody erected a tall tower on top of Munjoy Hill in Portland.

The former sea captain put up his 86-foot-tall wooden tower on one of Portland's highest spots, but it wasn't to warn of marauding pirates or enemy warships. The observation level stood 160 feet above sea level and had a clear view of Portland harbor out into Casco Bay and the broad Atlantic beyond. By squinting through a powerful telescope, Moody could identify merchant sailing ships that were still 30 miles out to sea, which meant they were a day away from docking at Portland. Moody would alert the merchants who subscribed to his service by raising a flag on his tower that signaled that their ships were literally coming in. They could prepare the docks for unloading, saving precious hours—and money.

The shorebound former sailor was also ahead of his time in other forms of media. Since he occupied the catbird seat in town, he used the heights to make weather observations, which he sold to a local newspaper. Not content with supplying both

the shipping news and weather, Moody expanded into entertainment. He surrounded his "ugly brown tower," as Portlanders apparently called it, with an entertainment complex that included both a dance hall and a bowling alley, effectively making Munjoy Hill the Orlando of its time.

Today, only the tower remains, and it is shoehorned among shops and homes. In 1807, Portlanders smugly predicted that the tower would topple in the first winter storms. But more than two centuries later, it the oldest known surviving maritime signaling tower in the United States, a testament

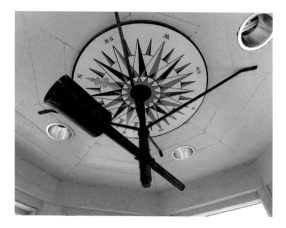

to Moody's sturdy design. He anchored the edifice with 122 tons of rock around the base and formed the octagonal frame with long timbers from tall pine trees cut near Sebago Lake and then floated down the Presumpscot River to Portland. The tower tapers as it rises, which allows strong coastal winds to flow around the structure rather than pushing it over. Indeed, the tower continued to operate until the advent of radio made it obsolete. The tower ceased "signalizing," as Moody put it, in 1923. The City of Portland purchased it in the 1930s, and it now operates as a museum of local maritime history under the aegis of Greater Portland Landmarks. It is open during the summer and early fall for guided tours.

Inside, a spiral staircase with several landings leads to the observation deck. There are only 86 steps from the reception area to the top, making it a pretty easy climb. The tours stop at each level to permit extended examination of the historical displays. One, for example, chronicles the Great Fire of 1866, which destroyed much of the city before it burnt out on the flanks of Munjoy Hill, thus sparing the wooden tower. The building's greatest enemy was time. Displays on one level detail the ambitious restoration project from 1998 to 2000 to rescue the structure from the punk rot caused by moisture and the alarming disintegration of timbers from a powder post beetle infestation. Restorers literally disassembled the building to replace affected pieces of wood. About 85 percent of the current tower, however, is original. By way of comparison, a restored naval vessel of the same era would likely have only the original hardware remaining.

The days of hanging complex flags to indicate which vessels would make port the next day are long over, but the view from the observation deck is as glorious as in Moody's era. Signage on the rails and cupola help visitors identify the lighthouses at Portland Head, Portland Breakwater (also called "Bug Light" because it is so small), and Spring Point Ledge. The aerie also provides clear views of Fort Scammel on House Island (built in 1808 and the only Portland fort to exchange fire in a battle) and Hog Island's granite pentagon of Fort Gorges (finished in 1865 just in time to be obsolete in the face of modern explosives). On a clear day, the distant north-northwest horizon is interrupted by the peaks of Mount Washington in the distance. But it's more historically satisfying to whirl around 180 degrees to emulate

Lemuel Moody by training binoculars, a telescope, or a telephoto lens southwest to spot the ships bound for Portland harbor.

Wadsworth Longfellow House, Portland
459 Congress Street, Portland; 207-774-1822; mainehistory.org; museum open year-round, house May through October; admission charged

When the ashes had cooled on the Great Fire of 1866 in Portland, native son and famous poet Henry Wadsworth Longfellow (1807–82) described the destruction: "Desolation! Desolation! Desolation!" he wrote. "It reminds me of Pompeii, the 'sepult city.'" He was not being merely histrionic. Some 1,800 buildings burned to the ground, leaving 10,000 people homeless.

The poet's boyhood home did survive the fire and is now the oldest building on Portland's peninsula. Opened as a museum in 1901, it chronicles the evolution of the city through the stories of three generations of a family of movers and shakers in the political and cultural life of America. It is also a poignant bridge between a Portland built on fishing and sea trade and the industrial city that rose from the ashes.

Peleg Wadsworth (1748–1829), the Revolutionary War general in charge of Maine's forces and later the congressional representative from the District of Maine 1793–1807, was a comrade-in-arms of Paul Revere and George Washington—a patriotic lineage that would loom large in family lore. He constructed Portland's first

all-brick house in 1785–86. The two-story farmstead with a pitched roof sat on a 1½-acre lot on Back Street (now Congress Street), which marked the edge of town and was the route on which traders brought their goods to Portland. To take advantage of the house's strategic location, Peleg set up a shop next to his barn. He and his wife, Elizabeth (1753-1825), raised 10 children here before they retired in 1807 to the family farm in Hiram, Maine.

Their eldest daughter, Zilpah (1778–1851), grew up in the house with her siblings and wrote eloquently of their happiness during her childhood. On January 1, 1804, Zilpah was married in the front parlor to up-and-coming young lawyer Stephen Longfellow IV (1776–1849), who had originally been betrothed to Zilpah's sister Eliza, who died of consumption. The young couple moved into the house in 1807, eight months after the birth of their second son. Compressing both family lineages into one moniker with a strong rhythmic line, they had christened him Henry Wadsworth Longfellow.

By all accounts, Henry and his seven siblings enjoyed a loving and nurturing childhood. Their father prospered as a lawyer and then a jurist, and the Longfellows added a third story and new trim to the house in 1815, providing a bit of Greek Revival dress to the house's classic Federal bones. Stephen Longfellow was often away, riding the circuit as a judge or serving in the Massachusetts General Court, the Maine state legislature, and in Washington as a representative to Congress. His law library collection fills a handsome bookcase in the study. Spiritually and politically progressive, Zilpah inculcated a lifelong love of learning in her children. They grew up reading widely, drawing and painting, and playing music. Avid letter and journal writers, Henry and his brothers and sisters all wrote poetry from an early age. The small desk where Henry penned "The Rainy Day" ("Into each life some rain must fall / Some days must be dark and dreary") sits in a room off the kitchen where family china is stored.

Longfellow left to attend Harvard and ultimately settled in Cambridge, Massachusetts (see p. 120). But he often returned to his boyhood home, where he had

developed the sensibilities that would make him arguably America's leading poet of the hearth ("The Children's Hour") as well as its greatest storyteller in verse ("The Song of Hiawatha," "Evangeline," "The Courtship of Miles Standish").

Walking into the kitchen from the dooryard garden, the most striking artifact is not the fireplace cooking apparatus or the Chinese export plates, but a well-worn and still-graceful rocking horse. During the cold Maine winters, the children would play in the warm kitchen, and it's easy to imagine a young Henry already rehearsing the galloping rhythm he would use decades later in "The Midnight Ride of Paul Revere."

Henry's younger sister, Anne Longfellow Pierce (1810–1901), ultimately became steward of the family home. Widowed in 1835 after only 3 years of marriage, she spent 87 of her 90 years living in the house, which was not even electrified until after her death. Because the property was always in family hands, most household items and artifacts are original to the Wadsworths and Longfellows. When Henry died in 1882, Anne decided to bequeath the home as a memorial to her famous brother and specified in her 1895 will that it should go to the Maine Historical Society, which her father had cofounded. She left eight pages of detailed instructions regarding the placement of objects and how the rooms should be maintained.

The Historical Society parted slightly from her wishes, making the home a memorial to the entire family. In 2002, the house was restored to its mid-19th-century heyday under Anne's watch. The downstairs parlor is dominated by a large lithograph of George Washington (one family heirloom was a lock of Washington's hair), and heavy, moody Victorian décor. Upstairs bedrooms look as they did when they were occupied by family members. One room even has a copy desk with quill pen resting in an inkwell—a reminder of the potential of words not yet written.

Sabbathday Lake Shaker Village, New Gloucester
707 Shaker Road, New Gloucester; 207-926-459;maineshakers
.com; open for tours Friday before Memorial Day through Columbus
Day; Sunday worship service only, 10 a.m. year-round; admission
charged for tours

Straddling Route 26 in the rural western edge of New Gloucester, Sabbathday Lake Shaker Village looks like the perfectly imagined version of New England's agricultural past. Stout-trunked, ancient sugar maple trees line the roadside where the village store with its welcoming, shaded front porch faces off across the blacktop from the simple Meeting House. Visitors pull into the dooryard behind the store, careful not to hit the mid-1950s red International Harvester Farmall 200 tractor at the driveway's edge. They park their cars beneath the spreading branches of an oak as old as the sugar maples.

One dirt road runs through the village from the red barn past the white-clapboard buildings, some in active use, some preserved for storage as part of the historic site. Hollyhocks grow up around the doorways, and hydrangeas as old-fashioned as a grandma's powdered cheek mark the turning of the footpaths. Nearby, an iron pump

is fastened on a well rock, which is a huge improvement over hauling water with a rope and bucket. A gray and white barn cat stretches out on the rock, catching the sun's warmth but keeping one eye open lest some visitor try to pet him. The sweet aroma of freshly cut timothy and clover mixes with the smell of manure from the sheep pen.

Sabbathday Lake Shaker Village was known, even during the religious movement's height, as "the least of Mother's children in the east" because it was the smallest, most remote, and poorest of the Shaker communities in the eastern United States. Dishonest business agents saddled the Sabbathday Shakers with debts that took the community decades to pay. Yet they persevered. Other Shaker communities have closed, but this one remains as the last active Shaker community in the world.

Now only about 40 minutes by modern roads from Portland, Sabbathday Lake Shaker Village is more modest than the showcase museum villages at Hancock (see p. 80) in Massachusetts or Canterbury (see p. 196) in New Hampshire. It was founded by Shaker missionaries in 1783, when the tract of land with five farming families was known as Thompson's Pond Plantation. Within a year, nearly 179 converts had gathered. Finally, in 1794, they formalized their organization as a Shaker community by making an oral covenant to consecrate their earthly belongings to God and follow the teachings of Mother Ann Lee. To mark the occasion, they raised the Meeting House with two separate sets of granite steps from the road and separate entrances for men and women. Shaker prayer services are still held here on

Sundays and are open to all who wish to attend. That may be as many as 50 people during the height of tourist season.

In 1795, the community began to expand its footprint by building the first communal Dwelling House and over the ensuing decades built barns, mills, and schools. Like other Shaker communities, Sabbathday Lake reached its peak in the third quarter of the 19th century and has contracted since to its current size of 17 buildings on 1,800 acres of land. The property is protected from development by a series of preservation and land conservation easements.

The younger of the two Shakers, Brother Arnold Hadd, is in his early 60s as this book goes to press, and he does much of the heavy lifting on the farm. Elderly Sister June Carpenter tends largely to indoor chores. Occasionally, a novitiate will spend a year with the community to decide if she or he wants to sign the Shaker Covenant and stay on for life.

It's hardly an easy life of ecstatic communion with the divine. Sabbathday Lake is an agricultural community—really a family farm—and there is work to do from first light to last. Although the Shakers lease out some of their farmland and all of their apple orchards, they continue to raise sheep and shaggy Scottish Highlands cattle. They maintain a sustainable wood lot for timber harvest. They grow vegetables and herbs—in part for the seeds that they sell—and keep bees and chickens. When they find a spare moment, they also weave cloth, make baskets, and turn wooden ware on the lathe. Mother Ann's admonition "Hands to work, hearts to God" remains their motto.

The Shaker community appears much like other rural Maine villages that depend on subsistence farming. The Shakers, though, have a mission. They carry forward their beliefs and the history of the movement. They are the last members of a once-large family, and along with the faith, they have inherited the furniture and the papers of other Shaker villages. As a result, Sabbathday Lake has the most extensive library of Shaker materials in the world. In fact, Sister June, a former librarian, came

in 1988 to catalog the library and felt such a sense of belonging that she decided to stay. Sabbathday Lake also owns a striking collection of Shaker artifacts, including "classic period" Shaker furniture.

Because they maintain a museum, the research library, and a gift shop, the Shakers employ a small year-round staff that swells to as many as

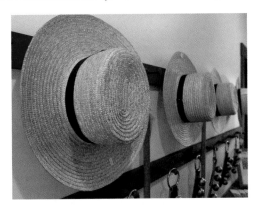

a dozen during the summer and fall tourist season. More than 500 people belong to the auxiliary Friends of the Shakers, many of whom assist Brother Arnold with the farming tasks or lead tours for visitors. Only a handful of buildings are open for touring, but the guides provide excellent narratives on the history of the Shaker movement, Shaker practices and furniture styles, and the tenets of the Shaker faith. In an active community, these theological abstractions seem a lot less abstract. Here they seem like words to live by.

Nickels-Sortwell House, Wiscasset
121 Main Street, Wiscasset; 207-882-6218; historicnewengland .org; open for guided tours June through mid-October; admission charged

Built in 1807 for a grand sum of $14,000 (in a period when a skilled workman earned $1 per day), the Nickels-Sortwell House was Captain William Nickels's bid for social prominence. He intended the home to outshine all others with its exquisite Palladian window, ornately carved woodwork, three-story flying staircase, and huge skylight to flood the interior with natural illumination. One of two historic houses in town operated by Historic New England, the property hits many of the high points of Wiscasset history.

The village was founded in 1729 on the site of an excellent natural harbor 11 miles from the open sea. For the next century and a half, a succession of blocky square-riggers and sleek schooners rolled down the ways from Wiscasset's shipyards, built from timber floated down the Sheepscot River. The town grew flush on the coastal and Caribbean trade just after the American Revolution, and from 1800 until the Civil War, it was the busiest shipping harbor in the country east of Boston.

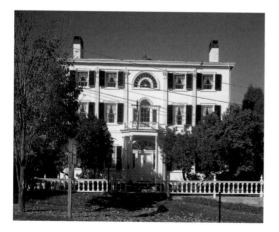

All the maritime wealth tended to find expression in the construction of ever-grander trophy homes. A surprising number of them remain, making the village a living museum of American vernacular architecture in the Federal and Greek Revival styles. (Much of Wiscasset was declared a National Historic District in 1973.) William Nickels owned no less than 30 ships when he decided to build the finest home in town. He erected his Federal manse on High Street in sight of the harbor, and he lavished his wealth on every conceivable flourish.

But his timing could not have been worse. In December 1807, President Thomas Jefferson's Embargo Act banned trade with British ports, hobbling most New England shipping. When the War of 1812 broke out despite the embargo, it dealt the *coup de grace* to Nickels and most other traders. To make matters even worse, Nickels's eldest daughter and his wife both died in 1812. Sinking beneath the weight of debt, two years later Nickels deeded the house to his business partner, who allowed the family to continue living there. But the captain didn't live to enjoy peace and the resumption of maritime trade in 1815. That year he died of tuberculosis, and everything he owned was sold to satisfy his debts.

The house soon became a tavern and inn for boatbuilders and sailors and by midcentury was refashioned as a hotel to capitalize on the early days of the tourist trade on the Maine coast. It was operating as the Belle Haven Hotel when banker and railroad and mining executive Alvin Sortwell and his wife, Gertrude, rented the top two floors in the summer of 1895. The Sortwell family had deep family roots in Wiscasset and fell in love with the landmark building. By 1899, they arranged to buy it and began restoring the property according to the principles of the Colonial Revival movement—an early preservationist effort that sought to preserve the America of the Founding Fathers.

They promptly painted the house white and began filling its rooms with antiques and Colonial Revival furniture. Alvin Sortwell died in 1910, but Gertrude and daughter Frances continued spending the summers here, and after researching the home's history, removed the front portico added during the hotel years and pared the structure back to its original lines. In 1925, they engaged Charles Eliot II of the famous Olmsted landscape design firm to create the gardens. (Eliot did not generally take on private commissions, but the Sortwells were his friends and neighbors in Cambridge, Massachusetts.)

In the late 1930s, Frances Sortwell relocated to Wiscasset year-round and spearheaded many of the village's efforts to celebrate its architectural heritage. She herself purchased and restored eight homes and several public buildings. She died in 1956, but not before willing the Nickels-Sortwell House to the Society for the Preservation of New England Antiquities, now Historic New England.

The Sortwell family decided to leave their belongings in the house, and Historic New England augmented the Sortwell family possessions with items from its own collections appropriate to the Nickels period. As a result, the house bears the marks of all its different eras—the striking carved woodwork and spiral staircase of the shipwrights William Nickels hired, the brass room numbers on some bedroom doors from the hotel period, and the gracious Colonial Revival décor of the Sortwells. The eras all mesh, of course, in that very New England mode of making everything old new again, proving that history doesn't just repeat itself—it never really goes out of style.

Olson House, Cushing
Hathorne Point Road, Cushing; 207-354-0102; farnsworthmuseum .org; open for guided tours Memorial Day through Columbus Day; admission charged

One of the most recognizable paintings in American art, Andrew Wyeth's *Christina's World* was first exhibited at the MacBeth Gallery in Manhattan in 1948. Alfred Barr, founding director of the Museum of Modern Art, snatched it up for the bargain price of $1,800—an investment MOMA has recouped untold times in sales of calendars, notecards, posters, and other reproductions. The painting was to be a cornerstone for building Wyeth's reputation.

Christina's World still hangs on the walls of Museum of Modern Art, now seeming far more "modern" than it might have appeared in the resolutely abstract art world of 1948. The image depicts Anna Christina Olson lying on the ground in a grassy field and looking up toward a weathered farmhouse atop the hill. A barn and some less distinct outbuildings stand near the house. That famous farmhouse also still stands, topping a rise in Cushing, Maine, on the tidal St. George River south of Thomaston. It is owned by the Farnsworth Art Museum in Rockland, which opens the plain, rustic 18th-century farmhouse to the public during the summer.

The Farnsworth celebrates Maine's role in American art as part of its mission and has long cultivated a relationship with the Wyeth family. It owns outstanding examples from three generations of the artistic family: N. C. Wyeth (1882–1945), Andrew Wyeth (1917–2009), and Jamie Wyeth (1946–). The Farnsworth was an early supporter of Andrew Wyeth's work, first purchasing six of his paintings in 1944 and mounting a major exhibition of his work in 1951.

The Wyeth family had a summer home in the area, and Andrew Wyeth first became acquainted with the Olson family—Christina and her younger brother,

Alvaro—in 1939 through another summer resident and neighbor of the Olsons, Betsy James. Within the year, Betsy and Andrew would marry, and the young painter began a three-decade friendship with the Olsons. Working mainly in watercolor or tempera, he would paint their house, their saltwater farm, and their buildings again and again between 1939 and 1968. The Olsons even let him use an upstairs bedroom as a studio.

It was in this studio that he was first inspired to make the painting. He was gazing out at the field and saw Christina looking up at the house. Unable to walk, Christina Olson often dragged herself along on the ground as she tended to her chores. As Wyeth noted for the MOMA label on his painting, although she had been crippled by polio, she "was limited physically but by no means spiritually. The challenge to me was to do justice to her extraordinary conquest of a life which most people would consider hopeless."

The painting is not an example of photorealism. Wyeth was a master of tempera, a technique that permits the artist to paint in minute detail, and he did exactly that. The painting renders single blades of grass and strands of Christina's hair. The play of light suggests the high-latitude sun of summer in Maine, and the rendering of the field shows the ripe sedges of late summer rather than the Indian paintbrush and wild alpine strawberries found there in June. But what appears to be excruciat-

ing realism is masterful painterly sleight of hand. Betsy Wyeth actually posed for the picture, not Christina Olson, and Wyeth took liberties with the landscape for his composition. The field stretches only half as far from Christina's position by the road, and Wyeth moved the barn and outbuildings away from the house for better effect.

Yet it is impossible to shake the sense of déjà-vu on viewing the house from the road. The Farnsworth has restored the property to look as Wyeth painted it, and the view seems to be missing something without a woman lying in the grass. The house is likewise haunted inside by images from Wyeth's *oeuvre*.

Every summer for 30 years he documented life on the saltwater farm—as much by the absence of people as by their presence. As Wyeth once commented, "I just couldn't stay away from there. I did other pictures while I knew them but I'd always seem to gravitate back to the house . . . It was Maine."

Windjammers of Rockland and Camden
**Maine Windjammer Cruises (*Grace Bailey* and *Mercantile*):
PO Box 617, Camden; 207-236-2938 or 800-736-7981;
mainewindjammercruises.com; most vessels sail from Memorial Day
weekend through September**

The Penobscot Bay harbors of Rockland and Camden rock with a mix of pleasure-craft sloops and the grittier half-cabin hulls of working lobster boats. But for a few hours on summer Saturday afternoons, the calendar flips back a century to the end of the Great Age of Sail. The schooners of the windjammer trade are in port to discharge passengers, load provisions, and welcome the next week's adventurers aboard.

Coastal Maine is famous for its sailing ships—China trade vessels from Searsport, five-masted schooners from Thomaston and Wiscasset that shuttled between New York and London, and the behemoth steel Downeasters out of Bath. But smaller sailing vessels of the type now used as windjammers are less well known. From the early 19th to the early 20th century, literally thousands of these two- and three-masted schooners plied Maine's coastal waters. They fished for mackerel, hand-lined for cod, and sieved for sardines. They hauled pulpwood to Bucksport, granite from Vinalhaven to New York, and timber from the log drives on the Penobscot, Kennebec, and Androscoggin Rivers to mills all up and down the eastern seaboard.

Steam and then gasoline or diesel engines made those coasting schooners obsolete. Why haul canvas when you could switch on an engine to drive a propeller? Many of the schooners had their masts cut down and spent their final days as nothing more than cargo barges. By the 1930s, thousands of hulls lay up against the rocks in harbors all along the Maine coast.

Captain Frank Smith had other ideas for these tall ships. He thought there might be a business in pleasure cruises aboard the old schooners. In 1936, he launched Maine Windjammer Cruises® with the *Mabel*. An industry was born. In the 80 years since, the sailing adventure trade in Penobscot Bay—which centers on the harbors of Camden and Rockland—has been responsible both for rehabilitating many great historical vessels and for introducing thousands of travelers to the sheer exhilaration of raising a sail and hearing it snap taut as the wind catches the canvas and sends a historic hull sailing swiftly once more on a course downeast. Eight schooners of the Penobscot Bay windjammer fleet have received National Historic Landmark status, including the following four.

Grace Bailey

Frank Smith first chartered this
two-masted schooner in 1939 to
try her out in the excursion trade.
He was so pleased with the results
that he bought the boat the following year, and she has served
as a windjammer ever since. One
of the few surviving two-masted
schooners with a wooden hull,
she was built in 1882 on Long
Island, New York, and sailed as
the *Grace Bailey* until a 1906
reconstruction, when she was
rechristened the *Mattie*. (She

returned to her "maiden name" after a 1989–90 restoration.) In a 50-plus-year career
as a cargo vessel, she sailed to the West Indies in the fruit trade and carried granite
from Penobscot Bay to help build Grand Central Station in New York.

With an 81-foot deck and an overall length of 123 feet, the *Grace Bailey* is long
and lean and carries four sheets: a mainsail, a foresail, and two headsails. The extensive sail area combined with the sharp hull make her one of the fastest of the Maine
windjammers in a stiff breeze. She has no engine aboard but does carry a yawl boat
with an engine to assist with docking maneuvers. The hull is planked with oak, but
the decks are pine and the cargo hold has been reconfigured to sleep 29 passengers.
One unique feature of the vessel is her restored 1882 main cabin with handcarved
paneling and a piano. The *Grace Bailey* is berthed in Camden.

Mercantile

Roughly the same size as the *Grace Bailey*, the *Mercantile* was Maine born and
bred. Members of the Billings family built her on Little Deer Isle on the east side of
Penobscot Bay. Framed and planked in white oak, she reaches 80 feet on deck, 115
feet overall. The *Mercantile* was built with a shoaling hull so she can enter shallow
harbors where deeper-draft vessels would run aground. Launched in 1916, *Mercantile* spent the first several decades in the coasting trade, serving island communities in
Penobscot Bay and farther downeast and spending one season fishing mackerel. Her
rigging is also similar to the *Grace Bailey*—a mainsail, foresail, and two headsails.

Mercantile began sailing as part of Maine Windjammer Cruises out of Camden
in 1942 and has been in service ever since. Last restored in 1989, her cargo hold
sleeps 29 passengers plus the crew.

The *Mercantile*

Stephen Taber

PO Box 1050, Rockland; 207-594-4723 or 800-999-7352; stephentaber.com

Also a veteran of the windjammer trade, the *Stephen Taber* is a rare example of a centerboard two-masted schooner. This adaptation of the hull and keel was created specifically for the demands of the rocky Northeast coast. With the centerboard raised, she draws just five feet of water and can access shallow channels and dockage. With the board let down, she is stable in deep water and strong winds.

Although her boom and bowsprit give her an overall length of 115 feet, the *Stephen Taber*'s deck is only 68 feet. The sharp-cut hull is agile and responsive to changes in the sail. (She has no auxiliary engine.) For example, part of her summer itinerary often takes her into the granite pond of Pulpit Harbor on North Haven, where after threading a course around Pulpit Rock, the captain must coax the ship into a narrow channel that is about 150 feet wide from sheer wall to sheer wall.

Constructed in 1871 on the north shore of Long Island, the *Stephen Taber* was a cargo workhorse in New York harbor for her early career. She was briefly fitted out as a yacht in 1900–02, but returned to service as a cargo carrier. In 1920, she was sold to a Maine captain and has sailed the waters of Penobscot Bay ever since. In 1946, she was converted to the tourist trade, and in 1981–83 received a major restoration under the current owners, who made her previously claustrophobic below-decks quarters considerably more comfortable. Although launched a few months later than the *Lewis R. French*, the *Stephen Taber* is considered the oldest two-masted schooner in continuous service. She sleeps 22 passengers and sails out of Rockland.

Lewis R. French
PO Box 992, Camden; 800-469-4635; schoonerfrench.com
Built just south of Penobscot Bay at Christmas Cove in the town of South Bristol, the *Lewis R. French* is a gaff-rigged two-masted topsail schooner. She was launched in April 1871, making her the oldest two-masted schooner still in service. Moreover, she has worked from Maine home ports her entire career.

Unlike most other windjammers, the *Lewis R. French* was also a fishing vessel from 1877–88 before returning to the coasting trade. She has not carried sail throughout her long service. She was demasted and fitted with an engine in 1924. Following a gasoline fire in Belfast harbor in 1929, she was rebuilt as a sardine carrier and worked out of Lubec from 1931 until 1969 carting tinned sardines between Maine and Nova Scotia. Sold in 1973, she was restored over the next three years to her original sailing condition and has worked the windjammer trade ever since. Now powered entirely by sail, she carries up to 21 passengers from her berth in Camden.

Her gaff rigging allows a relatively short hull—64 feet on the deck, 101 feet overall—to carry more sail than a conventional rigging would allow. She carries four lower sails and two topsails for a total of more than 3,000 square feet of canvas, which makes the *French* a sprinter in the wind.

Camden Amphitheatre and Public Library
55 Main Street, Camden; 207-236-3440; librarycamden.org;
grounds open dawn to dusk

Originally a ship-building center and mill village, by the end of the 19th century Camden was overrun with wealthy rusticators who had transformed a sleepy, salty seacoast town into a summer colony on a par with Bar Harbor and Newport (see p. 57). Part of the attraction was Camden's scenic harbor and deep anchorage, which appealed to yachtsmen from up and down the eastern seaboard. Among them was publishing tycoon Cyrus Curtis (*Saturday Evening Post* and *Ladies Home Journal*), who founded the Camden Yacht Club.

His daughter, Mary Louise Curtis Bok, had an even more lasting impact on the appearance of "Camden by the Sea," as village promoters took to calling the community early in the 20th century. At the end of the 1920s, Bok donated land on Main Street to the town to build the Camden Public Library. As soon as that Colonial Revival building was in place, she decided to do something about the undeveloped slope of land between the library and the harbor. Since she moved in fashionable circles and kept current with developments in art and design, she decided to grace the town with a garden landscape by the pioneering garden designer Fletcher Steele and a park by the famous Olmsted landscape design firm.

The Harbor Park was a popular success, since pleasure craft had already supplanted fishing boats and shipping vessels in Camden's harbor, and the parkland

seemed a natural extension of watery idylls. The Olmsted firm finished it in 1935. A year later, Frank Smith launched the windjammer cruise industry in Camden (see p. 230), cementing Camden's identity as a tourist destination.

But the real gem turned out to be the landscape design that Bok commissioned from Fletcher Steele for the library and the amphitheater on the adjoining slope. It is generally recognized as the first Modernist public landscape in the United States.

Construction of Steele's design began in 1928, and it reflected a sea change in his own thinking. Trained by Frederick Law Olmsted at Harvard's landscape architecture program before World War I, Steele was initially known as an American ambassador for the English Arts & Crafts–style garden exemplified in the work of Gertrude Jekyll—formal constructions with painterly strokes of color and massed flower border beds.

A 1925 trip to the Art Deco Exposition in Paris turned his head around. He was bowled over by the Cubist gardens. Embracing Modernism with the zeal of a fresh convert, Steele became a bridge between Neoclassical and Modernist garden design. Like Picasso, he found the affinity between formal classical order and the more radical geometry of Modernism.

Rather than seeing his landscape design as an adjunct to the new library, Steele ignored the northeast-southwest orientation of the building. He focused instead on the natural lay of the land—a glacial scoop coming down a hillside into the harbor. He oriented the curved seating of the amphitheater, which is cut into the slope below the library, at a 45-degree angle to the library's axis, then connected the two with a walkway and double staircase that eased the transition of both levels and orientation.

Since the amphitheater faced the sea, Steele planted trees on the hill behind it using only species that grew within a 5-mile radius. The center of the seating curve was a natural spot to mount a musical performing stage, while the semicircle opened onto a grassy plain ideally suited to theater in the round with the harbor as a backdrop. Steele retained some of the mature elms on the property and kept some boulder outcrops in place. By working the granite tiers of the amphitheater seating around the rocks, he was able to provide visual relief from the strict geometry.

The landscape appears almost indigenous, as if Steele had only modified it slightly with the concentric semicircles of stone to create the terraced seating. He did supply some truly decorative touches, however, incorporating a brick niche (which now holds a statue) on the double staircase up to the library and placing wrought iron rails, gates, arches, and elegant tripod lights in various Art Deco–inspired styles throughout the space.

The Camden Amphitheatre was finished in 1931, and despite the growth of its trees over the years, Steele's plan is still evident both in the ways in which he sculpted the topography and in the plantings he specified. The space continues to function both as a public park and as a summer gathering place for craft fairs, concerts, live theater, and even film screenings. It is especially popular for wedding ceremonies.

Fort Knox, Prospect
740 Fort Knox Road, Prospect; 207-469-6553; fortknox .maineguide.com; open May through October; admission charged

Located on a bluff above the mouth of the Penobscot River, Fort Knox might have been the most pleasant posting in the US Army. It sits at one of the prettiest spots on the Maine coast, and all foreign threats were over by the time it was built in 1844–69. The handsome granite coastal fortification perches on a green shelf surrounded by high trees on one side and a deep river gorge on the other. Ospreys, golden eagles, and bald eagles all ride the thermals of the gorge as they fish the teeming waters where the fresh water of the Penobscot River meets the deep-sea rift beneath Penobscot Bay. Views from the fort stretch all the way down the bay to its large islands and upriver past Orland.

But Mainers have long memories, and this stretch known as the Penobscot Narrows was the site of the worst American naval disaster until Pearl Harbor, the summer 1779 debacle known as the Penobscot Expedition. As the American colonies strove for independence, Britain buttressed its New Brunswick border by claiming everything east of the Penobscot River to the Bay of Fundy as "New Ireland." Since Maine was a district of Massachusetts, that state sent 44 ships and several hundred men to Castine to take the territory back. Overwhelming British sea power drove

them up the Penobscot River, where they were forced to scuttle and burn their ships and escape overland, tails between their legs. During the War of 1812, Britain again claimed New Ireland—and didn't give it back until 1815.

Mainers wanted a fort to protect themselves from those hostile Canadian Brits, and they finally got Fort Knox, named for Major General Henry Knox, a commander of artillery during the Revolution and the first US Secretary of War. (He also retired a short distance down the coast in Thomaston.) The five-sided granite fortification was the first stone, rather than wooden, fort built on the Maine coast, and ended up costing nearly $30 million in current dollars, even though the stone was quarried just 5 miles away. Congress grudgingly provided construction money in dribbles, and as a result, Fort Knox took 25 years to finish. Each of the two batteries had a furnace to heat cannonballs red hot so they would set ships ablaze when they struck.

The introduction of iron-clad warships made hot-shot cannonade obsolete by the time the fort was finished, and since no enemies broached the Maine coast, Fort Knox became a sleepy outpost. Last fully manned during the Spanish-American War, it retained but a single "keeper of the fort" until 1923, when it was declared surplus and sold to the state of Maine for $2,121.

Designated as a state historic site, the fort was open sporadically over the next many decades until the Friends of Fort Knox formed in the 1990s. The group undertook the maintenance and restoration of the site and was rewarded in 2012 with a state government contract to operate Fort Knox as a museum and make it the gateway to the Penobscot Narrows Observatory atop the Penobscot Narrows Bridge. The crisply laid granite, the green lawns of the parade ground, and the overall smart look of the fort make it seem ready for an inspector general to show up at any moment. Hardly a summer weekend goes by without some sort of open-air fair, Civil War reenactor encampment, Scottish Tattoo, pirate festival, or medieval tournament.

Penobscot Narrows Bridge, overlooking Fort Knox, p. 236

Thematic Index

Artists' Sites
Bush-Holley Historic Site, Cos Cob, Conn., 1
Chesterwood, Stockbridge, Mass., 85
The Epic of American Civilization Murals, Hanover, N.H., 202
Florence Griswold Museum, Old Lyme, Conn., 19
Winslow Homer Studio, Scarborough, Maine, 214
Olson House, Cushing, Maine, 228
Saint-Gaudens National Historic Site, Cornish, N.H., 199
Gilbert Stuart Birthplace, Saunderstown, R.I., 43

Carousels
Crescent Park Looff Carousel, Riverside, R.I., 53
Flying Horse Carousel, Watch Hill, R.I., 39
Flying Horses Carousel, Oak Bluffs, Martha's Vineyard, Mass., 156

Civil Rights History
African Meeting House, Boston, Mass., 128
Prudence Crandall Museum, Canterbury, Conn., 32
Rokeby Museum, Ferrisburgh, Vt., 167
Harriet Beecher Stowe House, Hartford, Conn., 14

Industrial History
Harrisville Historic District, N.H., 191
Locks and Canals Historic District, Lowell, Mass., 102
Slater Mill, Pawtucket, R.I., 45

Lighthouses
Block Island South East Light, New Shoreham, Block Island, R.I., 41
Cape Ann Light Station, Thacher Island, Rockport, Mass., 96

Maritime History
Block Island South East Light, New Shoreham, Block Island, R.I., 41
Cape Ann Light Station, Thacher Island, Rockport, Mass., 96
Battleship Cove, Fall River, Mass., 150
Fort Knox, Prospect, Maine, 236
Fort Warren, Georges Island, Boston, Mass., 143
Landmark Vessels of Mystic Seaport, Mystic, Conn., 27

Modern Architecture

Natural Sites and Farms

Presidential Homes

Shaker Sites

Submarines

Women's Sites

Birdcraft Sanctuary, Fairfield, Conn., 3
Prudence Crandall Museum, Canterbury, Conn., 32
Emily Dickinson Museum, Amherst, Mass., 92
Florence Griswold Museum, Old Lyme, Conn., 19
Hill-Stead Museum, Farmington, Conn., 12
Sarah Orne Jewett House, South Berwick, Maine, 211
The Mount, Lenox, Mass., 82
Louisa May Alcott's Orchard House, Concord, Mass., 112
Harriet Beecher Stowe House, Hartford, Conn., 14

Writers' Sites

Herman Melville's Arrowhead, Pittsfield, Mass., 77
Emily Dickinson Museum, Amherst, Mass., 92
Ralph Waldo Emerson House, Concord, Mass., 109
Robert Frost Farm, Derry, N.H., 189
House of the Seven Gables Historic District, Salem, Mass., 100
Sarah Orne Jewett House, South Berwick, Maine, 211
Longfellow House, Cambridge, Mass., 120
Wadsworth Longfellow House, Portland, Maine, 221
Monte Cristo Cottage, New London, Conn., 22
The Mount, Lenox, Mass., 82
Louisa May Alcott's Orchard House, Concord, Mass., 112
Harriet Beecher Stowe House, Hartford, Conn., 14
Mark Twain House, Hartford, Conn., 17
Walden Pond, Concord, Mass., 107

Photo Credits

Primary Photographers

Patricia Harris & David Lyon: cover, facing 1, 6, 7, 10, 11, 13, 15, 20, 21, 23, 24, 26, 27, 28, 30, 31, 32, 33, 35, 36, 37, 38, 39, 40, 43, 44. 47, 48, 49, 51, 52, 53, 54, 55, 56, 57, 71, 72, 76, 77, 78, 79, 80, 81, 83, 84, 85, 86, 87, 88, 92, 93, 94, 95, 101, 103, 107, 108, 109, 110, 111, 112, 113, 114, 115, 118, 119, 121, 122, 124, 125, 126, 127, 129, 130, 131, 132, 134, 135, 137, 138, 139, 130, 142, 144, 145, 146, 149, 154, 155, 157, 158, 159, 160, 161, 162, 164, 167, 168, 170, 171, 178, 179, 180, 182, 183, 184, 185, 186, 187, 188, 189, 190, 191, 192, 193, 194, 196, 197, 198, 199, 201, 202, 203, 205, 208, 209, 210, 212, 213, 219, 220, 221, 222, 224, 225, 229, 236, 238.

Additional Photography

Gavin Ashworth (courtesy Preservation Society of Newport County) 57, 59, 62, 64, 65, 67, 68, 73, 74; Trent Bell Photography (courtesy Portland Museum of Art) 214, 215; Block Island Tourism Council 41, 42; David Bohl (courtesy Victoria Mansion) 217; Camden Public Library 234; Connecticut Audubon Society 4, 5; John Corbett (courtesy Preservation Society of Newport County) 63; Don Couture (courtesy Yale University) 9; Caryn B. Davis Photography (courtesy Hill-Stead Museum) 12; Barbara Hatch (courtesy Maine Windjammer Cruises) 231; Greenwich Historical Society, 2; Carol Highsmith 105; Historic New England viii, 117, 226, 227; The House of the Seven Gables Settlement Association 100; Fred LeBlanc (courtesy the *Lewis R. French*) 233; Penny Leveritt (courtesy of Historic Deerfield) 89, 90; Mark Twain House 17, 18; Marsh-Billings-Rockefeller National Historical Park 166; USS *Massachusetts* Memorial Committee, Inc. archives 150, 151, 152; Mount Washington Resort 205, 206, 207; Old Slater Mill Association 45; Preservation Society of Newport County 75; Shelburne Museum 172, 173; Paul St. Germain (courtesy Thacher Island Association) 97, 98, 99; St. Johnsbury Athenaeum 174, 175, 176; Lee Stauer (courtesy the *Mercantile*) 232; The *Stephen Taber* 232; Victoria Mansion 216.

Acknowledgments

We would like to thank editor Amy Lyons for her enthusiasm for this project and the staff at the Globe Pequot Press for wrestling our manuscript into a book. Time after time as we worked on this book, people stepped forward to assist, to slip us into otherwise fully booked tours before the season ended, and to give us peeks behind the scenes that made it possible to learn just a little bit more than we might have picked up on our own. We cannot speak highly enough of the professionalism, curiosity, and enthusiasm of the staff at the National Park Service sites and all the other National Historic Landmarks. You know who you are—this book would not have been possible without your encouragement and assistance. Finally, we are indebted to our readers and only hope that this book repays them many times over.

About the Authors

Patricia Harris and David Lyon are authors of more than 30 books on travel, food, and art, including Boston, Massachusetts, Rhode Island, Vermont, and New Hampshire in the Food Lovers series published by the Globe Pequot Press. They live in Cambridge, Massachusetts, not far from the Longfellow House, and can be found online at HungryTravelers.com.